Pietro Gori
**Nietzsche's Pragmatism**

# Monoraphien und Texte zur Nietzsche-Forschung

Herausgegeben von
Christian J. Emden
Helmut Heit
Vanessa Lemm
Claus Zittel

Begründet von
Mazzino Montinari, Wolfgang Müller-Lauter, Heinz Wenzel

Advisory Board:
Günter Abel, R. Lanier Anderson, Keith Ansell-Pearson, Sarah Rebecca Bamford,
Christian Benne, Jessica Berry, Marco Brusotti, João Constâncio, Daniel Conway,
Carlo Gentili, Oswaldo Giacoia Junior, Wolfram Groddeck, Anthony Jensen,
Scarlett Marton, John Richardson, Martin Saar, Herman Siemens,
Andreas Urs Sommer, Werner Stegmaier, Sigridur Thorgeirsdottir,
Paul van Tongeren, Aldo Venturelli, Isabelle Wienand, Patrick Wotling

# Band 72

Pietro Gori

# Nietzsche's Pragmatism

A Study on Perspectival Thought

Translated by Sarah De Sanctis

**DE GRUYTER**

The translation of this work has been funded by SEPS

Segretariato Europeo per le Pubblicazioni Scientifiche
Via Val d'Aposa 7 - 40123 Bologna - Italy
seps@seps.it - www.seps.it

This work has originally been published in Italian language: Il pragmatismo di Nietzsche. Saggi sul pensiero prospettivistico © Mimesis Edizioni, Milano-Udine 2016.
www.mimesisedizioni.it.

ISBN 978-3-11-073685-4
e-ISBN (PDF) 978-3-11-059333-4
e-ISBN (EPUB) 978-3-11-059109-5

Library of Congress Cataloging-in-Publication Data: 2018967607

**Bibliographic information published by the Deutsche Nationalbibliothek**
The Deutsche Nationalbibliothek lists this publication in the Deutsche Nationalbibliografie; detailed bibliographic data are available on the Internet at http://dnb.dnb.de.

© 2020 Walter de Gruyter GmbH, Berlin/Boston
This volume is text- and page-identical with the hardback published in 2019.
Printing and binding: CPI books GmbH, Leck

www.degruyter.com

To the wanderers and Good Europeans

# Acknowledgements

My first acknowledgement goes to the publisher Walter De Gruyter and to the editor of the philosophy department Christoph Schirmer, who helped me so much during the whole editorial process. I would also like the editors of the series that hosts the volume to know that it is a sincere honour to see my book published within the *Monographien und Texte zur Nietzsche-Forschung*. I thank them all for this opportunity.

Financial support for the translation has been provided by SEPS – Segretariato Europeo per le Pubblicazioni Scientifiche. I would like to thank that institution for its work and for having funded the translation of this book. Finally, I am grateful to the translator, Sarah De Sanctis, for the remarkable work she did.

The work presented in this volume is the condensation of a decade of research on Nietzsche's engagement with modern science and epistemology, with a particular focus on his problematizing truth. It would not have been possible to carry out that research without the support of the Portuguese Fundação para a Ciência e a Tecnologia (FCT), that since 2011 funded my stay at the Institute of Philosophy of the Nova University of Lisbon (IFILNOVA). I am particularly grateful to the director of the IFILNOVA, prof. António Marques, for his constant support to my work. I owe much more to the vice director of that institution, my former supervisor and now colleague and friend João Constâncio, who since our first encounter stimulated my engagement with the international Nietzsche-scholarship and supported this editorial project from its very beginning.

The list of people that shaped my thought over years and influenced my work on this volume's topic could be long. Just to mention those whose commentaries have been crucial to me, I would like to thank Maria Cristina Fornari, Giuliano Campioni, Luca Lupo, Helmut Heit, Maria João Branco, Marta Faustino, Erik C. Banks, Mattia Riccardi and Massimo Ferrari. Paolo Stellino deserves a special place in this list, for both his contribution to the development of my ideas and the support he gave me during these years of academic wandering. I also owe a lot to the friends and colleagues of the *Lisbon Nietzsche Group* and the Italian *Seminario Permanente Nietzscheano*, for the stimulating discussions that take place during our meetings.

The English translation of the book gave me the opportunity to update the secondary literature, re-work on some sections (in particular, significant changes to the final chapter have been made, with a completely new fourth paragraph) and, more generally, to improve my argument. I would like to thank Anthony K. Jensen and Jack Bemporad for having proofread and reviewed the final version of the volume, providing fundamental remarks for the completion of my work.

As always, I cannot forget the people I love the most. I find it really hard to express with mere words what I owe to my wife Benedetta and our son Guido. I am pretty sure that without them my life would have taken different paths and I would have never become what I am.

*P. G. Lisbon, September 2018*

# Contents

**Abbreviations of Nietzsche's Writings —— XI**

**Introduction —— 1**

**1 Evolutionary Epistemology and the Critique of Truth —— 6**
1.1  A naturalistic approach to epistemology —— 7
1.2  Correspondence and adaptation to external reality —— 12
1.3  Nineteenth-century forerunners —— 17
1.4  The biological usefulness of knowledge —— 26
1.5  Questioning "Truth" —— 36

**2 Pursuit of Facts and Interpretations. A Contextual Reading of NL 1886–87, 7[60] —— 41**
2.1  Facts are just what there aren't, there are only interpretations —— 43
2.2  We cannot determine any fact "in itself" —— 46
2.3  The "subject" is not something given —— 51
2.4  Inasmuch as the word "knowledge" has any meaning at all, the world is knowable —— 59
2.5  Against positivism —— 67
2.6  "Perspectivism" —— 71

**3 Perspectivism and Herd Morality —— 77**
3.1  The "subjects" of perspectivism —— 78
3.2  Tones of appearance —— 84
3.3  Consciousness and language —— 90
3.4  The herd instinct —— 95

**4 Many Names for the Same Way of Thinking —— 101**
4.1  Nietzsche as phenomenalist and/or pragmatist —— 103
4.2  Fictionalism and critical thought —— 111
4.3  Artistic pragmatism and scientific pragmatism —— 118
4.4  Perspectivism as a "program of behaviour" —— 123

**5 A Pragmatist Conception of Truth —— 129**
5.1  Utilitarianism about truth —— 129
5.2  Anti-metaphysical principles —— 138
5.3  William James on truth —— 144
5.4  Nietzsche's pragmatism —— 151

**References —— 156**
    Nietzsche's writings —— 156
    Secondary literature —— 156
    Other texts —— 164

**Index —— 168**

# Abbreviations of Nietzsche's Writings

KGW  *Kritische Gesamtausgabe Werke*
KGB  *Kritische Gesamtausgabe Briefwechsel*
KSA  *Kritische Studienausgabe Werke*

AOM  *Assorted Opinions and Maxims*
BGE  *Beyond Good and Evil*
BT   *The Birth of Tragedy*
D    *Daybreak*
EH   *Ecce Homo*
GM   *On the Genealogy of Morality*
GS   *The Gay Science*
HH   *Human, All Too Human*
NL   *Posthumous Fragments*
TI   *Twilight of the Idols*
TL   *On Truth and Lies in an Extra-Moral Sense*

Detailed information on the German critical edition of Nietzsche's writings and letters which has been referential for the present work, as well as the list of the English translations of Nietzsche's writings which are cited within the volume, is provided in the final bibliography. Notes from the posthumous notebooks not available in English translation have been translated by the author.

References to the posthumous fragments are given as follows: NL year, KSA volume, note; e.g. NL 1886–87, KSA 12, 7[60]. For longer fragments, KSA page number is also provided.

References to Nietzsche's published works are given as follows: work abbreviation, section title or number (when available), aphorism or paragraph number, KSA volume, page number; e.g. GM III 12; KSA 5, p. 365. GS 354; KSA 3, p. 593. TI, "Improving" Humanity 1; KSA 6, p. 98.

All the excerpts from books whose English translation do not appear in the final bibliography (e.g. the works of Hans Kleinpeter, Afrikan Spir, Gustav Teichmüller etc.) have been translated by the author.

# Introduction

In his late period, Nietzsche focused on a fundamental question of Western thought: the problem of truth, or rather of the "will to truth." (GM III 24; KSA 5, p. 400) This question emerges from his reflections on European culture and her morality, a culture that, as Nietzsche observes, has always been animated by "the flames lit by the thousand-year old faith, the Christian faith which was also Plato's faith, that God is truth; that truth is divine." (GS 344; KSA 3, p. 577) In the age of the death of God, however, this faith can no longer remain undisputed; according to Nietzsche, the time has come to put up for discussion the value of this belief and to critically examine its role as the guiding principle of human theoretical and moral orientation. The fundamental issue that Nietzsche stresses therefore concerns the very possibility of believing in that "*metaphysical faith* [...] if nothing more were to turn out to be divine except error, blindness, the lie – if God himself were to turn out to be our longest lie." (GS 344; KSA 3, 577) Nietzsche focuses on this problem at the end of *On the Genealogy of Morality*. According to him, the very fact that, until today, "truth was not *allowed* to be a problem" was a "gap in every philosophy," and he took on the "task" of carrying out this criticism. As Nietzsche conclusively remarks, "the value of truth is tentatively to be *called into question*." (GM III 24; KSA 5, p. 401)

In *On the Genealogy of Morality* Nietzsche stresses the importance of this critique of the value of truth – not only for his own late thought, but also, more generally, for Western culture and its anthropology. It is possible to argue that, for Nietzsche, the question of the "will to truth" is the core of the nihilistic process of anthropological degeneration that characterizes European morality, which, according to him, is "to blame if the human type [*Typus Mensch*] never reached his *highest potential power and splendour*." (GM Preface 6; KSA 5, p. 253) That question plays a pivotal role in the editorial and philosophical project that Nietzsche outlines in his late period. In GM III 27, he in fact announces the forthcoming publication of *The Will to Power. Attempt at a Revaluation of all Values*, and refers his readers to the section "History of European Nihilism" of that book, where "the problem of the *meaning* of the ascetic ideal" would have been "addressed more fully and seriously." The actual development of that editorial project has been quite different from Nietzsche's original plan, but at the end of 1888 he still considered it as completed. In his letters, Nietzsche describes the *Revaluation of all values* as the most important "task" he ever dealt with, a task which he is destined to achieve, despite the huge effort it takes. This is also expressed in the *Preface* to *Twilight of the Idols*, a book that Nietzsche writes with the specific aim of preparing his (ideal) readers to the forthcoming *Revaluation*. As known, *Twilight of the Idols* deals with the principles of the Western worldview, the "eternal idols" that Nietzsche attempts to sound out, in order to reveal their fundamental lack of content. These idols are in fact the old truths and beliefs that, since Plato, have been accepted uncritically, and to which nowadays we attribute a metaphysical value: "What the word 'idols' on the title page means is quite simply what had been called truth so far. *Twilight of the Idols* – in plain language: the end of the old truth..." (EH, Twilight of the Idols 1; KSA 6, p. 354)

A critical approach to truth is therefore not merely a theoretical enterprise, for Nietzsche. Truth is not a matter for epistemology, solely; it rather involves the ethical, moral, even the aesthetic plane, for it rests at the basis of the whole European culture. That is why to "tentatively call into question [...] the value of truth" (GM III 24; KSA 5, p. 401) is so important. As Nietzsche argues, both the potentialities and the dangers of the Western worldview are intertwined in the notion of truth. Like a highly radioactive element, that notion has never revealed its destructive power only because no one explored it properly. Meanwhile, it slowly corroded the system it ignited, finally determining the destruction of that system itself. In other words, the collapse of "Christianity *as a morality*" that in GM III 27 Nietzsche announces as imminent, is the direct result of the "two-thousand-year discipline in truth-telling" that animated European culture. Nietzsche describes himself as prophet and privileged spectator of that collapse: for him, the final step will take place when "Christian truthfulness [...] will finally draw the *strongest conclusion*, that *against* itself; this will, however, happen when it asks itself, 'What does all will to truth mean?'." At that moment, concludes Nietzsche, the time will be ready for the last stage of Western culture as we know it: "That great drama in a hundred acts reserved for Europe in the next two centuries, the most terrible, most questionable drama but perhaps also the one most rich in hope..." (GM III 27; KSA 5, p. 410–1)

Nietzsche's view on this issue, however, contains the means for a possible solution of the problem at stake. At the end of the third essay of the *Genealogy*, Nietzsche observes that the "*kernel*" of the ascetic ideal that has dominated Western culture consists in "that unconditional will to truth," in that "faith in a *metaphysical value, a value as such of truth*" which can be encountered in any historical realization of that ideal (GM III 24 and GM III 27). This allows Nietzsche to set the objective of his late task, but also to determine the strategy for achieving that task itself. To call into question the notion of truth, in fact, means to reflect not merely on its theoretical content, but rather on the value that one ordinarily attributes to that content. The fundamental tool to contrast the effects of European morality on the human being (BGE 203) and finally determine the "countermovement" that Nietzsche calls *revaluation of all values* (NL 1887–88, KSA 12, 11[411]), is the type of critical thinking that abandons the "moral prejudice" according to which "the truth is worth more than appearance." (BGE 34; KSA 5, p. 53) This viewpoint is the opposite of the dogmatic conception that Nietzsche attributes to both the Platonic and the Christian view (the latter being "Platonism for the 'people'," BGE Preface; KSA 5, p. 12): it embraces "*perspectivism*, which is the fundamental condition of all life," (BGE Preface; KSA 5, p. 12) and attributes value to human knowledge not as a means to access the reality of things *in themselves*, but rather as an instrument for the preservation of life. At the basis of this viewpoint we find Nietzsche's idea of "perspectivism," which involves a two-fold relativism about human knowledge: firstly, on the "vertical" plane we find a multiplicity of viewpoints; secondly, on the "horizontal" plane, a relative value is attributed to "truths," for they are impermanent, they constantly change along with the conditions of experience (both physiological and cultural). Nietzsche's rejection of the idea of "objective" knowledge (of the very notion of "knowledge," in fact), follows from these observations on the fundamental inconsistency of the ordinary notion of truth. As known, Nietzsche defends a view of knowledge – and a moral conception consistent with that epistemology – according to which the realm of "appearances" is the only dimension within which it is possible to find (temporary) reference points for a theoretical and practical orientation.

Nietzsche's late perspectival thought thus arises as a reaction to a well-defined cultural attitude and consists in a critique to common-sense metaphysics, that is, to the ordinary faith in "logic and the categories of reason" as if one "possessed in them the criterion of truth and *reality*." (NL 1888, KSA 13, 14[153], my translation) In defending this anti-metaphysical view, Nietzsche is extremely consistent with some outcomes of late nineteenth-century science – the same science that in GM III 23 Nietzsche calls the *"most recent and noble manifestation"* of the ascetic ideal. This should not surprise, if one considers that, as it is now widely accepted within the Nietzsche-scholarship, Nietzsche's perspectival thought is inspired by evolutionism as much as by post- and neo-Kantian epistemology. In order to get rid of the remnants of the old metaphysics, modern science in fact developed a new approach to the problem of human knowledge; as a result, the very notion of knowledge was reconceived, and the idea that the value of concepts and theories is merely instrumental gained new upholders. In other words, it seems to be possible to interpret the Nietzschean "death of God" in a less poetic but nevertheless sticking way, namely as a post-positivist disenchantment towards our world-description. Consequently, Nietzsche's view could be compared with other positions following from those same principles, and whose approach to the problem of the value of truth also plays an important role in the history of Western philosophy.

The anti-metaphysical stance pertaining to late nineteenth-century culture is especially expressed by the American pragmatist movement. As William James observed (1909, p. 57), pragmatism arose from the profound transformations that took place in modern epistemology, and can therefore be considered as a reaction to the problem of meaning of scientific truth. In outlining this philosophical position, James especially focuses on the above-mentioned "vertical" relativism about truth, which, for him, follows from the "multiplication of theories" and the development of "so many geometries, so many logics, so many chemical and physical hypotheses." (James 1909, p. 58) Consequently, James argues that in modern times the idea "that even the truest formula may be a human device and not a literal transcript has dawn upon us"; therefore, scientific concepts, laws and theories are now "treated as so much 'conceptual shorthand,' true so far as they are useful but no farther." (James 1909, p. 58) It is worth noting that this view also implies the "horizontal" relativism which one encounters in Nietzsche's perspectivism. James, in facts, agrees with the view defended by representatives of scientific instrumentalism such as

Ernst Mach and Henri Poincaré, who stressed the historical and conventional character of scientific knowledge.

On this basis, it is possible to outline a viable research program aimed at comparing classic American pragmatism and Nietzsche's view. That research program would not try to make a pragmatist out of Nietzsche, but only let him dialogue with a philosophical perspective that – as happened with Nietzsche himself – has been soon simplified and misinterpreted, so that nowadays it is difficult to deal with it properly. As argued by Sergio Franzese (2009, p. 208), one should not be "deceived by the epistemological tone of pragmatism"; rather, it should be considered that "the underlying problem" that pragmatism faces "is the same [as Nietzsche's]: to get rid of metaphysics." The Jamesian approach to the problem of truth, as much as that provided by other early pragmatists, was capable to "produce a quake which shook the foundations of our traditional ontological and moral certainties" (Franzese 2009, p. 208), thus leading to the same outcomes announced by Nietzsche in the *Genealogy of Morality*, namely that "morality will be *destroyed* by the will to truth's becoming-conscious-of-itself." (GM III 27; KSA 5, p. 410)

The comparison between pragmatism and perspectivism will therefore deal with several elements, starting from the framework of these views and their consequences on European culture and its philosophy. But the research must also consider the principles of both James's and Nietzsche's approaches to the problem of truth, as much as their particular aims, that each one of them developed autonomously and in an original way. A fundamental premise concerns also the way pragmatism is approached in this volume, for I will try to take a step back from contemporary interpretations and engage directly with the Jamesian conception. More precisely, I would conceive pragmatism in a broad sense, as an attitude towards the problem of the meaning of truth rather than a method to solve that problem. In other words, what interests me most is the problem itself, the very fact that pragmatists approached that problem, and how (and why) they did it. And I am interested in that because I think that it is in the approach to that problem that the compliance between pragmatism and perspectival thought can be revealed.

One of the principles of classic pragmatism (in the version developed by William James in his 1907 essay) is the rejection of the correspondence conception of truth, the intellectualist idea that "truth" means "agreement with reality." (James 1907, p. 198–9) Accordingly to modern developments of neo-Kantianism, James also criticizes the "naïve realism" defended by common sense, which arises from an uncritical approach to knowledge. Moreover, it can be argued that pragmatism deals in a positive and fruitful way with the epistemological relativism that modern epistemology outlines. A problematic conception, for it can lead to sceptic and nihilistic results of the sort: no truth can be achieved; therefore, our activity cannot provide us with principles of orientation of any sort. But pragmatists aim precisely to avoid this conclusion and pay attention to the practical plane as the dimension where the value of logically irrelevant views can be assessed. This attitude can be found in a variety of positions belonging to the same cultural framework as Peirce's and James's. Such positions can be seen as comparable *strategies* for dealing with the same problem, which is ontological as much as epistemological insofar as it involves questions pertaining to realism vs. instrumentalism. But it also pertains to the field of ethics and morality, for truth is not a merely theoretical issue, and the way we approach the meaning of truth and knowledge strongly influences our life and practical behaviour. Among these forms of pragmatism, we find Ferdinand Schiller's humanism, Ernst Mach's empirio-criticism, and Hans Vaihinger's fictionalism – as well as, of course, Nietzsche's "perspectivism." All these authors – although each one in an original way and according to their own particular purposes – tackled the twilight of Western metaphysics and attempted to find a way out of the maze of relativism. For Nietzsche, this task is extremely important, given the consequences it has on the philosophical and anthropological plane. In his view, future philosophers are precisely "those few [...] whose eyes [are] strong and subtle enough for [...] the greatest recent event – that 'God is dead'." (GS 343; KSA 3, p. 573) These "fearless ones" will react positively to the collapse of Western metaphysics, to the obliteration of the old principles of orientation, which will be for them only the starting point of a new navigation. This is, for Nietzsche, the beginning of a renewed anthropological development of the human being, whose result will be a higher and finally health type of man (*Typus Mensch*).

The five chapters collected in this volume, which can be seen as five different but intertwined approaches to one fundamental problem, will deal with the various issues outlined thus far. The focus of the whole book is Nietzsche's perspectival thought, that is, Nietzsche's attitude towards philosophy that follows from his reflections on perspectivism. In dealing with this view, the framework of Nietzsche's approach to knowledge and truth will be outlined, thus determining the basis of the possible comparison between that approach and American pragmatism. What should be clear since the beginning, is that it is not my aim to argue that Nietzsche was a pragmatist, in the sense of reducing his philosophy e.g. to James's view. On the contrary, I will only try to show the "pragmatist feature" of Nietzsche's thought, a feature that, in my opinion, is far deeper and more substantial than what is ordinarily believed. Moreover, I will argue that Nietzsche's perspectivism and/or his "pragmatism" is not limited to the epistemological question – that is, to the pragmatist conception of truth as it has been traditionally (mis)interpreted by the Nietzsche-scholarship. Nietzsche's view is primarily concerned with European culture and civilization, and his attempt to put up to question the value of truth is in fact the expression of his non-nihilistic attitude toward the general crisis of Western thought, whose consequences can be assessed on both the practical and the anthropological plane.

# 1 Evolutionary Epistemology and the Critique of Truth

> Evolution destroyed the
> final foundations of traditional belief.
> To many people, it was evolution that would
> provide the foundations of a new belief-system.
> Evolution would lead to a deeper and truer
> understanding of the problems of knowledge.
> Ruse 1998, p. 30

Several scholars have explored Nietzsche's view of knowledge, from the very beginning of his reception. The majority of them have stressed his idea that our logical schemes are historically determined and that they played a fundamental role for the preservation of the species. This led some interpreters to consider Nietzsche as a supporter of an "evolutionary epistemology" (an exemplary case is Stack 1992). That view, however, is usually taken in a generic sense, and the interpreters rarely pay attention to the fact that the terminology adopted by Nietzsche only proves that he adhered to the evolutionary viewpoint already widespread in Europe before the publication of Darwin's *On the Origin of Species* – that is, when Darwinian evolutionism was not yet a dominant paradigm in the natural and social sciences. Moreover, Nietzsche scholarship overlooks the fact that, in the contemporary philosophical debate, "evolutionary epistemology" identifies a specific research program, which includes a defined position on the way both cognitive mechanisms (of animals in general and of human beings in particular) and scientific theories are generated and developed. To argue that Nietzsche defended – even only partially – that position is of course possible, but in order to do so it is necessary to compare his considerations on the adaptive value of logical schemes with the guiding-lines of that specific research program.

In the following pages I will engage with this investigation, which seems to be fruitful for several reasons. In terms of content, it leads to two main results. Firstly, it will be possible to clarify to what extent Nietzsche can be counted among the forerunners and early defenders of an evolutionary epistemology. As much as other thinkers of his time – such as Herbert Spencer, Ernst Mach, and William James – Nietzsche supports some of the theses that belong to the research program later formulated in detail by Donald Campbell and Karl Popper, albeit his view differs from that program on some crucial points. The theses that Nietzsche shares with evolutionary epistemologists include, for example, the above-mentioned general evolutionary conception of knowledge, that is, the belief that our logical schemes generated in the same way as other biological traits belonging to an organism. Another, more specific, thesis is that the categories of reason must be conceived as givens established *a priori* for the individual and *a posteriori* for the species.

The second and broader result concerns Nietzsche's attitude towards the notion of truth. The evolutionary conception of knowledge implies a problematization of the traditional view of truth as correspondence to the portion of reality it refers to. That problematization is of great importance for Nietzsche, and it played a fundamental role in the development of his late thought. Also on that point, therefore, it is possible to compare Nietzsche's view and the research program developed by Campbell and Popper.

In addition to these specific results, it is also possible to reflect on the usefulness of comparing Nietzsche's view of knowledge with contemporary evolutionary epistemology, for the sake of an interpretation of his thought. In that case, too, observations can be made both on the general and on the particular level. For example, the investigation to be carried out will highlight the currency of Nietzsche's conception of knowledge and the fact that it can be directly compared with positions discussed within the contemporary philosophical debate. Therefore, the image of Nietzsche that this book aims to outline is not that of a thinker that looks backwards, towards the romantic tradition that of course influenced his education and determined his philosophical interests, but rather primarily a "forward-looking" philosopher, who anticipated some contemporary views. As will be tentatively argued, Nietzsche was a proper son of his time, and from the early years he was inspired by questions that arose in the late nineteenth-century philosophical and scientific debate. That debate involved, among others, authors belonging to the schools of neo-Kantianism as much as Pragmatism, who may be considered as forerunners of contemporary evolutionary epistemology.

This research will therefore allow us to contextualize Nietzsche's observations within a specific epistemological discussion. As mentioned above, that discussion invites us to question the value and meaning of the traditional notion of truth and reflect, for example, on the validity of the scientific description of the world, as well as on the active and creative role of our sense organs. Moreover, the evolutionary conception of human knowledge calls into question the validity of a "correspondentist" epistemology and, as Michael Bradie (1986, p. 444) observes, leads to an "epistemological relativism" according to which "each kind of organism constructs, as it were, an image of reality based on its own needs and capacities." For those reasons, this view is quite closely related to Nietzsche's perspectival epistemology.

## 1.1 A naturalistic approach to epistemology

Although the biological conception of knowledge has been defended in modern time, especially during the nineteenth century, "evolutionary epistemology" is a contemporary concept coined by Donald Campbell in his 1874 seminal paper on the topic. The wide and complex discussion that paper triggered has been recently explored by Michael Bradie (1986 and 2011); given its clarity, the overview he provided can help introducing Campbell's position and, in general, the questions at issue within that debate. Bradie (2011) observes that, broadly speaking, evolutionary epistemology consists of a "naturalistic approach to epistemology, which emphasises the importance of natural selection" for the questions it poses. These issues, continues Bradie, can basically be traced back to the two thematic areas to which the term "epistemology" refers: the one related to the cognitive mechanisms of animal (and especially human) species, and the one related to the development of scientific ideas and theories. Bradie, therefore, argues that

> There are two interrelated but distinct programs which go by the name "evolutionary epistemology." One [EEM] is the attempt to account for the characteristics of cognitive mechanisms in animals and humans by a straightforward extension of the biological theory of evolution to those aspects or traits of animals which are the biological substrates of cognitive activity, e.g. their brains, sensory systems, motor systems, etc. The other program [EET] attempts to account for the evolution of ideas, scientific theories and culture in general by using models and metaphors drawn from evolutionary biology. (Bradie 1986, p. 403)[1]

Both these research lines are grounded on the idea that the animal cognitive capacities are a product of their evolutionary development and can, therefore, be analysed by applying the same principles adopted for the study of the biological features of a species. The model used by the main supporters of evolutionary epistemology is the Darwinian one, which is based on the notion of natural selection. The various positions that have been developed over the years depend on the greater or lesser adherence to that model, and on whether it is taken to be valid in a strictly descriptive sense or, on the contrary, only metaphorically (cf. Bradie 1986, p. 410).

The idea that the model of natural selection can be extended to all human intellectual activities is stated in the opening lines of the essay in which Donald Campbell first defined the notion of "evolutionary epistemology." In that text, published in a collection of papers dedicated to the thought of Karl Popper, Campbell presents some views that he had developed over the years, and that allowed him to reinterpret the model of scientific research defended by Popper in terms of "a natural selection epistemology." (Campbell 1974, p. 413)[2] Campbell starts by considering "man's status as a product of biological and social evolution" and maintaining that "evolution – even in its biological aspects – is a knowledge process, and that the natural-selection paradigm for such knowledge increments can be generalized to other epistemic activities, such as learning, thought, and science." (Campbell 1974, p. 413) Therefore, Campbell focuses on the cognitive mechanisms of the human being in order to reflect on the methodology of scientific research and its actual development. In particular – and

---

[1] I make use of the abbreviations adopted by Bradie (1986): EEM = *evolution of cognitive mechanisms program*; EET = *evolution of theories program*.

[2] Another author of reference for evolutionary epistemology is Stephen Toulmin (1967, 1972) whose position, however, Campbell does not discuss (see Ruse 1998, p. 45–6). Since my argument is based on Campbell's text, and considering that Toulmin basically agrees with the theses of EEM and EET that will be explored, I decided not to deal with this author here.

this demonstrates that Campbell is a quite radical upholder of the second research program identified by Bradie – Campbell argues that it is possible to apply the Darwinian evolutionary model in a strict sense to the process of formation and selection of scientific theories. In fact, his research focuses on the idea that the processes of "blind" or "unjustified" variation and selective preservation, which characterize the acquisition of knowledge in biological organisms, can be encountered in the development of scientific knowledge, too. In other words, according to Campbell, the way in which ideas are produced in a scientist's mind is closely related to the mechanism of random mutation and to the genetic recombinations that take place in the evolution of organisms (Campbell 1974, p. 420–1). Moreover, Campbell holds that even in the case of scientific research one can apply a formula adopted in evolutionary biology, namely 'the greater the number and the variation of attempts, the greater the probability of success.'

As one may guess, this position cannot be easily defended; indeed, several scholars have criticized it (see, for example, Richards 1977, Thagard 1980 and Ruse 1998, chapter 2). As Campbell himself stresses, "an essential connotation of 'blind' is that the variations emitted be independent of the environmental conditions of the occasion of their occurrence." (Campbell 1974, p. 421) Such conditions play a crucial role only in the second phase of the process, when the variations are selected on the basis of their greater or lesser fitness. Even if this idea has proved to work – and quite well – in the case of the development of cognitive mechanisms, its application to the methodology of scientific research is not trivial. Taking the issue to the extreme, it could be argued that the model of blind variations in epistemology implies that, during her research activity, a scientist can elaborate a series of theories without taking into consideration the problem she aims to solve. (Richards 1977, p. 496) But it is also possible to put it simply, and to interpret Campbell as stating just that theories arise before observation, and that the latter is but the "test field" of the former.[3]

This second option is at the basis of Popper's falsificationism, of which Campbell's evolutionary epistemology is a somewhat more detailed reformulation. In his 1974 essay, in particular, Campbell draws from the position expressed by Popper in his *Logic of Scientific Discovery* (1934), in which the inspiration to the Darwinian model of the survival of the kind who happens to be more fruitfully adapted to the environment is particularly clear. Indeed, Popper argues that

> what characterizes the empirical method is its manner of exposing to falsification, in every conceivable way, the system to be tested. Its aim is not to save the lives of untenable systems, but, on the contrary, to select the one which is by comparison the fittest, by exposing them all to the fiercest struggle for survival. (Popper 2002, p. 20)

---

**3** Ruse (1998, p. 58) distinguishes between the moment an idea arises and the time it gets into science. According to Ruse, Campbell admits that there is a directionality in the second case, while insisting that ideas are randomly generated and subsequently selected.

Moreover, according to Popper, in the end "the theory which best holds its own in competition with other theories [is chosen]; the one which, by natural selection, proves itself the fittest to survive." (Popper 2002, p. 91) Over the years, Popper will develop his position in broader and more articulate formulations. However, the general point can basically be summarized as one reads in the *Herbert Spencer Lecture* held in 1961 (later published in Popper 1972), according to which "the growth of knowledge proceeds from old problems to new problems, by means of conjectures and refutations." (Popper 1972, p. 258. Cf. also Popper 1969, chapter 1) In that occasion, Popper reiterated his disagreement with the way in which the scientific community judges the relationship between theory and observation and, against the traditional model of "verification," he set his own idea that a theory, in order to be scientific, must be "falsifiable." In other words, Popper believed precisely

> that a theory – at least some rudimentary theory or expectation – always come first; that it always precedes observation; and that the fundamental role of observations and experimental tests is to show that some of our theories are false, and so to stimulate us to produce better ones. (Popper 1972, p. 258)

According to Popper, who in a 1984 paper titled *Evolutionary Epistemology* reaffirmed his view, the development of scientific research runs through the formulation of theories that are tested by observation, in a way that corresponds strictly to the "trial and error" process that characterizes any biological adaptation to the environment. In defending that view, Popper explicitly refers to the Darwinian model, and stresses the descriptive value of the analogy adopted:

> We are always faced with practical problems; and out of these grow sometimes theoretical problems; for we try to solve some of our problems by proposing theories. In science these theories are highly competitive. We discuss them critically; we test them and we *eliminate* those theories which we judge to be less good in solving the problems which we wish to solve: so only the best theories, those which are most fit, survive in the struggle. [...] This view of the progress of science is very similar to Darwin's view of natural selection by way of the elimination of the unfit: of the errors in the evolution of life, the errors in the attempts at *adaptation*, which is a trial and error process. Analogously, science works by trial (theory making) and by the elimination of the errors. (Popper 1984, p. 240)[4]

---

[4] The reference to the Darwinian context that inspires Popper's outline of evolutionary epistemology is already present in the *Herbert Spencer Lecture*. In that paper, Popper insists especially on the non-metaphorical value of his description of scientific methodology. In fact, Popper argues that "the growth of our knowledge is the result of a process closely resembling what Darwin called 'natural selection'; that is, *the natural selection of hypotheses:* our knowledge consists, at every moment, of those hypotheses which have shown their (comparative) fitness by surviving so far in their struggle for existence; a competitive struggle which eliminates those hypotheses which are unfit. This interpretation may be applied to animal knowledge, pre-scientific knowledge, and to scientific knowledge. What is peculiar to scientific knowledge is this: that the struggle for existence is made harder by the conscious and systematic criticism of our theories. Thus, while animal knowledge and pre-scientific knowledge grow mainly through the elimination of those holding the unfit hypotheses, scientific

Popper states this within the reformulation of his own theory of knowledge in the light of the new notion introduced by Campbell. In the 1984 paper, Popper deals with some critical remarks to his view, and tries to sum it up in five theses. These theses concern in particular "the evolution of human language and the part it has played (and still plays) in the growth of human knowledge; the ideas of truth and falsity; the description of states of affairs; and the way states of affairs are picked out by language from the complexes of facts that constitute the world; that is, 'reality'." (Popper 1984, p. 239) It is not possible (and maybe not so interesting) to deal with Popper's whole argument and his response to his critics. I would only deal with the first two theses he presents in his paper, for they help us to stress his evolutionary conception of both human and scientific knowledge. In particular, the trial-and-error model is reaffirmed in the second one, which concerns the way science develops. For Popper,

> the evolution of scientific knowledge is, in the main, the evolution of better and better theories. This is, again, a Darwinian process. The theories become better adapted through natural selection: they give us better and better information about reality. (They get nearer and nearer to the truth). (Popper 1984, p. 239)

This thesis introduces an interesting issue for the aim of this chapter. Popper speaks of "best theories" and of a gradual and progressive approach to "truth." What does he mean with that? What is the evolutionary epistemologists' view on that matter? A clear and uncontroversial definition of what is meant here by "truth" can be inferred from Popper's 1961 *Herbert Spencer Lecture*. In that text, Popper mentioned the tendency of science to produce unified theories with the "aim of getting nearer to the truth," which he conceives as a *"correspondence with the facts."* (Popper 1972, p. 263–4) The primary purpose of human knowledge, which finds its most refined manifestation in science, is therefore to elaborate hypotheses and theories which are as close as possible to that truth, thus showing their superiority over the other theories in terms of adaptation to the environment – that is, to the facts they aim to describe and explain. According to Popper, "the fittest hypothesis is the one which solves the *problem* it was designed to solve, and which resists criticism better than competing hypotheses. If our problem is a purely theoretical one [...] then the criticism will be regulated by the idea of truth, or of getting nearer to the truth." (Popper 1972, p. 264) It may be argued that Popper entails a strong – perhaps exces-

---

criticism often makes our theories perish in our stead, eliminating our mistaken beliefs before such beliefs lead to our own elimination. This statement of the situation is meant to describe how knowledge really grows. It is not meant metaphorically, though of course it makes use of metaphors." (Popper 1972, p. 261) The passage can be compared with Toulmin's observation (1967, p. 470): "In talking about the development of natural science as 'evolutionary,' I have not been employing a mere *façon de parler*, or analogy, or metaphor. The idea that the historical changes by which scientific thought develops frequently follow an 'evolutionary' pattern needs to be taken quite seriously; and the implications of such pattern of change can be, not merely suggestive, but explanatory."

sive – optimism for the scientific enterprise, defending a scientific realism as much as a purely positivistic view of scientific progress. One cannot deny the fact that Popper is quite confident in the explanatory power of science, but it should not be neglected that the evolutionary perspective itself sets a fundamental limit to the progress of scientific knowledge. As observed by Hahlweg (1986, p. 173), if the metaphor of adaptation is applied strictly to the notion of truth, then one has to admit that, as much as "no organism is ever perfectly adapted, no theory can ever claim to be absolutely true." The scientific process would then consist in a tendency to elaborate theories with an increasing explanatory power, none of which would however be able to fill the gap between the theoretical model and the object it described. In other words, no scientific theory can ever acquire an absolute truth value, no matter how long it has "survived." (Holland/O'Hear 1984, p. 199)

These brief considerations show how problematic the evolutionary model is with respect to the problem of truth, although the concept of "adaptation" involves the idea of an adjustment – if not in terms of mirroring, at least of structural correspondence – with what the hypotheses and theories describe. This is a feature of both EET and EEM: in fact, the evolutionary interpretation of the development of scientific knowledge involves a fundamental metaphysical conception of the human cognitive mechanisms. That view has been defended, before Popper, by Campbell and Konrad Lorenz, and is known as *hypothetical realism*.

## 1.2 Correspondence and adaptation to external reality

To apply the Darwinian model of natural selection to the articulation of scientific research basically means to extend the biological conception of human cognitive mechanisms to a higher intellectual activity. Popper defends that view in the first thesis published in his 1984 paper, a thesis that broadly defines the naturalistic approach to epistemology:

> The specifically human ability to know, and also the ability to produce scientific knowledge, are the result of natural selection. They are also closely connected with the evolution of a specifically human language. (Popper 1984, p. 239)

According to Popper, "this first thesis is almost trivial." But, as a matter of fact, it implies a strong commitment to the relationship between knowledge and reality which is by no means trivial, and which cannot be neglected in defining evolutionary epistemology. Indeed, according to the upholders of that research program, the selection of the human cognitive apparatus which took place throughout the evolutionary history of mankind depended on the actual fitness (or adaptation) of that apparatus to external reality. Gerhard Vollmer is particularly clear on that point: according to him, our cognitive apparatus is a result of evolution. The subjective cognitive structures are adapted to the world because they have evolved, in the course of evolution, in adaptation to that world. And they match (partially) the real structures because only such matching has made such survival possible. (Vollmer 1975, p. 102. I owe this quotation to Bradie 1986, p. 403.)

That position has been defended in particular by Konrad Lorenz (1977, p. 4), according to whom one should "consider human understanding in the same way as any other phylogenetically evolved function which serves the purposes of survival, that is, as a function of a natural physical system interaction with a physical external world." In other words, the human cognitive apparatus would have developed consistently with the reality it describes, in the same way as an organ adapts to the environment (for example, the hoof of a horse to the ground). The fact that the relationship between the cognitive system and the external world is structured in terms of a (even partial) mirroring of the latter by the former, emerges from a previous study in which Lorenz had endorsed the "biologizing" of Kantian categories (Lorenz 1941). The starting point of that research was the idea that our inborn categories of thought fit the *thing in itself*, at least to some degree. Lorenz received and developed that idea, arguing in particular that it should be somehow possible to know the *thing in itself*, but that this could be done only through the categories of thought. Furthermore, he believed that "any validity or appropriateness of the categories to the *Ding an sich* is due to their status as a product of an evolution in which the *Ding an sich* has acted in the editorial role of discarding misleading categories." (Campbell 1974, p. 445) As one can easily see, this conception replicates the evolutionary model, as it conceives an *adaptation* of our cognitive mechanisms to reality, which is achieved through their *selection* by the external environment, depending on the capacity of those mechanisms to adequately reproduce reality. The conclusion of this argument is that "the *a priori* categorical structures which organisms use to form their cognitive pictures of reality are to be understood as the *a posteriori* evolutionary products of phylogenetic development." (Bradie 1986, p. 403–4) This is a crucial outcome, for, as Campbell (1974, p. 443) remarks, "this insight is the earliest and most frequently noted aspect of an evolutionary epistemology, perhaps because it can be achieved from a Lamarckian point of view, as well as from the natural selection model."

Lorenz thus develops an idea that other thinkers before him – e.g. Herbert Spencer – left unanalysed. In dealing with that, however, Lorenz makes other observations which are quite important in order to define contemporary evolutionary epistemology. In the paper on Kantian categories, Lorenz argues that

the realization that all laws of "pure reason" are based on highly physical or mechanical structures of the human central nervous system which have developed through many eons like any other organ, on the one hand shakes our confidence in the laws of pure reason and on the other hand substantially raises our confidence in them. (Lorenz 1941, p. 103)

In fact, even though

> the "keyboard" provided by the forms of intuition and categories [...] is something definitely located on the physicostructural side of the psychophysical unity of the human organism, [...] these clumsy categorical boxes into which we have to pack our external world "in order to be able to spell them as experiences" (Kant) can claim no autonomous and absolute validity whatsoever. (Lorenz 1941, p. 103)

To conceive the categories of reason as evolutionary adapted to the external world, therefore, irreparably undermines their validity. Although they "have proved themselves as working hypotheses in the coping of our species with the absolute reality of the environment" (Lorenz 1941, p. 103), they are nothing more than approximations and *attempts* to reproduce an adequate image of reality. In fact, Lorenz concludes that

> All the knowledge an individual can wrest from the empirical reality of the "physical world-picture" is essentially only a working hypotheses. And, as far as their species-preserving function goes, all those innate structures of the mind which we call "a priori" are likewise only working hypotheses. Nothing is absolute except that which hides in and behind the phenomena. (Lorenz 1941, p. 104)

This approach to human knowledge is two-fold. On the one hand, the existence of an "objective" dimension of the *thing in itself* is admitted, while on the other hand Lorenz maintains that it is not possible to describe it properly, that is, to refer to its actual attributes and features. In other words, as Campbell argues (1974, p. 447), "the *Ding an sich* is always known indirectly, always in the language of the knower's posits [...]. In this sense it is unknowable. But there is an objectivity in the reflection, however indirect, an objectivity in the selection from innumerable less adequate posits." Bradie calls that position "hypothetical realism." Its basic postulate is that "there is an objective world of objects and relations which exists independently of any knowing and perceiving organism. The organisms which inhabit and interact with this world, however, have only indirect, fallible knowledge, which is 'edited' by the 'objective referent'." (Bradie 1986, p. 444) This view prevents the epistemological relativism implied by evolutionary epistemology from turning into an ontological relativism. Indeed, it is possible to admit that "each kind of organism constructs, as it were, an image of reality based on its own needs and capacities" (Bradie 1986, p. 444), and that, consequently, each of them describes the reality in its own way, with its own language. But both Popper and Campbell admit that reality has particular features that cannot be described by any of these possible existing – perspectival – languages. They conceive an objective referent that allegedly underlies the "subjective, provincial, approximate and metaphoric" language of science, which is "never the language of reality in itself." (Campbell 1975, p. 1120) This position is well expressed in another text written by Lorenz, *Behind the Mirror* (1977, p. 7), in which one reads that what we experience [when we look through the "spectacles" of our modes of thought and perception which are "functions of neurosensory organization that has evolved in the service of survival"] is indeed a real image of reality – albeit an extremely simple one, only just sufficing for our practical purposes; we have developed "organs" only for those aspects of reality of which, in the interest of survival, it was imperative for our species to take account, so that selection pressure produced this particular cognitive apparatus.

Thus, by stressing the parallelism with the adaptation of the organs to the environment, Lorenz defines hypothetical realism as the view that

> the categories and modes of perception of man's cognitive apparatus are the natural products of phylogeny and thus adapted to the parameters of external reality in the same way, and for the same reasons, as the horse's hooves are adapted to the praire, or the fish's fins to the water. (Lorenz 1977, p. 37. Both these last excerpts are quoted in Bradie 1986, p. 445)

The example of the horse's hoof (already published in Lorenz 1941, p. 99) makes the whole discourse particularly clear. Furthermore, it shows the actual Darwinian imprint of evolutionary epistemology. Indeed, the fundamental idea is that there is a direct relationship between the developing organ and the environment to which it must adapt, and this connection is so strongly bound that from the organ's observable features one can infer *objective* attributes that pertain to the reality it fits.[5] If, as Lorenz holds, the evolution of the mind complies the development mechanisms of the other parts of the body, then it can be argued that our intellect has been shaped according to the attributes of the world with which it copes. Therefore, a correspondence between our cognitive structures and the structures of reality can be affirmed. Moreover, an investigation of the former can reveal objective, *real* existing features of the latter, although a complete and absolute knowledge of reality cannot be achieved.

Finally, it is possible to see once more that evolutionary epistemology calls into question the value of the ordinary notion of truth. In fact, it "abandons 'literal truth' while retaining the 'goal of truth'," (Bradie 1986, p. 444) as the hypothetical realism defended by Campbell clearly shows. Thus, it can be argued that "while admitting the fallibility of our current theories and the consequent probability that they are not the final truth about the matter, nevertheless [hypothetical realism] does not abandon the idea that there is a final truth to the matter to which our current theories are groping approximation." (Skagestad 1981, p. 85) According to Bradie (1986, p. 447), "hypothetical realism is the view that there is a real world which scientific theories approximately 'fit'. As science 'progresses', it converges on a 'true descrip-

---

5 A particularly interesting example is the "Darwin's Orchid" (*Angraecum sesquipedale*), a flower from whose characteristics Darwin inferred the existence of a specific insect (a lepidopter with a sufficiently long proboscis to be able to collect the nectar from that flower). After Darwin's death that insect has been in fact discovered, thus strengthening the Darwinian theory, for she proved to have predictive and not only descriptive power.

tion' of that world."⁶ Thus, if Campbell defended that view, it is possible to infer that he also rejected the epistemological relativism several authors accepted, at the time. Campbell's insistence in speaking of an *objective* truth, of a *correspondence* with the real features of the external world – to which we have no access, since knowledge is the result of cognitive and perceptive processes – shows us how different his view is from, for example, William James's. The latter, in fact, conceived truth as a relationship between experiences, and admitted that nothing remains to be questioned once the scope and origin of a certain belief is defined.

On the other hand, as has been recently stressed, it is possible to call into question the evolutionary epistemologists' argument for the correspondence between most of our beliefs and reality. Firstly, it can be observed that it "concerns only perceptual knowledge and the inheritable patterns that one encounters at the basis of common-sensical reasoning, while it seems not [...] to be applicable to scientific knowledge." (Buzzoni 2011, p. 81) Moreover – perhaps this observation is broader as much as more relevant – the fundamental view of evolutionary epistemology does not necessarily require that the organs of a species *always* lead to true conclusions. Indeed, as Buzzoni argues (2011, p. 81), it can be admitted "that in some cases even beliefs that we know to be false have proven to be useful for the preservation." This aspect (which is particularly interesting if one deals with Nietzsche's thought) is coherent with some observations developed by Lorenz. In fact, Lorenz can be seen as a realist about the existence of an external world, since he stresses that the selection of a given perceptual scheme depends on its capacity to adapt to the reality it reproduces. On the other hand, however, Lorenz holds that the categories of reason are only "working hypotheses," "approximations" that can never be considered true in the sense of a complete adaptation to the world. Only a "mirroring" of that kind would allow us to speak of a real and objective correspondence of (scientific) knowledge with reality. Finally, Lorenz believes that correspondence to remain unattainable, and it can be argued that it is precisely the metaphor of adaptation, if strictly applied, which leads to that moderate relativism (cf. Hahlweg 1986, p. 173–4).

What has been said so far will be clearer when Nietzsche's thought will be considered. As I will try to show, several points of agreement (and disagreement) between Nietzsche's conception of knowledge and the contents of evolutionary epistemology (in particular, of course, regarding EEM) can be encountered. But, before turning to Nietzsche's view on that matter, other thinkers of his time must be considered, authors whose work Nietzsche knew and who, in various ways, anticipated and influenced Campbell, Lorenz and Popper.

---

6 This idea is consistent with Popper's claim (pronounced in his *Herbert Spencer Lecture*) that science aims to produce unified theories.

## 1.3 Nineteenth-century forerunners

As Campbell observes in his 1974 paper (p. 437), "what we find in Popper [...] is but one type of evolutionary epistemology, perhaps best called a natural selection epistemology. [...] Theories of pre-Darwinian type generated the major evolutionary input into epistemology, even though their acceptance was furthered by the authority of Darwin's work." Therefore, when Nietzsche lived and worked the evolutionary approach to epistemology was a widely discussed issue. The evolutionary model in general, and the Darwinian model in particular, were adopted in many fields, deeply inspiring science, literature, and philosophical studies (see for example Kelly 1981). The authors that Campbell mentions as the most important forerunners of evolutionary epistemology in the nineteenth century include thinkers that Nietzsche knew directly or whose ideas can be meaningfully compared with his own. In this section, I will follow Campbell's paper, that would allow me to cast light on the cultural context of Nietzsche's position and focus on some views that may have influenced him (albeit their influence on Nietzsche was not always direct as it can be).[7]

The first author which is worth considering, and to whom Campbell pays attention, is William James.[8] In the 1880 paper *Great Men, Great Thoughts, and the Environment*, James applies the natural selection model to the view of the blind variation of ideas, as later did Campbell.[9] In that text, James critically discusses some funda-

---

[7] My path will of course differ from Cambpell's on more than one point. I will consider the same authors he indicates as early historical perspectives on evolutionary epistemology, but I will deal with some of them more extensively, given their relevance for my own research. Moreover, I chose to follow a reverse path, from more recent to early thinkers, with the aim of tracing back evolutionary epistemology to her origin, that is, to the general evolutionary and biological conception of knowledge which I believe we can also find in Nietzsche. My purpose is therefore *not* to show that authors such as Herbert Spencer or Friedrich Lange already defended an evolutionary epistemology, but rather to argue that Campbell's and Popper's conception of the development of both human and scientific concepts and theories is an *original* development of ideas elaborated within a context shared by Nietzsche himself. In other words, although it can be shown that the seeds of evolutionary epistemology rest in modern post- and neo-Kantian epistemology, I think that we are not allowed to argue that "evolutionary epistemology" has been defended properly before Campbell. Thus, Nietzsche is not an evolutionary epistemologist, since he only defended that conception *partially*, as most of his sources did.

[8] In this book I will focus almost exclusively on James, among the representatives of the American pragmatist movement. As argued by Massimo Stanzione (1981, p. 26), the pragmatists "applied evolutionary biology to human ideas and emphasised the study of ideas as instruments of the organism." (On this, see also Wiener 1944. In general, on the relationship between Darwinism and pragmatism, cf. Hofstader 1945; Sini 1972; and Franzese 2009, chapter 1.) Moreover, Stanzione (1981, p. 25) stresses that "Peirce, Baldwin and James inferred from the evolutionary perspective the principles that allowed them to develop a theory of human and scientific creativity."

[9] The essay, originally published in *Atlantic Monthly* n. 46 (1880), was then included in *The Will to Believe* (1896) under the title *Great Men and their Environment*. For the purposes of this research, it is worth noting that Nietzsche most likely knew the position defended by James in that essay, for a discussion of it was published in H. Joly, *Psychologie des grands hommes*, which Nietzsche read. A French translation of James's paper was also published in the journal *Critique Philosophique* on

mental ideas of Herbert Spencer, and it is therefore in the light of the latter philosophy that the essay must be interpreted. Firstly, James focuses on the genesis of great men and on the role that brilliant individuals play in the development of society; secondly, he turns his attention to the evolution of the mind, contrasting the Spencerian image of a totally passive mind with the Darwinian conception. James, in particular, observes that Darwin's distinction between "spontaneous variations, as the producer of changed forms, and the environment, as their preserver and destroyer, [does] not hold in the case of mental progress." (James 1992, p. 640)[10] According to James, indeed, the human brain is highly dynamic and continuously active; therefore, it constantly produces images and ideas. Most importantly, all that nervous activity takes place *independently* of the environment, which is why we can speak of *spontaneous or random variations*. (James 1992, p. 643) Thus, the starting point of James's reflection is an evolutionary view of human cognitive mechanisms. From that viewpoint, he argues that

> the new conceptions, emotions, and active tendencies which evolve are originally produced in the shape of random images, fancies, accidental out-births of spontaneous variation in the functional activity of the excessively instable human brain, which the outer environment simply confirms or refutes, adopts or rejects, preserves or destroys – selects, in short, just as it selects morphological and social variations due to molecular accidents of an analogous sort. (James 1992, p. 641)

On the basis of these naturalistic and biological reflections, which are fully consistent with EEM, James elaborates a conception of the development of scientific research that largely anticipates Campbell's position on "blind variations," thereby also defending EET. In fact, James argues that scientific ideas and theories arise spontaneously and completely at random in the researcher's mind. In addition to the fact that each brain constantly produces a great amount of ideas, James observes that the same intuition in the mind of two different researchers would not produce the same result. That is, therefore, a highly "unstable" situation – to say it in the language of chemistry – which does not allow for any form of prediction based on the (physical or intellectual) environment within which a given theory is developed. Thus, as James conclusively remarks,

> the conceiving of the [scientific] law is a spontaneous variation in the strictest sense of the term. It flashes out of one brain, and no other, because of the instability of that brain in such as to tip and upset itself in just that particular direction. But the important thing to notice is that the good flashes and the bad flashes, the triumphant hypotheses and the absurd conceits, are on exact quality in respect of their origins. (James 1992, p. 642–3)

---

January 22–29 and February 5, 1881 (I owe to Giuliano Campioni 2009, p. 43, this information). A commentary on James's paper can be found in Franzese (2009, p. 41–3 and 73 ff.)

**10** The idea that the mind is the product of the random and spontaneous variation of natural development is reaffirmed by James in the concluding chapter of his *Principles of Psychology* (1890), *Necessary Truths and the Effects of Experience*.

Other authors in addition to James used the image of "trial and error" or "blind variation" to describe the creative character of the human intellect. Campbell (1974, p. 428 ff.) cites, for example, Alexander Bain, William S. Jevons, and Henri Poincaré, whose thought, unfortunately, cannot adequately be explored here. Conversely, it is worth dealing with Ernst Mach, a referential figure of the late nineteenth- and early twentieth-century epistemology, who deeply influenced James and was known by Nietzsche.[11]

It can be demonstrated that, like James, Mach adhered to both EEM and EET, paying special attention to the latter. Moreover, the way Mach refers to the Darwinian model, insisting on the non-metaphorical value of its application to epistemology, makes his view akin to Popper's in several respects.[12] An introduction to Mach's *biological theory of knowledge* is provided by Milič Čapek, who in a 1968 paper investigated Mach's epistemological conception in the light of Herbert Spencer's (Čapek 1968, p. 172).[13] For Čapek, Mach's theory of knowledge is "the belief that the cognitive functions of the human mind are not static and immutable entities but, like all other physical and psychological features of man, are subject to gradual growth and development." (Čapek 1968, p. 172) Čapek focuses on Mach's adhesion to Spencer's conception (which makes him akin to the early Poincaré), in order to stress two well-defined points. Firstly, he holds that Mach accepted the idea that the process of adaptation of the human mind to the external environment was complete (this is a controversial statement whose further discussion would lead us beyond the scope of the present research). In fact, Čapek argues that Mach "was firmly convinced that the present – or rather the 19th century – structure of the human mind reflected more or less faithful and without serious distortions the structure of the reality independent of the human mind." (Čapek 1968, p. 173 – 4)[14] The second aspect that char-

---

**11** Mach's influence on James concerns especially two issues. The first one is the approach to the relation of the physical to the psychical, which both Mach and the late James (the James of the *Essays in Radical Empiricism*) explored from a point of view that Bertrand Russell (1921, 1927) called "neutral monism" (cf. Banks 2003, chapters 7 and 9; and Banks 2014). The second issue is purely epistemological and involves the evaluation of concepts in terms of truthfulness and falsity. As will be thoroughly argued in the fifth chapter of this volume, James's pragmatist conception of truth – which in several respects can be compared with Nietzsche's – was in fact deeply inspired by Mach's epistemology. Finally, we know that Nietzsche bought the first edition of Mach's *Analysis of Sensations* (*Beiträge zur Analyse der Empfindungen*), but only after 1886, that is, when he already developed and expressed his view on human knowledge. On Nietzsche's interest in Mach and on the possibility of comparing their views, see for example Hussain 2004b; Gori 2009a and 2012a.
**12** An element of comparison, in this sense, is Mach's observation that "science in its development moves among surmises and parables, there is no denying it; but the more it approaches perfection, the more it goes over into description of fact only." (Mach 1976 [1905], p. 181)
**13** On Mach's theory of knowledge see also Banks 2003; Gori 2009a, p. 18 ff.; and Gori 2018b.
**14** Campbell criticizes Čapek's conclusion, and argues that the latter "attribution to Mach of Spencer's belief in the completeness and perfection of the evolutionary process is contradicted by this quotation from Mach's contemporary, Boltzmann, 'Mach himself has shown in a most ingenious way that no theory is either absolutely true or absolutely false, and that, moreover, every theory is constantly

acterizes Čapek's interpretation of Mach's evolutionary approach to epistemology concerns the *a priori* validity of concepts. For Čapek, Mach thinks that concepts are the result of the evolutionary development of the species, and they are *a priori* only for the individual subject. (Čapek 1968, p. 178)[15] Finally, Čapek argues that, for Mach, "none of [our concepts] is inborn in the Kantian sense;" on the contrary, all of them, "even those which are the most abstract, are the result of adaptive experience." (Čapek 1968, p. 177–8)

This epistemological conception, clearly inspired by the evolutionary theory widely popularized during the second half of the nineteenth century, is developed by Mach in an original way and thus applied to the methodology of scientific research. The result of that reflection is what Mach, in his 1910 article written on the occasion of the controversy with Max Planck,[16] calls a "biological-economical representation of epistemology":

> I had become acquainted with the teaching of Lamarck from my esteemed teacher F. X. Wessely already in 1854 while a *Gymnasium* pupil. This made it easy for me to accept Darwin's ideas on evolution which were published in 1859. These ideas were already present in my Graz lectures from 1864 to 1867, and were expressed through conceiving the competition of scientific thoughts as a life and death struggle resulting in the survival of the fittest. This view does not contradict my theory of economy, but helps enlarge it by merging it into a biological-economical representation of epistemology. Expressed in the briefest way, the task of scientific knowledge appears to be: *Fitting thoughts to facts and thoughts to each other*. (Mach 1991, p. 133–4)[17]

The idea that the development of scientific research can be described as a process of mutual adaptation between facts and thoughts, follows from Mach's fundamental view of human knowledge, according to which our thoughts fit experiences in the same way as the organisms fit the environment. An entire chapter of *Knowledge and Error* (1976 [1905]) is dedicated to the *adaptation of thought to facts and to each other*. In that chapter, Mach argues that "ideas gradually adapt to facts by picturing them with sufficient accuracy to meet biological needs," although, due to several reasons, "the accuracy goes no further than required by immediate interests and

---

being improved just as are organisms as described by Darwin'." (Campbell 1974, p. 455) On Mach's epistemological position and his conclusion that concepts do not have an absolute truth-value, see below in this section.

15 Cf. Mach (1895, p. 222): "It is not to be denied that many forms of thought were not originally acquired by the individual, but were antecedently formed, or rather prepared for, in the development of the species, in some such way as Spencer, Haeckel, Hering, and others have supposed, and as I myself have hinted on various occasions."

16 For a history of this article, see Guzzardi 2002.

17 To understand the conception of the "competition of scientific thought" that Mach lectured in Graz between 1864 and 1867, one can read his paper *Die Geschwindigkeit des Lichtes* (1866), later included in the *Popular Scientific Lectures* (1895): "Slowly, gradually, and laboriously one thought is transformed into a different thought, as in all likelihood one animal species is gradually transformed into new species. Many ideas arise simultaneously. They fight the battle for existence not differently than do the Ichtyosaurus, the Brahman, and the horse." (Mach 1895, p. 63)

circumstances." (Mach 1976 [1905], p. 120) Since these interests and circumstances vary from case to case, continues Mach, "the adaptive results do not quite match," and this requires a "mutual correction of the pictures to adjust the deviations in the best and most profitable way." (Mach 1976 [1905], p. 120)[18] What remains unclear in these pages is what Mach actually means when he talks of "adaptation." To understand this – and, therefore, to see to what extent Mach's epistemology adheres to the natural selection model – one must take into account the lecture *Transformation and adaptation in scientific thought*,[19] where Mach deals with Darwin's theory.

Mach mentions Darwin in the very beginning of his speech. Just a few decades after the popularization of Darwin's ideas, Mach writes, "yet, already we see his ideas firmly rooted in every branch of human thought, however remote. Everywhere, in history, in philosophy, even in the physical sciences, we hear the watchwords: heredity, adaptation, selection." (Mach 1895, p. 217) The impact of Darwinian theory on scientific culture has been profound, and it rapidly changed the way several different disciplines approached their objects of study. Based on this, it is legitimate to apply that model to the study of cognitive processes and, by extension, to the investigation of scientific knowledge. Mach continues:

> I wish simply to consider the growth of natural *knowledge* in the light of the theory of evolution. For knowledge, too, is a product of organic nature. And although ideas, as such, do not comport themselves in all respects like independent organic individuals, and although violent comparisons should be avoided, still, if Darwin reasoned rightly, the general imprint of evolution and transformation must be noticeable in ideas also. (Mach 1895, p. 217–8)

What is worth stressing, in this passage, is the consideration of human knowledge as a "product of organic nature." This idea, which Mach applies to cognitive mechanisms as well as to scientific knowledge (since he conceives the latter as a more elaborate version of the former), leads us to evolutionary epistemology, and shows that Mach adhered to both EEM and EET.[20] Moreover, in perfect agreement with Popper, Mach seems to adopt the model of natural selection in the strict (not metaphorical)

---

[18] In the same section, Mach also defines *observation* as "adaptation of thoughts to facts," and *theory* as "mutual adaptation of thoughts." (Mach 1976 [1905], p. 120) Furthermore, he remarks that theory and observation influence each other.

[19] The conference, held in 1883 on the occasion of Mach's rectorship at the University of Prague, has been published in two slightly different versions in *Popular Scientific Lectures* (1895) and in *Principien der Wärmelehre* (1896).

[20] The extension of EEM to EET is better clarified in the version of this conference published in *Principles of the Theory of Heat* (*Principien der Wärmelehre*). In that volume, Mach observes that "our entire psychical life, and especially our scientific life consists in a continual revision of our notions. [...] Thoughts are organic processes. The alteration of our mode of thinking is the most delicate reagent for our organic development that there is, and this development, when we regard it from this point of view, is immediately certain to us. [...] Thus, our whole scientific life appears to us as one side merely of our organic development." (Mach 1986 [1896], p. 358)

sense, focusing on a particular aspect of the parallelism between ideas and physical features of an organism:

> The ideas that have become most familiar through long experience, are the very ones that intrude themselves into the conception of every new fact observed. In every instance, thus, they become involved in a struggle for self-preservation, and it is just they that are seized by the inevitable process of transformation. Upon this process rests substantially the method of explaining by hypothesis new and uncomprehended phenomena [...] We substitute for new ideas distinct and more familiar notions of old experience – notions which to a great extent run unimpeded in their courses, although they too must suffer partial transformation. The animal cannot construct new members to perform every new function that circumstances and fate demand of it. On the contrary it is obliged to make use of those it already possesses. When a vertebrate animal chances into an environment where it must learn to fly or swim, an additional pair of extremities is not grown for the purposes. On the contrary, the animal must adapt and transform a pair that it already has. (Mach 1895, p. 228–9)

According to Mach, the process through which ideas adapt to facts (and to each other) takes place in the same way as when an organism adapts its members to a new environment. Just as, under certain circumstances, the function of an organ simply changes, without the organ atrophying,[21] so scientific theories that, from time to time, have to account for the new data collected empirically, are not eliminated but corrected, integrated, and therefore improved in terms of explanatory capacity. Everything is part of an "economic" conception of scientific thought and activity, that is, the idea that concepts are schematizations of complex facts, thus making possible an efficient management and communication of knowledge. In order to be successful in the struggle for survival, therefore, a new theory must offer us a broader and simpler explanation, gathering a greater amount of data than the previous theories, without losing operational efficacy and predictive power.

The consequences of the model adopted by Mach in epistemology concern primarily the value of (scientific) concepts. These are the product of a given historical and cultural epoch, and therefore are subject to a development which is mainly historical (see Mach 1911 [1872]). According to Mach – he repeatedly stressed this point in his works – the function of the notions adopted both in the ordinary description of the world and in the "high-level" investigation of the kind pursued by the most advanced scientific research, is essentially to gather information and sets of events. No ontological or metaphysical value can be attributed to those notions; that is, we must not conceive our conceptualization as an expression of the "truth" of things. This ob-

---

[21] Cf. Darwin 2008, p. 143: "An organ originally constructed for one purpose [...] may be converted into one for a wholly different purpose." The term "exaptation" has been recently adopted in the case of physical characteristics performing a function different from the one for which they were selected (see Gould/Vrba 1982). Darwin's example (2008, p. 143) is that of the swimbladder in fishes, which originally had a hydrostatic function (flotation) and was subsequently used for respiration. Another example is that of birds' feathers, developed by natural selection for thermal insulation (*adaptation*), to be subsequently used to fly (*exaptation*).

servation leads us back to the above-mentioned correspondence theory of truth. Although Mach's view is closer to Campbell's and Lorenz's hypothetical realism than to a radical form of nominalism, one can argue that he still denies that concepts can adequately reproduce the reality they only describe. Moreover, Mach seems not even interested in facing the problem of whether we may have any access to an objective knowledge – whether we can reach the plane of the *reality* of things, the realm of the *thing in itself* – or we are stuck within the boundaries of our intellectual mechanisms (cf. Mach 1959, p. 30). According to Mach, concepts are involved in a process of adaptation to facts and of reciprocal adaptation that – as seen also in the case of Popper or, even better, of Lorenz, who argues that our categories are merely "working hypotheses" – never leads to a final stage of complete (that is, *objective*) mirroring. As Mach conclusively remarks (Mach 1976 [1905], p. 102), "although concepts are not mere words, but are rooted in facts, one must beware of regarding concepts and facts as equivalent, confusing one with the other." Concepts "bear the imprint of the culture of their period," and, furthermore, they "must always be expected to incur correction by the facts." Finally, and maybe most importantly, "one cannot assume that our concepts correspond to absolute constancies, since enquiry can find only constantly conjoined reactions."[22]

Speaking of the power of our concepts to provide us with a *true* account of the external world, a power which the evolutionary model strongly limits, rather leading us to a form of epistemological relativism, another prominent figure among the precursors of evolutionary epistemology should be mentioned, thus further enriching Nietzsche's philosophical context. Herbert Spencer, to whom both Mach and (albeit polemically) James made reference, cannot be left aside, indeed.[23] For Campbell (1974, p. 437 ff.), Spencer is in fact the main spokesman of an epistemology based on natural selection. Furthermore, Spencer's view exemplifies a non-Darwinian evolutionary approach to human knowledge that had become dominant around 1890. Roughly speaking, one can say that Spencer believed that our cognitive mechanisms

---

**22** The evolutionary model therefore imbues the criticism of metaphysical knowledge that Mach defended throughout his research. According to him, "metaphysical" are those concepts that are isolated from the historical path of their creation, and which therefore one ordinarily attributes an absolute value (see on this Gori 2014, and below in this volume, chapter 5). In *Transformation and Adaptation in Scientific Thought*, Mach defends a position that can be compared with James's and Campbell's shared view of the "blind variations" of ideas. In fact, Mach argues that "the construction of a hypotheses is not the product of artificial scientific methods. This process is unconsciously carried on in the very infancy of science. Even latter, hypotheses do not become detrimental and dangerous to progress except when more reliance is placed on them than on the facts themselves; when the contents of the former are more highly valued than the latter, and when, rigidly adhering to hypothetical notions, we overestimate the ideas we possess as compared with those we have to acquire." (Mach 1895, p. 229)

**23** As known, Spencer was known and discussed also by Nietzsche. But he only read Spencer's *Principles of Sociology*, and not the *Principles of Psychology* where Spencer expressed his epistemological conception.

have evolved by adapting to the external environment, and defended a conception of the mind as a *passive* mirror of that environment. This view is problematic, as the above quoted James's critical remarks already showed. In fact, Spencer's endorsing a specific version of the Lamarckian theory prevents him from achieving the most important goal of evolutionary epistemology, that is, to call into question the ordinary conception of truth. As Campbell observes (1974, p. 437),

> What Spencer missed was the profound indirectness of knowing necessitated by the natural selection paradigm, and the inevitable imperfection and approximate character of both perceptual and scientific knowledge at any stage. Instead, believing that an infinitely refinable and sensitive human cognitive apparatus had in the course of evolution adapted perfectly to the external environment, he became a naïve realist accepting the givens of the cognitive processes as fundamentally valid.

Beyond the difficulties raised by this form of realism, Spencer adheres to EEM in many respects. According to Campbell's reconstruction, indeed, he not only supports a biological conception of our cognitive mechanisms, but also defends the idea that the adaptation of these mechanisms to the environment consists in their ability to reflect external data in an increasingly refined manner. Spencer's position should therefore be considered as an anticipation of the "biologizing of Kant" later endorsed by Lorenz, which, according to Bradie (1986, p. 403), links EEM and EET. In fact, Spencer's view allows one to extend the evolutionary model from the cognitive to the epistemological level.[24] Therefore, it can be argued that Spencer agrees with evolutionary epistemology in rejecting "any view of an *ipso facto* necessarily valid synthetic a priori." (Campbell 1974, p. 441) For Höffding 1955, contrarily to that conception, in his *Principles of Psychology* (1855) Spencer applies for the first time the genetic and evolutionary model to the study of the mind. Höffding, in particular, argues that for Spencer

> those conditions and forms of knowledge and of feeling which are original in the individual, and hence cannot be derived from his experience, have been transmitted by earlier generations. The forms of thought correspond to the collective and inherited modifications of structure which are latent in every new-born individual, and are gradually developed through his experience. (Höffding 1955, p. 475; quoted in Campbell 1974, p. 443)

In other words, Spencer holds that the categories of reason are *a priori* for the individual, but *a posteriori* for the species.

That thesis is particularly important, and allows us to include Spencer among the precursors of evolutionary epistemology although his position is not perfectly consistent with the two research programs outlined by Bradie. Indeed, one must admit that

---

[24] This passage is well described in Wuketits 1984, p. 8f.: "Since the human mind is a product of evolution, [...] the evolutionary approach can be extended to the *products of mind*, that is to say to epistemic activities such as *science*."

Spencer is not an evolutionary epistemology in the contemporary sense, but his biological conception of knowledge is close enough to that defended by proper evolutionary epistemologists – and, most importantly, expressly discussed by them – to consider him as a forerunner of that view. The most important difference rests on Spencer's evolutionary model, which is not the Darwinian one followed by both Popper and Campbell. But it is also possible to argue that the seeds of evolutionary epistemology do not pertain to evolutionism only. A biological interpretation of the intellectual process and the fundamental idea that the categories of reason are the product of a well-defined physiological structure have been developed by other authors who in the first half of the nineteenth century discussed Kantian epistemology.

As a final step of what has been explored so far, and in order to finally introduce Nietzsche, it is worth mentioning two authors that fall within that line of thought: Friedrich A. Lange and Hermann von Helmholtz.[25] The first of them, author of the fundamental *History of Materialism* ($^1$1866, $^2$1875) that deeply influenced Nietzsche,[26] was one of the most important supporters of neo-Kantianism. His research focused in particular on the physiology of perception, and aimed to analyse some of the psychological issues left open by Kant by relying on the most recent results of the natural sciences.[27] Starting from these premises, Lange rejected the innate character of categories, rather seeing them as the product of the psycho-physiological structure of the mind. Anticipating the subsequent investigation carried out by Lorenz, Lange explicitly aimed to "translate Kant's *Critique of Pure Reason* in physiological terms, thus making it more comprehensible." (Lange 1882 [1875], vol. 2, p. 69)

The last step of this "reverse path" tracing evolutionary epistemology back to its nineteenth-century inspirations is Helmholtz, one of Lange's most important precursors and main reference (and, for that reason, also well-known to Nietzsche; cf. e.g. Reuter 2006). The main reason Helmholtz is worth to be mentioned in this rough outline of Campbell's conception is that he held a position that was consistent with Spencer's.[28] In his paper on Mach's biological theory of knowledge, Čapek especially stresses this compliance, and argues that Helmoltz "explicitly challenged Kant's view that the axioms of Euclid are *a priori* necessities of thought." (Čapek 1968, p. 175) In so doing, Čapek continues, Helmholtz elaborated a psycho-physiological reinterpre-

---

[25] My aim in this section is only to outline Campbell's evolutionary epistemology and the framework out of which it arose. For that reason, I will not explore Lange's and Helmholtz's view of knowledge thoroughly, although that would be an interesting research to be done within the Nietzsche scholarship. What interests me here is just to show that evolutionary epistemology rests on some modern developments of Kantianism, which are not evolutionary epistemologies themselves. In the next section, I will turn to Nietzsche and explore his view, in order to discuss how much it is consistent with Campbell's and if Nietzsche only defends a general biological conception of knowledge. The way neo-Kantianism has been debated at Nietzsche's time and to what extent it influenced him are two interesting topics which I prefer to leave for another study.
[26] Cf. Stack 1983 and Salaquarda 1978.
[27] Cf. Martinelli 1999, p. 52–3, and Lehmann 1987.
[28] See Helmholtz 1921 and 1924, vol. 2.

tation of Kant's categories of reason – which, for Čapek, is not adequately supported by an evolutionary explanation. Čapek conclusively remarks that

> if the *a priori* forms are merely parts of our psycho-physiological organization, and if this organization is our phylogenetic heritage – and both of these theses were accepted by Helmholtz – can we escape Spencer's conclusion that "what is *a priori* for an individual is *a posteriori* for a species"? Although this conclusion has never been formulated by Helmholtz, he could have hardly rejected it. (Čapek 1968, p. 175–6)

These last examples show that the fundamental ideas endorsed by evolutionary epistemology arose in a context in which human knowledge was a widely debated issue, and within which a naturalistic inquiry of mind and thought – though not necessarily based on the evolutionary model – had already called into question the value of logical and categorial forms. The evolutionary conception of knowledge therefore found an environment favourable to its diffusion, as well as an intellectual milieu prepared to draw its philosophical consequences. The limitation of the truthfulness of ordinary notions, and the consequent relativization of their explicative power, fell within – and, in some respects, ignited – the crisis of the Western world view the European intellectuals faced in the late nineteenth century. It is within that context that Nietzsche developed his ideas, and his engagement with Kant, the Kantian and, especially, the neo-Kantian legacy cannot be underestimated anymore. Several souls coexisted in Nietzsche, and the stances expressed in his writings came from various fields of interest. Among them, modern epistemology and the studies on the physiology of the sense organs play an important role. Nietzsche merged them with the widespread evolutionary ideas that he encountered in the writings of both supporters and critics of Darwin and, as a result, he developed a philosophical reflection well anchored to his time which provides an original look at the cultural development of Western civilization.

## 1.4 The biological usefulness of knowledge

What can be said about Nietzsche in the light of what has been argued so far? He certainly did not adhere to EET. Although in his writings one finds observations on the value of the scientific world-description, it can be argued that the question about the way scientific theories are created and developed – in the strict sense debated by Popper, Logical Empiricists and contemporary philosophers of science – did not interest him.[29] For what concerns EEM, things are rather different. In dealing

---

[29] In his writings, Nietzsche demonstrates to take care of the way our knowledge and world-description come to be held, but this is not the same interest that contemporary epistemologists devote to science. Bradie's EET concerns the way science develops and the relationship between new and old theories. Of course, this is grounded on a broader account of human knowledge and implies questions on the value, fruitfulness and operational efficiency of natural laws and scientific concepts,

## 1.4 The biological usefulness of knowledge — 27

with human knowledge, Nietzsche famously expresses some statements which are consistent with that research program, even though he never defended the crucial ideas of contemporary evolutionary epistemology. The following remarks therefore aim to discuss whether one can properly speak of "evolutionary epistemology" in describing Nietzsche's view of knowledge (that is, whether he can be included among the forerunners of that conception), or if such an assumption would be a false inference from the textual evidences which instead merely account for Nietzsche's adherence to a general biological conception of knowledge.

First things first. Let's start from two of the best-known passages in which Nietzsche deals with the question of knowledge from an evolutionary point of view. The first one is *Gay Science* 110 (*Origin of Knowledge*), an aphorism in which Nietzsche argues that the human intellect has a fundamental role for the preservation of life, and considers the product of its activity from an instrumental point of view. In particular, Nietzsche observes that the ordinary view affirming the existence of substantial entities, free will and a universal "good in itself" are only "erroneous articles of faith" inherited in the course of the evolutionary history of mankind, and that have been preserved due to their usefulness for life. "Through immense periods of time – argues Nietzsche – the intellect produced nothing but errors; some of these turned out to be useful and species-preserving; those who hit upon or inherited them fought their fight for themselves and their progeny with greater luck." (GS 110; KSA 3, p. 469) Therefore, according to Nietzsche, the value of the notions elaborated by our intellect must be judged in the light of their fruitfulness as species-preserving tools. That is, they merely have an instrumental value.

This leads us to a particularly important issue, which is actually crucial for what will be further argued in this section. The idea that the truth-value of the products of intellectual activity is not a matter of correspondence between our world-description and external reality is grounded on a view contrasting the very idea of "*adaequatio rei*," as Nietzsche repeatedly shows.[30] As will be argued, it is possible to say that, in talking of "errors," Nietzsche refers to the fact that our concepts do not *correspond* to the external world, that is, they do not reproduce it *adequately*. In fact, Nietzsche believes that our cognitive activity implies that we constantly intervene on the external data, modifying them both through our senses and through our intellect. For example, in the 1881 notebooks (the year in which he was working on *The Gay Science*) Nietzsche argues that this mechanism belongs to human physiology and, consequent-

---

which one can also find in Nietzsche. But EET works, so to say, at a secondary level, which is grounded on the biological and cultural account of knowledge Nietzsche is primarily concerned with. The primary level is that of EEM, which is in fact the research program which can be compared with Nietzsche's view, as I will show in what follows.

**30** Nietzschean critique of the "correspondence theory" has been widely debated. See for example Danto 1965, p. 54ff.; Grimm 1977; Stack 1981a; Figl 1982, p. 181ff.; Wilcox 1986; Simon 1989, p. 244ff.; Clark 1991, chapters 2 and 4; Gemes 1992; and Cox 1999, p. 28ff.

ly, we cannot bypass it.³¹ With that in mind, Nietzsche reflects on the dichotomy between truth and error, and elaborates a new definition of these notions focused on the role played by the intellectual products on the preservation of the species. He then claims that the kind of knowledge which prevails over the others, thus becoming part of the conceptual system that will be inherited by future generations, is not the one that provides us with a better – i.e. *more adequate* – access to reality, but rather the most beneficial for our orientation in the world. The value which is attributed to a given knowledge, to a given notion, therefore only reflects its fruitfulness and operational efficacy in the struggle for survival.³² In other words, as Nietzsche concludes, "the *strength* of knowledge lies not in its degree of truth, but in its age, its embeddedness, its character as a condition of life." (GS 110; KSA 3, p. 469)

Nietzsche develops these reflections in GS 111, *Origin of the Logical*. In that aphorism, too, Nietzsche adopts the terminology of evolutionism, talking about preservation and struggle for survival. In his opinion, "all the foundations for logic" arose from the usefulness in species-preserving that a certain type of knowledge proved to have. That knowledge is the one affirming the existence of unchanging substantial elements, that is, "the predominant disposition to treat the similar as identical – an illogical disposition, for there is nothing identical as such." (GS 111; KSA 3, p. 471) That tendency, concludes Nietzsche, favoured the adaptation of the human being, and guaranteed him a greater "probability of survival."

In these sections Nietzsche reflects on human cognitive mechanisms from an evolutionary point of view but he does not go into detail, providing elements that allow us to explore his view thoroughly. Nietzsche speaks of preservation of the species, of survival, but, for example, he never mentions "natural selection." For what concerns the development of the "errors" produced by the intellect, we are in the same situation: although the content of GS 110 suggests that Nietzsche could have conceived the idea of a random production of concepts and notions of various kinds, which are subsequently selected on the bases of their usefulness for the species, the Darwinian model is never outlined clearly.³³ If one wants to discuss

---

**31** For instance, Nietzsche wrote that, "in order to make any kind of knowledge possible, an unreal world had to arise, the world of errors. [...] This error cannot be extinguished without extinguishing life, too: [...] our ORGANS (for *life*) are structured for the error." Moreover, in the same fragment he observes: "To live is necessary for knowing. To err is necessary for living. [...] We must love and cultivate the error, for it is the matrix of our knowledge." (NL 1881, KSA 11, 11[162]; my translation)
**32** Nietzsche reaffirms that position in a posthumous note from the period of the *Gay Science*: "The *life preserving principle* consists in fact in the way the first organic forms perceived the externa stimuli and judged what was outside themselves: that belief prevailed and preserved *what made it possible to continue living: not the truest, but the most useful belief.*" (NL 1881, KSA 9, 11[270]; my translation)
**33** There is little textual evidence to support the idea that the evolutionary model which Nietzsche refers to is the Darwinian one. For instance, in the 1881 note 11[270] (which is another draft version of what Nietzsche later published in GS) Nietzsche states that cognitive error is necessary for a species to be preserved. The way in which organisms originally reacted to the stimuli of the external environment is defined as "the life-preserving principle," and the error is called "the father of life." At the

Nietzsche's adhesion to EEM, only two points can be explored: a) the consideration of human knowledge from an evolutionary point of view; b) the reiterated affirmation of the "erroneous" character of the products of our cognitive activity, and the claim that their truth-value is based on their usefulness for the species. As will be argued, if a) constitutes a point of contact with EEM, as it involves a reflection on the becoming nature of Kantian categories, b) is not consistent with the restricted application of the adaptive model, according to which the cognitive mechanisms should at least fit the structure of external reality.

Nietzsche reflected on both these elements since his early years, as *On Truth and Lie in an Extra-Moral Sense* and the first volume of *Human, All Too Human* show. In the famous text from 1873, that Nietzsche left unpublished and that appeared only after his death, Nietzsche addresses for the first time some fundamental questions on language which he dealt with in his later writings. Among them, particularly interesting for the present research is Nietzsche's idea – inspired by Schopenhauer – that our intellect plays a fundamental role in the preservation of life.[34] According to Nietzsche, in fact, the capacity to cognitively manage the world has been fundamental in the struggle for survival, for it allowed mankind not to succumb to animals naturally endowed with organs far more lethal than the ones our species inherited:

> The intellect, as a means of preserving the individual, unfolds its main powers in dissimulation [*Verstellung*]; for dissimulation is the means by which the weaker, less robust individuals survive, having been denied the ability to fight for their existence with horns or sharp predator teeth. (TL; KSA 1, p. 876)

Nietzsche thus develops his first epistemological considerations with reference to a general evolutionary position, and this already can help us to discuss the consistency between his view and the research program later formulated by Campbell. But the above quoted passage contains something more which is worth stressing, namely an observation concerning the intellectual relationship of the human being with the external world. In fact, Nietzsche claims "dissimulation" to be the characteristic activity of the intellect, and maintains that this allows mankind to win the struggle for life. That view is closely related to the perhaps most famous passage of *On Truth and Lie on an Extra-Moral Sense*, namely the definition of truth as "a mobile army of metaphors, metonymies, anthropomorphisms, in short, a sum of human relations which have been poetically and rhetorically intensified, transferred, decorated and which, after lengthy use, seem firm, canonical and binding to a people." (TL;

---

end of this note, Nietzsche observes that "this *fundamental error* must be seen – must be imagined! – as a sheer *chance!*" On this, see Gori 2009a, p. 9–10.

**34** In *The World as Will and Representation* I, § 27, for example, Schopenhauer describes knowledge as "a means for both individual- and species-preserving, like any other organ of the body" (my translation). An evolutionary theory can be also encountered in *Parerga and Paralipomena*, another text that Nietzsche knew quite well, and that inspired *On Truth and Lie in an Extra-Moral Sense*. See on this Lovejoy 1911; Stack 1992, p. 76; and Gori 2009a, p. 42–3.

KSA 1, p. 880) As known, in this early writing Nietzsche discusses for the first time the ordinary confidence in human knowledge, that is, the belief that she produces "truths" to be conceived as *adequately corresponding* to the reality they reproduce (see Müller-Lauter 1999, p. 61; and Figl 1982, p. 181). According to Nietzsche, "what matters about words is never the truth, never an adequate expression […]. To the creator of language too, the 'thing-in-itself' (which would be precisely the pure truth without consequences) is quite incomprehensible and not at all desirable." (TL; KSA 1, p. 879)[35] Our language is therefore nothing more than a collection of signs for the aim of designation. It is a mere human instrument which does not provide us with an immediate and objective access to reality. The only reason why we are so confident in our language rests in its great efficacy for the purpose of communication.[36] This determined that the language's fruitfulness had been soon mistaken for its truthfulness, and that we finally "believe we know something about the things themselves" (TL; KSA 1, p. 879) when we use terms and concepts of a general kind. Nietzsche therefore famously concludes that "truths are illusions that are no longer remembered as being illusions, metaphors that have become worn and stripped of their sensuous force" (TL; KSA 1, p. 881); they are the product of both cognitive and sensorial processes that actively intervene on the world, returning an altered – or, as Nietzsche later said, *falsified* – image of the original.[37] The "metaphorical" character of what we know is specified by Nietzsche in this way: "A nerve stimulus first transformed into an image – the first metaphor! The image then reproduced in a sound – the second metaphor! And each time a complete overleaping of the sphere concerned, right into the middle of an entirely new and different one." (TL; KSA 1, p. 879) According to this view, every step leading from external reality to its conceptualization involves an intervention, a modification of the original datum. For that reason, Nietzsche affirms that we cannot know reality as it is *in itself* – or that, at least, we cannot verify the adequateness of our world-description.[38]

Nietzsche's observations on metaphors and dissimulations – that we also encounter in *Human, All Too Human I*, in which, as will be shown, Nietzsche speaks of cognitive "errors," too, adopting a terminology that he will maintain in the following years (cf. e. g. GS 110) – are deeply inspired by Friedrich A. Lange's *History of Materialism* (1866¹).[39] In that text, Nietzsche found a thorough examination of the mechanisms of human perception from a physiological viewpoint. Lange particularly

---

[35] On Nietzsche's early anti-realistic criticism of the ordinary view of language, see Gori 2017b.
[36] On this, see GS 354, KSA 3, p. 590–3.
[37] On the definition of truth in TL see Reuter 2006, and below, the fifth chapter of this volume. Nietzsche's "falsificationism" has been debated e. g. by Clark 1990; Leiter 2002; and Riccardi 2011. On Clark's interpretation of Nietzsche's view of truth, see also Anderson 1996.
[38] An interesting account of Nietzsche's view of language (in TL particularly) in the light of nineteenth-century physiology, is provided by Emden 2005, chapter 4.
[39] It is worth remembering that Nietzsche read Lange's work when it first appeared, and he later bought the second, revised and extended edition.

stresses the selective activity pursued by our sense organs on the external stimuli – an observation that Nietzsche roughly presents in TL and which is in fact the principle of his later conception of knowledge. In HH I 16, for example, Nietzsche argues that our perceptive organs actively intervene on reality and, consequently, defines knowledge as a creative process and the phenomenal world as "the idea of the world spun out of intellectual errors we inherited." (HH I 16; KSA 2, p. 37) Continues Nietzsche:

> That which we now call the world is the outcome of a host of errors and fantasies which have gradually arisen and grown entwined with one another in the course of the overall evolution of the organic being, and are now inherited by us as the accumulated treasure of the entire past – as treasure: for the value of our humanity depends upon it. (HH I 16; KSA 2, p. 37)

In this excerpt an evolutionary conception of knowledge is clearly stated. The concepts through which we describe the world are, for Nietzsche, the product of a long-lasting intellectual process of elaboration of possible world-descriptions. These intellectual attempts have subsequently been selected on the basis of their usefulness for our species-preserving. In HH I 16, Nietzsche especially focuses on the relationship between the thing in itself and the phenomenon, and he is even more interested in the ordinary evaluation of the latter. Nietzsche in fact stresses that the phenomenon is an intellectual creation, that is, it was "the human intellect that made appearance appear and transported its erroneous basic conceptions into things." (HH I 16; KSA 2, p. 37) Secondly, given that this creation is the result of a historical process, of an ongoing development, Nietzsche criticizes the philosophers who "are accustomed to station before life and experience – before that which they call the world of appearance – as before a painting that has been unrolled once and for all." (HH I 16; KSA 2, p. 37) On the contrary, Nietzsche invites us to consider "the possibility that this painting [...] has gradually *become*, is indeed still fully in course of *becoming*." (HH I 16; KSA 2, p. 36) It is worth noting that, starting from these premises, Nietzsche relies on "the steady and laborious process of science, which will one day celebrate its greatest triumph in a *history of the genesis of thought [Entstehungsgeschichte des Denkens]*." (HH I 16; KSA 2, p. 37) This history would be *de facto* an evolutionary epistemology (as EEM), since it aims to reconstruct the origin of ordinary concepts and, more generally, of our cognitive mechanisms, starting from the biological development of the human species. Nietzsche attributes great importance to that *Entstehungsgeschichte*, for he believes it would be able to "illuminate the history of the genesis of this world as idea" (HH I 16; KSA 2, p. 37) and show that the traditional – metaphysical – conception which grants an ontological value to the phenomena, is inconsistent. A theory of knowledge based on the evolutionary model would therefore put up for discussion the way we look at the phenomena we daily deal with, and involve a revaluation of the very meaning of ordinary words such as "real," "imaginary," "true," and "false."

Nietzsche deals with the history of the genesis of thought a few pages later, in HH I 18 (an aphorism whose content will be later explored in GS 110). Here Nietzsche focuses particularly on both the "belief in freedom of will" and the "belief in unconditional substances and in identical things," which he conceives as original errors committed by "everything organic." (HH I 18; KSA 2, p. 40) In so doing, Nietzsche embraces the view defended by Afrikan Spir in the 1877 volume *Denken und Wirklichkeit*. In that book, Spir develops Kant's critical philosophy in an original way, and, as the title suggests, focuses on the relationship between our intellect and the reality we aim to know.[40] At the beginning of HH I 18, Nietzsche quotes a passage from that volume (Spir 1877, p. 177): "The primary universal law of the knowing subject consists in the inner necessity of recognizing every object in itself as being in its own essence something identical with itself, thus self-existent and at bottom always the same and unchanging, in short as a substance." What is worth noting, for the aim of discussing Nietzsche's adhesion to EEM, is that, while embracing Spir's view and, consequently, admitting that human knowledge is grounded on a set of principles such as the existence of substantial entities, identical things, and freedom of the will, Nietzsche maintains that all these principles are not absolute *a priori*. According to him, even the law formulated by Spir has "evolved: one day it will be shown how gradually, in the lower organisms, this tendency comes into being." (HH I 18; KSA 2, p. 39) This observation allows us to argue that Nietzsche adhered to a biological and evolutionary conception of the categories of reason, according to which the logical forms and cognitive mechanisms inherited by the individual have in fact generated gradually during the evolutionary history of the human species.[41]

It is now possible to draw some conclusions on the possibility of relating Nietzsche with contemporary evolutionary epistemology. Given what Nietzsche writes in TL and HH I, the content of GS 110 and GS 111 can actually be seen as a defence of a biological theory of knowledge. In fact, Nietzsche believes that the intellect plays the same role as the other organs in the preservation of humankind, and it is there-

---

**40** On Nietzsche's interest in Spir's *Denken und Wirklichkeit*, cf. D'Iorio 1993; Green 2002; and Gori 2009a, p. 52–3. Nietzsche implicitly refers to Spir also in HH I 16 (KSA 2, p. 36), when he deals with the "concept of the metaphysical as that of the unconditioned" elaborated by "rigorous logicians." The fact that Spir is inspired by Kant has led many commentators to consider him a neo-Kantian. However, since neo-Kantianism is a philosophical movement with peculiar features that cannot be encountered in Spir, that consideration seems to be incorrect. Of course, this does not limit the importance of Spir for Nietzsche. On the contrary, it is worth stressing that post-Kantians of various kinds such as Spir, Gustav Gerber, Karl von Baer, Friedrich Lange and Hermann von Helmholtz are the primary sources of Nietzsche's biological conception of knowledge. Furthermore, it can be argued that these authors also influenced thinkers such as Mach and the other "forerunners" of evolutionary epistemology that Campbell takes into account and whose views have been explored in the previous section.
**41** Nietzsche's biological conception of knowledge is formulated in other paragraphs from *Human, All Too Human*. E.g. in HH I 2 (KSA 2, p. 24) Nietzsche argues that "man has become [and even] the faculty of cognition has become," and in HH I 10 (KSA 2, p. 30) he speaks of a "history of the evolution of organisms and concepts."

fore possible to deal with it by applying the same principles that we use to describe the biological development of the species. That means that the genesis of our cognitive processes should be investigated in the light of the evolutionary theory – which is an EEM claim. Moreover, as above shown, Nietzsche defends a view of logical forms which is consistent to the one advocated by Spencer and Lorenz. According to Nietzsche, these forms are fundamental intellectual patterns which arose and developed throughout the evolutionary history of our species. The individual only inherits them as an "innate" structure of his cognitive faculty.[42] This is further stressed in an 1888 notebook, where Nietzsche argues that the "*categories of reason* [...] might, with much tentative feeling and reaching around, have proved their worth through relative usefulness." (NL 1888, KSA 13, 14[105]) Moreover, Nietzsche observes: "From then on they counted as a priori ... as beyond experience, as not to be denied ... And yet perhaps they express nothing but the particular expediency of a race and species – their 'truth' is merely their usefulness." (NL 1888, KSA 13, 14[105]) This view is perfectly consistent with the ideas defended by evolutionary epistemologists, namely that the categories of reason are *a priori* for the individual and *a posteriori* for the species. As Stack (1992, p. 80) observes, Nietzsche most likely derives this idea from the neo-Kantian framework which profoundly influenced him. In fact, authors such as Lange and Helmholtz reconsidered the value of the Kantian categories in both a physiological and a biological sense – without however adhering to the kind of evolutionism contemporary epistemologists take into account.[43]

If, on the one hand, neo-Kantianism allows Nietzsche to hold a position quite close to EEM, on the other hand it creates a gap between his view and the conception endorsed by Spencer, Lorenz and Campbell. Lange's view on the role played by the sensory and intellectual apparatus in the creation of the phenomenal world leads to an anti-realistic theory of knowledge, according to which concepts are mere falsifications or "intellectual errors."[44] In the same 1888 notebook mentioned above,

---

[42] This conception can also be compared with James's observation on common-sense published in *Pragmatism*. According to James, "our fundamental ways of thinking about things are discoveries of exceedingly remote ancestors, which have been able to preserve themselves throughout the experience of all subsequent time." (James 1907, p. 170) See also below in this volume, chapter 5.
[43] It can be argued that both Lange and Helmholtz hold an evolutionary framework, although they do not defend that viewpoint explicitly. Most importantly, they did not adhere to the Darwinian conception, which is the one Campbell, Popper and other evolutionary epistemologists defend, and which they apply to the development of both cognitive mechanisms and scientific theories. As I tried to show in the previous paragraphs, it is precisely the adherence to that conception which characterizes evolutionary epistemology. Stack's remark, which I basically support, is precisely this: some fundamental conceptions of evolutionary epistemology pertain also to a framework whose origin does not rest on evolutionism – but which must be distinguished from evolutionary epistemology *tout court*. That post- and neo-Kantian framework is the primary source of Nietzsche's biological view of knowledge, although of course the influence of evolutionism of some sort on Nietzsche's thought cannot be neglected.
[44] In this regard, Stack (1992, p. 88) argues that Nietzsche "defines 'truth' (inherited 'truth') as that kind of *error* without which a certain species could not have survived."

Nietzsche observes with particular clarity that the truth-value of logical forms consists only in their usefulness for the preservation of the species, and argues that they cannot be seen as an adequate description of reality. Moreover, Nietzsche considers this misinterpretation as the fundamental error of philosophy (i.e. Western metaphysics), which mistakes the logical plane (conceptuality) with the ontological one (reality):

> The aberration of philosophy rests on the fact that, instead of seeing in logic and the categories of reason means toward the adjustment of the world for utilitarian ends (basically, toward an expedient *falsification*) one believed one possessed in them the criterion of truth or *reality*. The "criterion of truth" was in fact merely the biological utility of such system of systematic falsification; and since a species of animals knows of nothing more important than its preservation, one might indeed be permitted to speak here of "truth." (NL 1888, KSA 13, 14[153]; my translation)

In reflecting on – and developing – his evolutionary conception of knowledge, Nietzsche stresses a crucial point: namely, that the truth-value of logical forms rests on their usefulness as means of species-preserving, which does not imply their adequateness to external reality.[45] That means that, contrary to the defenders of EEM, Nietzsche does *not* strictly apply the evolutionary model. As argued in section 2, for both Lorenz and Campbell (but also for Spencer), to apply the evolutionary model to the study of cognitive mechanisms means to conceive the relationship between the intellect and the external world in terms of *an actual adaptation* of the former to the latter. That conception leads to a form of realism – hypothetical in the case of Campbell and Lorenz, *naive* in the case of Spencer – according to which the categories of reason reflect more or less adequately at least the structure of the external world and, therefore, allow us to infer some objective information about reality. Nietzsche strongly rejects that view, rather holding that our perceptive and cognitive apparatus *falsifies* the world.[46] Nietzsche's insistence on the mediated (anthropomor-

---

[45] Species-preservation is only one of the several criteria of "truth" (or "value") that one can find in Nietzsche. As known, in other passages Nietzsche rejects the Darwinian species-preserving principle (misinterpreted as a form of Spinozian self-preservation), and contrasts it with the will to power. Furthermore, in the late years, in particular in *On the Genealogy of Morality*, Nietzsche focuses on the species-enhancement (better, the "*Typus Mensch*"-enhancement; see GM Preface 6) as criterion of moral evaluation. I will deal with this in the fifth chapter of this book, where it will be argued that Nietzsche's perspectivism is intertwined with the anthropological question.

[46] The way Nietzsche supports his "falsification thesis" is problematic. On the one hand, he holds that our sensorial and intellectual apparatus modify the original data and that, consequently, what we know is only a humanly-created world-image. His acceptance of fundamental physiological considerations on the limitations of human perception developed by authors such as Gustav Fechner, Johannes Müller and Hermann von Helmholtz (two important sources of Nietzsche's thought such as Friedrich Lange's *History of Materialism* and Friedrich Überweg's *Grundniss der Geschichte der Philosophie* deal with those views) let Nietzsche believe that no Truth can be reached, namely that any claim that our concepts adequately replicate the external world is in principle ill-funded. Nietzsche's

phic) character of our knowledge eventually leads him to embrace an agnostic position with respect to the truth-value of logical forms. According to him, they are the only tool we have to describe reality and, therefore, we cannot ignore them. Since we have no access to the "thing in itself," any statement about it is simply meaningless. However, Nietzsche does not deny the very existence of an external world (which, on the other hand, would contradict Lange's cognitive model presupposing that the senses react to an external stimulus). He simply leaves aside the problem of whether and to what extent our senses and our intellect "adequately" replicate the contents and/or structures of that dimension.[47]

---

reaction to the metaphysical view of ordinary realism is probably naïve, and he may not have considered the logical implications of his defence of an anti-realist conception: "Every concept is a *false* world-representation, an *error*." How can he state that, if he rejects the very possibility of a correspondence theory? If there is no Truth, if one cannot compare the world we know with the world as it is "in itself," how can Nietzsche affirm that our cognitive apparatus *falsifies* the world? I mostly agree with the scholars who reflected on this issue (first of all Maudemarie Clark 1990) and stressed how problematic it is. But I also think there is a way to make sense of it, and modern epistemology and the actual scientific practice play an important role in that. As I tried to argue in the last years – and as I am also arguing in this volume – Nietzsche has been deeply influenced by modern science. That means that, most of the times, the meaning of the words he uses can be understood properly only by referring to the scientific conceptions that imbedded his views, that is, to the *paradigm* Nietzsche clearly adheres to. This is the case of *truth, falsification, error, realism* etc. In modern times, the notion of truth has been put up to question, precisely because science demonstrated that the ordinary world-description is *false*. With this, scientists did not mean that we were able to compare our picture with the actual features of external reality, but rather that what *we expected* external reality to be was not confirmed by experiments. This is the case of the notion of *aether*, but also of that of the *subject as a material soul*. Both these notions played an important role, but modern science finally rejected them as *false* and *erroneous*, for they did not fit the results of new experiments. In Nietzsche, I think that we can find a similar way of reasoning. Furthermore, he apparently believed that, given the way science demonstrated how the perceptual and cognitive apparatus works, we can affirm that there is no *immediate* reproduction of the external world. In the terms of the ordinary accepted correspondence theory, that means that every knowledge is *false*. Nietzsche probably failed in maintaining that language. He also probably failed in expressing his ideas with a too strong rhetorical passion: "If you claim that our concepts are true although you cannot demonstrate it, why cannot I affirm that they are false, given that this is a better funded stance?" – one can image him arguing. On this, I agree that Nietzsche cannot be defended. But one should focus on the way *he* considered his own argument, and especially on what was the aim of his rejection of the correspondence theory. Although Nietzsche did not develop his argument properly, I think that we all can see what he tried to teach us, and the value of his teaching cannot be underestimated because of his mistakes in pure logical reasoning. For more on this, see also chapter 2.2; and chapter 5.1.
**47** Early considerations on that issue can be found in HH I 9; KSA 2, p. 29–30. In that aphorism Nietzsche admits that "the absolute possibility of [a metaphysical world] is hardly to be disputed." But he continues by arguing that "we behold all things through the human head and cannot cut off this head; while the question nonetheless remains what of the world would still be there if one had cut it off. This is a purely scientific problem and one not very well calculated to bother people overmuch."

If one wants to discuss Nietzsche's adhesion to EEM, therefore, one faces two contrasting elements. On the one hand, Nietzsche defends an evolutionary conception of knowledge and agrees with EEM on the *a priori* value of the categories of reason for the individual. On the other hand, Nietzsche does not strictly apply the metaphor of adaptation as Spencer, Lorenz and Campbell do, and he does not endorse any form of realism either. Since the latter is a crucial aspect of contemporary evolutionary epistemology, we are at best allowed to include Nietzsche among its precursors, together with the vast number of authors who supported a generic evolutionary position in epistemology.[48]

Despite this perhaps unsatisfactory result, however, there is a further element to be considered: namely, Nietzsche's general view of truth, which can be compared with some theses inferred by evolutionary epistemologists. Nietzsche's agnosticism can indeed be compared to the epistemological relativism which, according to Bradie (1986, p. 444), directly follows from Campbell's observations. Moreover, one can say that, in claiming that it is not possible to reach a complete and adequate knowledge, Nietzsche endorses a view similar to Popper's. Broadly speaking, Nietzsche shares with EEM as well as with EET the idea that there is no absolute truth, and that, therefore, the traditional notion of truth must be called into question and, if possible, reformulated on completely new principles.

## 1.5 Questioning "Truth"

A good starting point to develop some conclusive remarks on Nietzsche's conception of truth and its philosophical consequences is *Beyond Good and Evil*. At the very beginning of that work, Nietzsche focuses on the "will to truth," an issue that has always seduced philosophers and that posed questions that none of them has ever been able to answer (BGE 1; KSA 5, p. 15). The problem that Nietzsche addresses almost programmatically is precisely that of "the *value* of this will. Granted, we will truth: *why not untruth instead?* And uncertainty? Even ignorance?" (BGE 1; KSA 5, p. 15)[49] This question arises from the reflections that Nietzsche made since his early years. *Beyond Good and Evil* takes up a series of themes and topics which Nietzsche addressed in the works published before *Zarathustra* (above all *Human, All Too Human*, of which *Beyond Good and Evil* was planned to be a continuation), developing them in the light of his mature thinking. Among them, of course, one

---

[48] The judgement expressed at the end of George Stack's paper on *Nietzsche's Evolutionary Epistemology* (1992, p. 99), according to which Nietzsche's thought "is compatible with a number of recent interpretations of evolutionary epistemology even in regard to specific details," should therefore be rejected. A thorough analysis reveals that, except for the question of the categories of reason, it is precisely on specific details that Nietzsche deviates from the upholders of that research program!
[49] On Nietzsche's notion of "will to truth," which I cannot exhaustively deal with here, cf. Gori 2015c and 2017a.

finds the epistemological question concerning the intellectual relationship between man and world, and – more important for the aim of the present research – the value of our knowledge for the preservation of the species. We encounter these issues e.g. in *Beyond Good and Evil* §§ 3, 4 and 11, which are included in the first section of the book, devoted to *The Prejudices of Philosophers*. According to Nietzsche, metaphysicians are to be blamed for they ordinarily divide the world into dichotomies such as "good" vs. "bad," "true" vs. "false," and for their belief that these "oppositions of values" replicate a truly existing structure (BGE 2; KSA 5, p. 16). Within this context, Nietzsche speaks of the truth-value of judgements, observing that it is not important whether a given judgement corresponds to reality or not – that is, whether it is called "true" or "false" in the traditional metaphysical sense. Rather, the question is

> how far the judgment promotes and preserves life, how well it preserves, and perhaps even cultivates, the type. And we are fundamentally inclined to claim that the falsest judgments (which include synthetic judgments *a priori*) are the most indispensable to us, and that without accepting the fictions of logic, without measuring reality against the wholly invented world of the unconditioned and self-identical, without a constant falsification of the world through numbers, people could not live – that a renunciation of false judgments would be a renunciation of life, a negation of life. (BGE 4; KSA 5, p. 18)

In this aphorism Nietzsche deals with several issues that have been considered so far. Firstly, he mentions the fictitious nature of logical forms, even including a little stab at Kant, whose *a priori* synthetic judgements are for Nietzsche "the falsest," insofar as they are the most artificial intellectual creation. Secondly, and perhaps most importantly, Nietzsche focuses on the value of those judgements for the preservation of the species. Therefore (perhaps, without being actually aware of it) Nietzsche contrasts the idea that our cognitive mechanisms developed according to their actual adaptation to external reality with his view that what is fundamental is their instrumental role as species-preserving. In other words, it can be argued that, for Nietzsche, our sense organ reproducing the external world adequately is not necessarily a contribution to the preservation of the species. The fruitfulness and operational efficiency of our sensorial and intellectual apparatus can be evaluated from another standpoint, e.g. in the light of how much it helps to preserve life (or enhance life, as Nietzsche argues in other writings). But Nietzsche develops his argument within the context of the ordinary conception of truth; thus, in BGE 4 he invites his readers to "acknowledge untruth as a condition of life," which would mean "resisting the usual value feelings in a dangerous manner." (BGE 4; KSA 5, p. 18)

The ordinary confidence in *a priori* synthetic judgements is further discussed in BGE 11, where Nietzsche reaffirms that "such judgments must be *believed* true for the purpose of preserving beings of our type; which is why these judgments could of course still be *false*!" (BGE 11; KSA 5, p. 25) It is particularly worth stressing that Nietzsche insists in adopting the traditional dichotomy between "true" and "false," of which he apparently tries to show the contradictory nature, believing that it can no longer be sustained in the light of the progress of contemporary philosophy. One possible explanation of this could be the fact that Nietzsche speaks at an audience educated – as Nietzsche himself was – by those philosophers that still believed in these dichotomies. Nietzsche therefore attempts to change the meaning of the ordinary language, with no need to give up fundamental notions such as "truth," "good," or even "soul."[50]

This position is further explored in BGE 34, a crucial aphorism for the present investigation because it represents an actual link between the epistemology that Nietzsche had elaborated since 1873 and a central theme of his mature reflection – namely, *perspectivism*. In that aphorism, Nietzsche argues that "the *erroneousness* of the world we think we live in is the most certain and solid fact that our eyes can still grab hold of." (BGE 34; KSA 5, p. 52) Therefore, our knowledge cannot trespass the boundaries of the "world of appearances" that traditional metaphysics defines in contraposition to the "'true' world," that is, the realm of unchanging and absolute forms.[51] Given that one cannot go beyond the phenomenal dimension, Nietzsche observes:

> It is no more than a moral prejudice that the truth is worth more than appearance; in fact, it is the world's most poorly proven assumption. Let us admit this much: that life could not exist except on the basis of perspectival valuations and appearances; and if, with the virtuous enthusiasm and inanity of many philosophers, someone wanted to completely abolish the "world of appearances," – well, assuming *you* could do that, – at least there would not be any of your "truth" left either! Actually, why do we even assume that "true" and "false" are intrinsically opposed? Isn't it enough to assume that there are levels of appearance and, as it were, lighter and darker shades and tones of appearance? [...] Why shouldn't the world *that is relevant to us* – be a fiction? (BGE 34; KSA 5, p. 53–4)

Once it is acknowledged that what we know is the product of both sensory and intellectual elaboration, we can no longer speak of "truth" in the ordinary sense, as an unconditioned access to reality. Moreover, if one considers that the phenomenal dimension played a fundamental role in the evolutionary history of mankind, then it is necessary to completely reassess the value of appearances. As mentioned above, according to Nietzsche it is no longer fruitful, nor even possible, to distinguish between "true" and "false" *in the ordinary sense*, since our whole knowledge is confined within the phenomenal plane – which, in terms of the correspondence theory, is the realm of falsehood and illusion. According to Nietzsche, future philosophy must abandon the old valuational system, but that does *not* mean that we are des-

---

[50] On this see Gori 2015d; and below in this volume, chapter 2.3 and 2.4.
[51] Nietzsche addresses the relationship between "true" and "apparent" world especially in two sections of *Twilight of the Idols*: *"Reason" in Philosophy* and *How the "True World" Finally Became a Fable*. In this latter section Nietzsche especially argues for the elimination of both these realms, in the same way as he does in BGE 34 (see on this Gori/Piazzesi 2012, p. 160 ff.). Finally, it is worth noting that Nietzsche's considerations on this issue are influenced by Gustav Teichmüller's *Die wirkliche und die scheinbare Welt*. In that volume Nietzsche found the terminology he later adopted to define the notion of "perspectivism" (cf. below in this volume, chapter 2.6 and chapter 3.2).

tined to an epistemological and axiological nihilistic relativism – the sort of relativism which claims that there is really *no truth*, no objective facts, and no universal validity claims.[52] On the contrary – as I will try to show in the following chapters – Nietzsche argues that truth and falsehood can still be determined, but from a different viewpoint, namely on the basis of a pragmatic evaluation of the most fruitful and operationally efficient among the several "erroneous" world-representations.[53] As Nietzsche puts it in a notebook compiled shortly before the publication of *Beyond Good and Evil*, "truth does not signify the antithesis of error but the status of certain errors vis-a-vis others." (NL 1885, KSA 11, 34[247])

One can call it Nietzsche's agnosticism. A view which follows from the epistemology elaborated since the early years and which is linked to – and indeed defines – Nietzschean perspectivism.[54] The latter is in fact grounded on the idea that the "reality" we deal with is the final result of a process of intellectual and sensorial schematization, generalization and falsification of the original datum (see GS 354), and that each one of us accesses to the world from his own viewpoint.[55] On the basis of what has been stated in the previous sections, it can be argued that this "perspectival epistemology" arises from a well-defined context: namely, the nineteenth-century debate on human knowledge, which provided modern science with a new paradigm to guide her interpretation of our intellectual activity. That discussion firstly involved neo-Kantian thinkers, many of whom also combined their ideas with the popular Darwinian model (the case of Mach particularly exemplifies this). On the philosophical plane, the most important result has been a relativization of the explanatory power of human (especially scientific) knowledge. This means that the reference points traditionally adopted for our world-description must be called into question, and that we have to re-define the boundaries of our knowledge. The disorientation that follows from these outcomes is well expressed by Nietzsche's pro-

---

52 Richard Bernstein (2010, p. 109) calls that view a "bad relativism."
53 Of course, fruitfulness and operational efficiency depend on the aim and scope of the evaluator. The metaphysical world-conception can be considered fruitful, for it allowed the species preservation. Logic, too, is a system of beliefs that proved to be extremely efficient, as Nietzsche himself admits. But at the same time Nietzsche argues that the development of science demonstrated that these conceptions were only useful tools, which must be abandoned insofar as theories with a greater explicatory power have been developed. Or, better, the *value* of these conceptions must be re-assessed, and their validity as *truthful i.e. adequate* world-description must be rejected. Furthermore, I believe that Nietzsche's interest in the problem of truth is not merely theoretical. His criticism toward that notion is clearly inspired by modern epistemology, but "truth" for him is a wide notion that includes also our valuational activity. That given, the problem of the value of truth involves primarily morality, and Nietzsche in fact deals with that in the final sections of *On the Genealogy of Morality* (GM III 24–7). Within that context, the evaluation of a belief-system in terms of fruitfulness and operational efficacy will take into account the anthropological development of the human being, what Nietzsche calls the "type of man" (*Typus Mensch*). I will deal with this in the fifth chapter.
54 On the relationship between Nietzsche's perspectivism and his agnosticism about "the possible existence of unknowable truths," cf. Leiter 2002, p. 278.
55 For more on this, see the third chapter of this volume, section 1.

nouncement of the "death of God," which can meaningfully be conceived, in a less poetic but equally effective way, as a post-positivist disenchantment with our world-representation.

An attempt to compare Nietzsche's thought with the research program of evolutionary epistemology thus makes more sense, for, as Bradie (1986, p. 446) points out, that program in fact tackles *epistemological relativism*. That relativism is well-expressed in Popper's observation that a scientific theory that "survives" for a longer period than others is not necessarily "truer" (in the ordinary sense of that term), but also in Lorenz's consideration that neither cognitive mechanisms nor scientific theories will ever completely or *adequately* adapt to the object they reproduce and describe, thus remaining at most "working hypotheses." An even clearer example of that epistemological relativism is expressed by Campbell, according to whom descriptive epistemology, which studies how organisms acquire and process knowledge, leads to "debunking of the value of 'hard facts' [*hard facts*]" (Campbell 1979, p. 195–6) and, consequently, forces us to abandon the very idea of a "literal truth." (Bradie 1986, p. 444) As shown above, inspired by the evolutionary model, Campbell describes a world of organisms which "constructs, as it were, an image of reality based on its own needs and capacities." (Bradie 1986, p. 444)

There is no need to be an expert in Nietzsche to see the similarities between that position and his perspectivism, especially if one considers the philosophical consequences of their positions. One fundamental difference between Nietzsche and Campbell rests in their attitude towards epistemological relativism. In fact, while Campbell admits a form of hypothetical realism, although aiming not to ascribe an *ontological* dimension to that relativism, Nietzsche does not even address the question, and develops his mature philosophy on the basis of the fundamental result of modern epistemology. To call into question the value of ordinary truth, which, from an evolutionary point of view, is something unattainable, is the starting point of Nietzsche's path leading to an "open see" full of possibilities for the human being. In that dimension, it would be possible to develop a renewed practice of life, thus producing a "higher" type of man capable of creating his own values without looking at them as absolute principles. That type of man would consequently orient himself within a world whose reference points – both epistemic and axiological – have proven to be only of a relative value.[56]

---

[56] On the anthropological value of Nietzsche's late philosophy, see Schacht 2006 and Gori 2017c. On Nietzsche's "philosophy of orientation" see Stegmaier 2008.

# 2 Pursuit of Facts and Interpretations.
## A Contextual Reading of NL 1886–87, 7[60]

The dichotomy between "facts" and "interpretations" is a heated topic in Nietzsche-studies as much as in the broader contemporary philosophical debate. As known, Nietzsche considers that dichotomy in the famous posthumous fragment NL 1886–87, KSA 12, 7[60], where, driven by an anti-positivistic urge, he outlines the principles of a perspectival epistemology:

> Against the positivism which halts at phenomena – "There are only facts" – I would say: no, facts are just what there aren't, there are only interpretations. We cannot determine any fact "in itself": perhaps it's nonsensical to want to do such a thing. "Everything is subjective," you say: but that itself is an *interpretation*, for the "subject" is not something given but a fiction added on, tucked behind. – Is it even necessary to posit the interpreter behind the interpretation? Even that is fiction, hypothesis.
> Inasmuch as the word "knowledge" has any meaning at all, the world is knowable: but it is variously interpretable; it has no meaning behind it, but countless meanings. "Perspectivism".
> It is our needs *which interpret the world*: our drives and their for and against. Every drive is a kind of lust for domination, each has its perspective, which it would like to impose as a norm on all the other drives.

In spite of the preparatory character of this passage (which, it is worth remembering, is taken from a notebook and was not intended for publication), the sweeping – and, for this reason, captivating – observation that "facts [*Thatsachen*] are just what there aren't, there are only interpretations [*Interpretationen*]" intrigued both scholars and the general public. Its impact has been so widespread that, sadly too often, the readers see it not only as a concise as much as meaningful definition of Nietzschean perspectivism, but also as a *motto* exemplifying Nietzsche's late philosophical view. Of course, this is not completely unfunded, especially if one considers that remark in the light of other considerations published for example in *Beyond Good and Evil* or in the fifth book of *The Gay Science*. As has been duly stressed in the past, the notion of "interpretation" plays an important role in Nietzsche's thought, indeed. Moreover, it is closely related with his "perspectivism," whose deepest philosophical meaning, which goes far beyond the mere theoretical sphere, can be ascertained precisely in the light of that notion.[1] On the other hand, however, two highly problematic (if not completely mistaken) assumptions pertain to that view – both of them still determining the superficiality of some bad interpretations of Nietzsche's thought that apparently consider it acceptable, in the philosophical studies, to isolate an author's sentences from their context and build upon them arbitrary as much as ill-founded readings. Firstly, the aim and scope of Nietzsche's observation is limited to the theoretical sphere only; secondly, the dichotomy between "facts" and "interpretations" is consid-

---

[1] On this cf. for example Figl 1982.

ered (I would say, *interpreted*) exclusively in a negative sense, as the obliteration of the reference points that help man orienting in the world. As a result, the complexity of Nietzsche's perspectival thought is neglected, for that philosophical view is reduced to a sterile relativism and epistemological nihilism.

But to deal with Nietzsche's text without falling into mistaken readings of this sort is possible, and it can be done precisely by supporting the philosophical interpretation with a strong historico-philological methodology. That is, in addressing both Nietzsche's published and posthumous writings, we should primarily try to shed light on the content of any single aphorism and fragment, in order to understand properly the actual meaning of the terms that Nietzsche uses in each passage. More specifically, this approach consists of an analysis of the texts which presupposes their contextualization within Nietzsche's writings, his readings, and the broad historical and cultural context within which Nietzsche developed his own reflections. It is not a mere commentary what I am talking of, for this approach aims primarily to clarify and interpret concepts – a result which I believe can only be attained when a philological work on the genesis and occurrence of these concepts has been completed.

The worth of a *contextual reading*[2] is particularly evident in the case of the posthumous note 1886–87, 7[60], given the abundance of philosophical implications that the dichotomy between "facts" and "interpretations" there stated proves to have. Indeed, if one aims to assess the value of that dichotomy and understand it properly, one must first consider its narrower context, that is to say, the overall content of the posthumous note where that observation appears. As can be easily seen, in that note one finds several interesting ideas on which Nietzsche reflected throughout his philosophical activity, most of which found space in published works (in some cases – it is worth stressing – only after having been subjected to significant modifications). In some respects, the fragment 1886–87, 7[60] can be seen as an actual thematic junction of Nietzsche's mature production, for it includes several issues that he addressed in greater detail in other texts (written both before and after that posthumous note). As said, the context that sheds light on the investigated dichotomy is in fact multifaceted: it involves Nietzsche's own writings, his readings, and the general cultural debate that interested and inspired him. As will be shown in what follows, with no reference to that context, the proper meaning of the observations that one encounters in the note 1886–87, 7[60] remains largely hidden.

In this chapter I will follow the single paths starting from each issue mentioned in that posthumous fragment. By so doing, I will try to outline the complex as much as rich reflection which these elements are part of. As a result of this investigation, the hidden content of that fragment will be unveiled, and it will be possible to pursue Nietzsche's view on "facts" and "interpretations" from an original point of view.

---

[2] My approach is inspired by the methodology that Werner Stegmaier adopted to provide his thorough *contextual interpretation* of the fifth book of *The Gay Science* (Stegmaier 2012, p. 75 ff.).

The research does not only aim to achieve that goal, of course. On the contrary, my purpose is to provide a more accurate interpretation of that dichotomy, on the one hand by circumscribing its thematic range and, on the other, by showing its function and relevance within Nietzsche's late philosophy. Finally, the contextual reading of NL 1886–87, 7[60] will help achieve a further result. Since a few lines below the dichotomy between "facts" and "interpretations" one finds outlined the philosophical conception that, here for the first time, Nietzsche calls "perspectivism" (a conception whose importance for his mature thought is indisputable), the exploration of the single statements included in that note will allow me to better determine that view – and, consequently, to interpret it properly.

## 2.1 Facts are just what there aren't, there are only interpretations

In order to understand the meaning, function and relevance of the formula "facts are just what there aren't, there are only interpretations," one can firstly consider how that formula changes in its various occurrences within Nietzsche's writings. In fact, this dichotomy does not appear only in the posthumous note 1886–87, 7[60]. Rather, Nietzsche presents it two other times, in two published works – albeit in a slightly (but significant) different form and context. The comparison of these occurrences allows us to trace the development of Nietzsche's reflection on that particular issue and, consequently, to evaluate both the quite provisional character of the view expressed in the notebook,[3] and the role that view plays in Nietzsche's late philosophy. As will be argued, despite his observation on the dichotomy between facts and interpretation is closely connected with the ideas on the interpretative and perspec-

---

[3] The fact that Nietzsche's notebooks contain draft observations which, consequently, can only be considered as steps of a still developing reflection, should be an indisputable premise of any scholar or ordinary reader who deals with Nietzsche's thought. Unfortunately, instead of using the posthumous notes as a tool to better understand Nietzsche's writings, the interpreters often ascribe to the fragments the same value they attribute to a published text. What's worse, sometimes they even compare ideas that Nietzsche included in these published texts with some views that he merely sketched in his private papers and that he then left there, as rough and incomplete as any record that we ourselves write down on our notebooks every day; and they do that pretending to have found the proof of a contradiction within Nietzsche's thought, while in fact they only encountered the trace of a ceaseless reflection. Of course, in that extraordinary laboratory for testing ideas which are Nietzsche's notebooks and scattered papers, it is also possible to find refined observations that, despite having remained unpublished, were probably (at least almost) ready to be included in a forthcoming work. For the sake of clarity, it is important to say that this is not the case with the posthumous note I am dealing with in this chapter. The Mp XVII 3b notebook from the end of 1886 – spring 1887, containing the fragments of group 7, includes a series of long notes titled and subsequently listed within the final draft index of *The Will to Power* (cf. KSA 12, p. 246 ff., and NL 1888, KSA 13, 18[17]). Anyway, the note 1886–87, 7[60] is not one of these. Rather, it is part of a group of short notes on various topics, which are written after the more structured ones.

tival nature of existence that Nietzsche defends in his mature period, it is not possible to consider it as the capital synthesis and point of arrival of his thought – all the more so, because in the 1886–87 note that observation appears in a generic form, which apparently (at first sight) is oriented towards a pure epistemological nihilism.[4] Only by contextualizing Nietzsche's claim that there are no "facts" it is possible to see that it is but the first step of a reflection that Nietzsche develops in moral terms, and that morality is the proper domain of the dichotomy we are investigating. Moreover, if one looks at that issue in the light and context of Nietzsche's writings, one realizes the "creative" and positive significance of his affirmation of the interpretative character of existence. Instead of leading to a strong as much as sterile relativism, the idea that Nietzsche defends especially in the fifth book of *The Gay Science* (e.g. GS 343; KSA 3, p. 573–4 and 374; KSA 3, p. 626–7) outlines a philosophy capable of reacting to the death of God with courage and "cheerfulness" (*Heiterkeit*), and to conceive the "new infinite" disclosed by that crucial event as an open space full of possibilities.

If read in the context of the posthumous note 1886–87, 7[60], Nietzsche's idea that "facts are just what there aren't, there are only interpretations" appears much less general in scope than what is ordinarily believed. In fact, it falls within a very specific thematic framework, which includes epistemological questions that were debated by authors read by Nietzsche, most of whom were engaged in a discussion and development of Kantianism. The fragment opens with a critique of the confidence that, according to Nietzsche, positivists had in the phenomenal level (a confidence that, in his opinion, was completely ill-founded); subsequently, we find a rejection of the Kantian view on the possibility of encountering or even conceiving "facts in themselves"; just after that observation, Nietzsche critically deals with what is believed to lay at the core of our cognitive relationship with the external world: the subject (whose existence as a substance entity is ordinarily taken for granted, and whose mere fictional character is rather stresses by Nietzsche, as it is well-known); finally, the reflection becomes more general, for Nietzsche addresses the very possibility of a "knowledge" of reality and reflects on the fact that the former notion should be entirely reconceived. Only at this point Nietzsche introduces the concept of "perspectivism" (a name that he himself coined, although inspired by another author, as will be shown) and explores the possibility of "variously" *interpreting* the world and to find "countless meanings" within it. All these elements will be examined in detail

---

[4] Any attempt to read Nietzsche's thought in the light of this dichotomy is mistaken, insofar as it isolates that sentence from its context, attributing to it a wide meaning that it does not have (see below). Unfortunately, this case is not isolated. In the history of Nietzsche's reception, both scholars and ordinary readers have extrapolated several sentences from his writings in an equally debatable manner, thus neglecting how complex and articulated his thought actually is. A remarkable example, given its relationship with the dichotomy I am considering and, more generally, with Nietzschean perspectivism, is that of the *motto* "nothing is true, everything is permitted," whose very attribution to Nietzsche is debatable – to say the least! (see on this Stellino 2015a and Gori/Stellino 2018)

in the following sections. As for now, the posthumous fragment will be considered in its entirety, in order to focus on the general meaning and scope of Nietzsche's reflection.

In his private reflections, Nietzsche develops a critique of traditional epistemology, which believes in the existence of a subject capable of adequately knowing the external world, or at least of constructing an image of it based on objective fixed points (i.e. "facts"). Conversely, in the published works, the discourse concerning the exclusive existence of "interpretations" pertains to a different thematic field. In *Twilight of the Idols*, "Improving" Humanity 1, in fact, Nietzsche writes:

> You have heard me call for philosophers to place themselves *beyond* good and evil, – to rise *above* the illusion of moral judgement. This call is the result of an insight that I was the first to formulate: *there are absolutely no moral facts* [*es gar keine moralischen Thatsachen giebt*]. What moral and religious judgements have in common is the belief in things that are not real. Morality is just an interpretation of certain phenomena [*eine Ausdeutung gewisser Phänomene*] or (more accurately) a *misinterpretation*. Moral judgements, like religious ones, presuppose a level of ignorance in which even the concept of reality is missing and there is no distinction between the real and the imaginary; a level where "truth" is the name for the very things that we now call "illusions." (TI, "Improving" Humanity 1; KSA 6, p. 98)

This passage opens a particularly important section of *Twilight of the Idols*, which also plays a fundamental role in Nietzsche's mature thought. In that passage, Nietzsche in fact deals with issues that he introduces in the previous chapters of that same book, issues that concern the degenerative effects that rational (and metaphysical) thought had on the Western human type, and on whose basis Nietzsche develops his argument against the idea that morality and religion (especially the Christian one) would be capable of "improving" the human being through "domestication" and "breeding" practices. This criticism in especially grounded on the idea that there is no objective referential moral principle, and that morality is only an interpretation of living conditions, physiological states and sensations, to which we attribute an artificial (and therefore fictional) meaning and explanation.[5]

For Nietzsche, morality follows the perspectival model which he described elsewhere and which acquires its most proper meaning in the light of the context outlined in *Twilight of the Idols*. That this is the case can be deduced from the fundamental conception which Nietzsche refers to in the quoted passage – and of which he pretends to be the original discoverer. That idea is first published in *Beyond Good and Evil* § 108 (KSA 5, p. 92), in a sentence quite similar to the dichotomy that one encounters later, in the 1886–87 note: "There are absolutely no moral phenomena, only a moral interpretation [*Ausdeutung*] of the phenomena..."[6] According to

---

[5] On this, see Gori/Piazzesi 2012, p. 197f. On Nietzsche's view of Christian morality and her role in the anthropological degeneration of "*der Typus Mensch*," see Schacht 2006.

[6] Nietzsche reflected on this contraposition already in the early 1880s. In NL 1882, KSA 10, 3[1], § 374, one reads the same sentence one finds in BGE 108, with a couple of differences. Nietzsche affirms that

Nietzsche, this observation – thus formulated – can actually be seen as a principle of his mature thought, as the very ground of his philosophical project of a *revaluation of all values*.[7]

In the light of this textual evidence it is therefore possible to say that, if we want to assess the value and meaning of the dichotomy between "facts" and "interpretation" within Nietzsche's thought, we must consider his own remarks. And on this issue he seems to be particularly clear: the thematic range of that dichotomy is morality! The discourse on the perspectival character of our relationship with the world must therefore be consistent with that viewpoint, that is, it should focus on the plane of human agency and moral behaviour. At the same time, however, the theoretical questions within which the investigated dichotomy was originally formulated cannot be neglected, but that does not contradict what has been argued so far. That is to say, the two thematic ranges are not necessary separate, as the detrimental prejudice of ordinary philosophy, according to which epistemological questions have nothing to do with practical (i.e. moral) philosophy, suggests. On the contrary, the content of the posthumous note 1886–87, 7[60] can be *genetically* connected with the considerations that Nietzsche expresses in TI. More precisely, the latter can be seen as the final moment of a reflection that, starting from purely theoretical considerations, draws broader conclusions involving the theme of the interpretative nature of existence.

The contextual reading of the note, which has not yet shown all its potential, already allowed us to achieve a useful result. In fact, at least some of the fundamental principles of Nietzsche's perspectival thought has been outlined, and it is already possible to see which is the actual range of application of that view. The foundations of this philosophical position must however be further explored, and this would be possible only once all the terms involved have been contextually analysed.

## 2.2 We cannot determine any fact "in itself"

The first element to be considered is precisely the term "fact" (*Thatsache*) that appears in the explored dichotomy, followed by the statement that "we cannot deter-

---

"there are absolutely no moral phenomena, only a moral interpretation of the phenomena," but he uses the term "*Interpretation*" instead of "*Ausdeutung.*" Furthermore, he adds that this interpretation is erroneous ("– *eine irrthümliche Interpretation!*"). In 1885, Nietzsche deals once more with that idea, which, for him, is his "main proposition [*Hauptsatz*]: there are no moral phenomena, there is only a moral interpretation [*Interpretation*] of those phenomena. This interpretation itself is of extra-moral origin." (NL 1885, KSA 12, 2[165]) Apparently, within this context Nietzsche talks of "facts" or "phenomena" without sharply distinguishing between them, as if they have the same meaning. An explication of this could be that, etymologically speaking, a "factum" is a product as much as a "phenomenon," e.g. the result of a cognitive process (that would also explain why Nietzsche argues that one cannot encounter facts "in itself").

**7** Cf. TI Preface (KSA 6, p. 57–8) and Gori/Piazzesi 2012, p. 126–7.

mine any fact (*Factum*) 'in itself'." At first glance, it seems that in this posthumous fragment Nietzsche aims to undermine our world-conception by criticizing the principles whose certainty we assume as indisputable and which constitute the basis of both our theoretical and practical activity. The "fact" (*Thatsache* or *Factum*) is a datum one should not put up to question, the "brick" of our conceptual – epistemological or axiological – constructions. It can therefore ground our knowledge as much as our moral behaviour; it can be a scientific datum, or a moral principle. Anyhow, at least in principle, a "fact" is an absolute and inalterable element. And it is precisely with this supposed but illusory absoluteness and inalterability of ordinary notions that Nietzsche engages from the very beginning of his philosophical activity. In *Human, All Too Human I*, for example, he writes that "there are no *eternal facts* [*ewigen Thatsachen*], just as there are no absolute truths" (HH I 2; KSA 2, p. 25), suggesting that we should contrast metaphysical thought with a "historical philosophizing." This approach would make it possible to radically criticize those concepts that, despite having developed throughout the evolution of humankind and his cultural history, are mistakenly seen as "*aeternae veritates*" (HH I 11; KSA 2, p. 30) and finally become "*eternal* idols" (TI Preface; KSA 6, p. 58).[8]

This way of thinking can be encountered again, albeit in a different form, in the years following the publication of *Human, All Too Human*. In 1881 Nietzsche elaborates his first interesting considerations on self-observation, an issue on which he basically remains sceptic.[9] In particular, reflecting on the fundamental feelings of pleasure and pain, Nietzsche observes: "These are not 'immediate facts' [*unmittelbaren Thatsachen*], as the representation." (NL 1881, KSA 9, 11[314]; my translation) According to Nietzsche, we call "pleasure" and "pain" the mere result of an activity of our intellect, which processes the data – a set of representations – giving them a unitary form (NL 1881, KSA 9, 11[314];). Nietzsche further reflects on that issue in 1884, as we read in the posthumous note 26[114]. This fragment begins with an incisive remark: "There are no immediate facts [*unmittelbaren Thatsachen*]!" and then Nietzsche argues that we cannot have a direct – i.e. non-mediated – relationship with our "feelings and thoughts: in the very moment I become conscious of them, I made an extract, a simplification, an attempt of structuring out of them; *this is actually to acquire consciousness:* that is, organize in an absolutely *active* way." (KSA 11, p. 179–80; my translation) In both these passages Nietzsche deals with our awareness of an inner state.[10] According to him, whether we experience a feeling (such as that of pleasure and pain) or a thought, in both cases an inner state, a physiological condition, has passed to a "higher level" of consciousness and is thus modified

---

[8] On historical philosophizing and the criticism of eternal idols cf. Gori 2012b.
[9] On this, see e.g. Stellino 2015b.
[10] It is not possible to explore the extremely rich as much as interesting topic of consciousness in Nietzsche. For a thorough discussion of the ontological status and on the mechanism and function that Nietzsche attributes to consciousness, cf. Lupo 2006.

or "translated" by the intellect according to its own categories.[11] This is the reason why Nietzsche thinks that there cannot be "immediate facts." As he writes in *The Gay Science* § 354 (KSA 3, p. 593), "all becoming conscious involves a vast and thorough corruption" and, therefore, it is physiologically impossible for us to gain any access to the "original datum."

This reflection recalls – and to some extent reproduces – the observation on the notion of "unconditional" (*Unbedingt*) that Nietzsche made after having read Afrikan Spir's *Denken und Wirklichkeit* (1877). Broadly speaking,[12] the problem concerns the ontological status of the metaphysical world, which Spir defines "unconditional," and especially the possibility of stating a relationship between phenomenon and noumenon (cf. D'Iorio 1993, p. 3). What is worth stressing, for the purposes of the present chapter, is that Nietzsche immediately criticizes that concept (see HH I 16 and HH I 18): for him, it is a simple logical construction that does not correspond to anything "real." More precisely, Nietzsche thinks that the very idea of an "unconditioned" lies far beyond the limits of our knowledge. Since our intellect actively intervenes on the data received from the external world, we can always only know something that is mediated and, therefore, *conditioned*. Hence the fundamental question – not only for Nietzsche, but for all post-Kantian philosophers – of the *thing "in itself."* As known, Nietzsche rejects the ontological value of that notion, by arguing that, since it belongs to the sphere of the unconditioned (*ab-solutus*, i.e. "in itself"), it does not pertain to the reality we actually know and within which we act.[13] As for Nietzsche, the thing in itself is a purely logical concept resulting from the hypostatization of features that do not belong to the phenomenal world, due to the human fundamental "metaphysical need" to seek permanence in a becoming world (see e.g. BGE 12). The thing in itself belongs to the "true" world, which is unreal and fictional insofar as it is an intellectual product. According to Western metaphysics, whose origin Nietzsche traces back to Plato, the "true" world has been set in opposition to the "apparent" realm of ordinary knowledge (cf. TI, "Reason" in Philosophy, and How the "True World" Finally Became a Fable), which has been subsequently devalued, as if it were a mere imperfect image of the former. According to Nietzsche, the "true" world is the realm of the substance-concepts, the absolute "truths" and "eternal idols" to be blamed for the degenerative anthropology they determined, and which one finds as final product of

---

[11] On the non-innate and evolutionary character of the categories of reason and the fact that they cannot be valid as a "criterion [...] of reality" (NL 1888, KSA 13, 14[153]) see above, Chapter 1.4.
[12] Given its complexity, it is not possible to deal with this issue adequately in this section. For more on this, see D'Iorio 1993 and Green 2002. D'Iorio especially explores the notion of unconditioned in Spir and Nietzsche.
[13] On "thing in itself" and "appearance," cf. Figl 1982 and Riccardi 2009. The latter (p. 216 ff.) especially compares the notion of "true" world mentioned by Nietzsche and that of "real" world that can be encountered in the works of M. Drossbach and G. Teichmüller (both authors who inspired Nietzsche's late views).

the two-thousand-years European cultural history.[14] The "true" world is the realm of the *unknowable* thing in itself – which cannot be known because knowledge entails the active intervention of the intellect and, consequently, a modification of the original datum. But it is also the world of the facts "in themselves" that "we cannot determine": according to the same line of reasoning, in fact, any attempt to observe something "unmediated" is contradictory, and Nietzsche can thus argue that "perhaps it's non-sensical to want to do such a thing." (NL 1886–87, KSA 12, 7[60])

Our starting point, namely the investigation of the "facts" that Nietzsche mentions in his 1886–87, 7[60] note, therefore leads us to the more general problem of "knowledge"; a particularly important topic of Nietzsche's thought, which he mentions a few lines later in the same note (I shall come back to this in the fourth section of this chapter). This already allows us to show that the considerations synthetically expressed in this posthumous note are linked to broader topics on which Nietzsche reflected for a long time. But the epistemological issue is not the only one related to Nietzsche's criticism of the existence of "immediate facts." At least two other issues connected with the 1886–87, 7[60] fragment are worth to be stressed, for they both involve pivotal ideas of Nietzsche's (especially late) thought.

The first of these topics is mentioned in an 1887 posthumous note, and concerns a fundamental internal "fact" in which we ordinarily believe without reservation: the "subject." In the fragment 1887, 11[113], titled *On psychology and theory of knowledge*, Nietzsche develops the ideas on pleasure and pain he explored in 1881 and, before reaffirming that these feelings are "late and derivative phenomena of the intellect," he draws his early-stated conclusion that we cannot have access to uninterpreted "facts." More precisely, Nietzsche argues that

> the *inner* world is phenomenal as well: everything *we become conscious of* has first been thoroughly trimmed, simplified, schematised, interpreted – the *real* process of inner "perception," the *causal association* between thoughts, feelings, desires is absolutely hidden from us, like that between subject and object – and may be just a figment of our imagination. This "apparent *inner* world" is managed with quite the same forms and procedures as the "outer" world. We never encounter "facts." (NL 1887, KSA 13, 11[113])[15]

Thus, six years later Nietzsche still believes that our introspection is mediated by our consciousness, and that the result of that process cannot be, by definition, a pure, simple i.e. unstructured data. That is why our knowledge of the inner world cannot be grounded on any "fact". Moreover, we need to put up to question the entity that, since Descartes, is ordinarily seen as the indubitable starting point of every introspective knowledge. If the "inner world" is in fact "apparent," then the same goes

---

14 On the anthropological question of *décadence* in *Twilight of the Idols*, cf. Gori 2015a.
15 This note is particularly well-known in contemporary secondary literature, because its second part contains a reflection that has started a discussion on Nietzsche's *epiphenomenalism*, that is, on the causal value to be attributed to the (presumed) subject of the acts of thought (see Leiter 2002, Katsafanas 2005, Constâncio 2011 and Riccardi 2018. See also *infra*, chapter 3.3).

for what we suppose or imagine to be the author of the events that take place at a purely physiological level. At the end of the note 1887, 11[113], Nietzsche famously observes that the idea that there is "the 'mind,' *something that thinks*" is in fact "a derivative, second consequence of the false self-observation that believes in 'thinking:' here *first* an act is imagined that doesn't occur, 'thinking,' and *secondly* a subject-substratum is imagined in which every act of this thinking, and nothing else, originates; i.e., *both doing and doer are fictions*." (NL 1887, KSA 13, 11[113])[16] As will be thoroughly argued in what follows, this reflection already appears in the posthumous fragment 1886–87, 7[60], where Nietzsche writes that "the 'subject' is not something given." Therefore, it is possible to argue that the idea that the subject is a fictional and illusory concept follows from the fundamental criticism of the immediate value of "facts," an issue that, as shown, Nietzsche develops since 1881 in connection with the problem of self-observation.

The second topic that the discussion on "facts" invites us to consider – and which, as in the case of the subject, will be thoroughly considered in the following sections – arises from an 1888 posthumous fragment, in which Nietzsche speaks explicitly of "facts in themselves" and "interpretations," once again exploring the problem of our access to the "*internal* factual world." In this note one reads:

> Mechanistic language is just a sign language for the *internal* factual world of quanta of will that struggle and overcome each other? All the presuppositions of mechanistic language – matter, atom, pressure and impact, gravity – are not "facts-in-themselves" [*Thatsachen an sich*] but interpretations aided by *psychological* fictions. (NL 1888, KSA 13, 14[82])

Two things are worth stressing, in this excerpt. Firstly, Nietzsche's referring to the "quanta of will" (*Willens-Quanta*) shows that his reflection must be contextualized within his view of the purely necessary – that is, not involving a causal agent or "acting subject," and, therefore, not "voluntaristic" in the ordinary sense – principle of natural dynamics (better known as the "will to power"; see on this Gori 2007, chapter 3, and Abel 1998). Secondly, Nietzsche speaks of "mechanism," thus revealing that his criticism focuses on *a quite specific scientific world-description*. This aspect must not be overlooked, and is especially important in order to reflect on the antipositivist attitude that Nietzsche assumes in NL 1886–87, 7[60]. In fact, the 1888 note 14[82] allows us to argue that the context of the dichotomy between "facts" and "interpretations" that we are dealing with is well-defined and narrow, for in that passage Nietzsche refers to a view that, at his time, was discussed by scientists and epistemologists that he knew (directly or indirectly, see Gori 2014 and 2009a).

Since they involve other elements that Nietzsche addresses in the posthumous note 1886–87, 7[60], these issues will be analysed separately, starting from the illusory character of the "subject," which is the topic of the next paragraph.

---

**16** For a discussion on the problem of self-observation in Nietzsche, cf. Stellino 2015b and Katsafanas 2015.

## 2.3 The "subject" is not something given

After having criticized the idea that "there are only facts," Nietzsche considers another element that he ascribes to positivism: the idea that "everything is subjective." In his opinion, that view is inconsistent, and it simply disappears once we realize the ontological lack of content of its fundamental concept. The "subject," the unavoidable principle of self-observation and self-description, as much as the origin of our practical activity, is not "something given," according to Nietzsche. Rather, as has been shown above, that concept is only an illusion resulting from a *"false self-observation"* (NL 1887, KSA 13, 11[113]) which determines that we believe that concept to be fixed and immutable – that is, a "fact."

The idea that the posthumous note 1886–87, 7[60] is a thematic junction of Nietzsche's mature production, and that therefore a contextualization within his work is the key to properly understand its content, is corroborated by an investigation assessing the importance of the problem of the subjectivity in Nietzsche's thought. During the second half of the nineteenth century, that classic issue of modern philosophy (starting from Descartes) was widely debated by neo-Kantian thinkers who developed a scientific psychology (see Martinelli 1999). From the philosophical point of view, one of the many relevant aspects of this problem, and perhaps the element on which Nietzsche focuses the most, concerns the role the notion of subjectivity plays in the development of European culture. The existence of a subject as the cause of our actions, in particular, is the kernel of Christian morality. Given that Nietzsche's aim, during his late period, was to overcome that morality and, consequently, educate a "higher" (non-*décadent*) human type, his interest in the problem of subjectivity is easily explained.

As Nietzsche observes in *Beyond Good and Evil* § 54, the idea that the primary referent of human actions (the subject) is not a substance with causal efficacy has important cultural consequences. In that aphorism, Nietzsche argues that "modern philosophy is, covertly or overtly, *anti-Christian*," because "all the philosophers have been out to assassinate the old concept of the soul, under the guise of critiquing the concepts of subject and predicate. In other words, they have been out to assassinate the fundamental presupposition of the Christian doctrine." (BGE 54; KSA 5, p. 73) To affirm that "'I' was a condition and 'think' was a predicate and conditioned – thinking is an activity, and a subject *must* be thought of as its cause" (BGE 54; KSA 5, p. 73) means to believe in a "soul," that is, in a voluntary cause of thinking, a hypothetical and fictional agent who is supposedly separated from its activity.[17] But, continues Nietzsche, the faith in such a cause belongs to traditional phi-

---

[17] Cf. this famous passage from *On the Genealogy of Morality:* "It is just as absurd to ask strength *not* to express itself as strength [...] as it is to ask weakness to express itself as strength. A quantum of force is just such a quantum of drive, will, action, in fact it is nothing but this driving, willing and acting, and only the seduction of language (and the fundamental errors of reason petrified within it), which construes and misconstrues all actions as conditional upon an agency, a 'subject', can

losophy, while modern thinkers try to "get out of this net – wondering whether the reverse might be true: that 'think' is the condition and 'I' is conditioned, in which case 'I' would be a synthesis that only gets produced through thought itself." (BGE 54; KSA 5, p. 73) Thus, concludes Nietzsche, one could admit "the possibility that the subject (and therefore 'the soul') has a *merely apparent existence*" (BGE 54; KSA 5, p. 73) and, consequently, undermine any morality grounded on the notions of "free will" and "responsibility" – such as Christianity (BGE 21; KSA 5, p. 35–6). According to what Nietzsche argues in *Twilight of the Idols*, in fact, without the reference to a soul as the cause of our actions, we could not "be considered free, and nobody could really be held responsible for [them]." (TI, The Four Great Errors 3; KSA 6, p. 90. On this, see also Gori 2015a, § II. B.)

These considerations follow from some reflections on consciousness that Nietzsche carried out since his early years (see for example D 119; KSA 3, p. 111–4, and GS 11; KSA 3, p. 382–3). Subsequently, during his philosophical maturity, Nietzsche developed those ideas and called into question the ordinary conception of subjectivity, according to which we have "the right to speak about an I, and, for that matter, about an I as cause, and, finally, about an I as the cause of thoughts." (BGE 16; KSA 5, p. 30) Nietzsche's well-known conclusion is that no substance-notion can be encountered as grounding psychical phenomena, and the I is only one of the several "eternal idols" produced by the "metaphysics of language." In *Twilight of the Idols* Nietzsche in fact blames the "basic presuppositions […] of *reason*" for clearing the way to a "crudely fetishistic mindset. It sees doers and deeds all over: […] it believes in the 'I', in the I as being, in the I as substance, and it *projects* this belief in the I-substance onto all things. […] Being is imagined in everything – *pushed under* everything – as a cause." (TI, "Reason" in Philosophy 5; KSA 6, p. 77) Thus, Nietzsche holds that the I is ontologically inconsistent, and that we should consider it as "only a *regulative fiction* with the help of which a kind of constancy and thus 'knowability' is inserted into, *invented into*, a world of becoming." (NL 1885, KSA 5, 35[35]) Consequently, the legitimacy of using the proposition "I think" as an immediate certainty is put up for discussion, as Nietzsche observes in the first section of *Beyond Good and Evil*.[18] In BGE 16 Nietzsche especially deals with that issue, arguing that, in order to be able to discuss it, one would have to answer

---

make it appear otherwise. And just as the common people separates lightning from its flash and takes the latter to be a *deed*, something performed by a subject, which is called lightning, popular morality separates strength from the manifestations of strength, as though there were an indifferent substratum behind the strong person which had the *freedom* to manifest strength or not. But there is no such substratum; there is no 'being' behind the deed, its effect and what becomes of it; 'the doer' is invented as an afterthought, – the doing is everything." (GM I 13; KSA 5, p. 279) On this, see also the posthumous fragment 1887, 11[113] above quoted, where Nietzsche develops the same argument. On the problem of the relationship between agent and action, cf. Pippin 2010, chapter 4.

**18** The Nietzschean and Kantian critiques of Descartes's "I think" have been recently addressed by Peter Bornedal 2010, chapter 3. On this, see also Loukidelis 2005 and 2013.

a set of bold claims that are difficult to establish – for instance, that I am the one who is thinking, that there must be something that is thinking in the first place, that thinking is an activity and the effect of a being who is considered the cause, that there is an "I" and finally, that it has already been determined what is meant by thinking, – that I *know* what thinking is. (BGE 16; KSA 5, p. 30)

In short, "in place of that 'immediate certainty' which may, in this case, win the faith of the people, the philosopher gets handed a whole assortment of metaphysical questions, genuinely probing intellectual questions of conscience," (BGE 16; KSA 5, p. 30) that any true critical thinker must face, if she wants to contribute to the development of European culture, and move it away from the verge of nihilism it has dangerously approached.

A couple of years later, in *Twilight of the Idols*, Nietzsche further reflected on the epiphenomenal character of the I. Two sections are especially worth to be considered. *"Reason" in Philosophy*, which contains the above quoted passage against the metaphysics of language, and *The Four Great Errors*, whose third paragraph, titled *Error of false causation*, is particularly significant for the aims of the present research. In that paragraph, indeed, Nietzsche focuses on the "famous realm of 'inner facts', none of which has ever proven factual," and claims that "the 'inner world' is full of illusions and phantasms." (TI, The Four Great Errors 3; KSA 6, p. 91) Among these illusory entities one finds the I (the "subject"), which, according to Nietzsche, becomes "a fairy tale, a fiction, a play on words," (TI, The Four Great Errors 3; KSA 6, p. 91) once we admit that a thought does not require the existence of a cause of any kind as its origin and conductor of its development. To admit that is the first step of an intellectual process that would make it possible to get rid of the common-sense view believing in the existence the "three 'inner facts'" which "people projected [...] out of themselves and onto the world – [...] the will, the mind, and the I." (TI, The Four Great Errors 3; KSA 6, p. 91) On the contrary, according to Nietzsche

> there are no mental causes whatsoever! All the would-be empirical evidence for this goes to hell! [...] – And we really botched this "empiricism" – we used it to *create* the world as a world of causes, wills, and minds. The oldest and most enduring psychology was at work here, doing absolutely nothing but this: it considered all events to be deeds, all deeds to be the result of a will, the world became a multitude of doers, a doer ("subject") pushed its ways under all events. (TI, The Four Great Errors 3; KSA 6, p. 91)

Nietzsche's talking of "inner facts" leads us directly to his critique of the notion of "subject" in the posthumous fragment 1886–87, 7[60], and sheds some light on the content of that note. The *ego* in fact falls within the "inner world" and is one of those "facts of consciousness" that we ordinarily assume as the basis of our world-description, believing that "this world is *more familiar to us*." (GS 355; KSA 5, p. 594) But, as Nietzsche observes, "facts are what there aren't," and that can be said especially of the inner world, which we can access only through a self-observation that turns out to be *false* (NL 1887, KSA 13, 11[113]). The "subject," therefore, is an illusory "fact" as much as all the others of the same kind. It is not an immutable basis voluntarily causing our thoughts and actions; rather, it is a merely human projection, something which is "imagined into everything, *pushed under everything* – as a cause." That is, the subject is the product of a "psychology [...] in its most rudimentary form" that distinguishes between agent and action and pushes being under a process which is in fact necessary and non-voluntary. (TI, "Reason" in Philosophy 5; KSA 6, p. 77) In other words, the subject is part of that same process of *interpretation* that dissolves the "facts in themselves." More precisely, the subject is the last and maybe the most important "fact" we must get rid of, in order to allow European culture to turn completely anti-metaphysical. This process of dismission of the fundamental prejudices of reason and, therefore, of the substance ontology inherited by the Platonic and Christian world-conception, can be accomplished only when we critically de-construct the last "article of faith" (GM I 13; KSA 5, p. 281) still standing: namely, the "interpreter" that man, driven by a fundamental metaphysical need as much as by the instinctive fear of leaving without reference points for his orientation, posits "behind the interpretation." (NL 1886–87, KSA 12, 7[60])[19]

Nietzsche's conclusive remark on the artificial distinction between interpreter and interpretation leads us back to the above-mentioned issue about how the relationship between actor and action, or thinker and thinking, should be considered. The fragment 7[60] therefore falls fully within the context of Nietzsche's reflections on the epiphenomenalism of consciousness and subject. A further – and final – confirmation of all this can be found in a fragment belonging to the same 1886–87 notebook. The fragment is part of a group of highly elaborated annotations, which, as far as can be judged by their classification, were supposed to be included in the *Will to Power* (at the time, Nietzsche was in fact working at that editorial project. See KSA 12, p. 246ff., and footnote 3 of this chapter). This posthumous note is especially related to the paragraph of *Twilight of the Idols* on the *Error of False Causation* and, according to what Nietzsche states there, it puts up to question our ordinary tendency to attribute a causal principle to any type of activity:

> Opposition to the alleged "facts of consciousness." Observation is a thousand times more difficult, error perhaps a condition of observation in general. [...] "Cause" and "effect:" calculated psychologically, this is the belief which expresses itself in the *verb*, in active and passive, doing and being done to. In other words: it is preceded by the separation of what happens into a doing and a being done to, by the supposition of something that does. Belief in the doer is behind it: *as if once all doing were subtracted from the "doer," the doer itself would remain*

---

**19** See also NL 1885–86, KSA 12, 2[151]: "One mustn't ask: 'So *who* interprets?' – instead, the interpreting, as a form of the will to power, itself has existence (but not as a 'being'; rather as a *process*, as a *becoming*) as an affect." Figl (1982, p. 81) especially focuses on the notion of will to power as a "dynamic" concept, which overcomes the dichotomy between being and becoming by gathering these two elements within itself. Based on this view, Figl describes interpretation an "ontological principle." (Figl 1982, p. 74)

*over.* Here we are always prompted by the "notion of I:" all that happens has been interpreted as doing: with the mythology that a being corresponding to the "I" – – – (NL 1886–87, KSA 12, 7[1])[20]

In the light of what has been argued so far, this passage should not need further comments. However, it presents some original aspects, if compared to the above quoted fragments. For example, Nietzsche speaks of "facts of consciousness," an expression that leads us to GS 355 and shows how strongly the topic of the subject is related to the issue this chapter is devoted to.[21] Secondly, Nietzsche dismisses as "mythology" the idea that substantial entities can be encountered beneath psychic phenomena. This is particularly interesting because, before Nietzsche, Friedrich A. Lange made the same remark in his *History of Materialism*, denouncing the risk that physiological studies of the brain might go beyond the scope of scientific research (Lange 1882 [1875], vol. 2, part 3. Cf. Gori 2015b, § 3).[22] It might be worth having a brief digression on the general debate about this topic, for it influenced Nietzsche's view of subjectivity and provides further elements for a contextualization and a better understanding of the posthumous note 1886–87, 7[60].

---

**20** Further considerations on these issues can be found in a slightly later note (NL 1887, KSA 12, 9[91]), in which Nietzsche presents an exhaustive reflection on determinism. Here, firstly, Nietzsche observes that "'mechanical necessity' is not a fact [*Thatbestand*]"; moreover, "necessity is not a fact but an interpretation [*die Nothwendigkeit ist kein Thatbestand, sondern eine Interpretation*]." According to Nietzsche, we ourselves introduced that notion, by interpreting "the fact that what happens *can be expressed in formulae* as resulting from a necessity that governs what happens." (NL 1887, KSA 12, 9[91]) Furthermore, Nietzsche argues that this has been possible because we "interpreted subjects, 'doers,' into things," thus creating that connection, which is now impossible to avoid in any description of natural processes. Nietzsche, therefore, observes that "cause and effect" is "a dangerous concept if one conceives of a *something* that *causes* and a something upon which there is an *effect*." (NL 1887, KSA 12, 9[91]) He then continues by considering the purely illusory character of the notion of subject (especially that of "*effecting* subject," which for Nietzsche "is not something that *effects* but merely a fiction"). Clearly, together with the subject, one must also give up the notion of "the object on which effects are exerted. Duration, conformity with itself, being, inhere neither in what is called subject nor in what is called object. They are complexes of what happens which appear to have duration in relation to other complexes – for example due to a difference in tempo (rest-motion, fixed-slack: all these are oppositions which don't exist in themselves and in fact only express *differences of degree* that look like oppositions when viewed through a particular prism." (NL 1887, KSA 12, 9[91]) This reflection is quite important for Nietzsche, for it involves the collapse of a whole series of substance-notions lying at the basis of the Western traditional world-description. In the same posthumous fragment 1887, 9[91], Nietzsche argues that, "yet we have understood that the subject is fictitious," thus falls "the world of atoms that exert effect, the assumption of which always presupposes that one needs subjects, [as much as] the 'thing-in-itself' […] because at bottom this is the concept of a 'subject-in-itself'." Finally, "the antithesis of 'thing-in-itself' and 'appearance' is untenable; with this, however, the concept "*appearance*" collapses too."
**21** Nietzsche uses the expression "*Thatsachen des Bewußtseins*" quite rarely. He uses it in this fragment, is GS 355, and then we encounter it only in other two 1885 posthumous notes, number 2[87] and 2[204] (KSA 12).
**22** Lange's influence on Nietzsche has been clearly demonstrated by Salaquarda 1978 and Stack 1983, and later confirmed by several studies from the *Quellen-Forschung*.

As has been recently shown (cf. Loukidelis 2013 and Gori 2015b), Nietzsche's criticism of Descartes's "I think" should be interpreted in the light of neo-Kantianism and, more particularly, of the discussion on "scientific psychology" that included Lange as one of the contenders. The I of which Nietzsche speaks in BGE 16 and BGE 17 does not differ from the soul discussed by Lange in his *History of Materialism* (where Nietzsche found a detailed, updated exposition of the latest publications in psychology), nor is it different from what the Austrian physicist Ernst Mach called, in the same years, the "supposed psychic unity" that science claimed to be able to locate within the brain. (Mach 1914 [1886], p. 26)[23] Mach especially stresses the dependence of philosophical and scientific knowledge on a religious tradition of thought and deplores the fact that science insists on seeking a "seat of the soul" (*Seele*) in the ganglia of the brain, thereby failing to raise the hypothesis that no substantial entity of that kind actually exists. The main problem that Mach addresses is the relation between "body and I (matter and spirit)" (Mach 1914 [1886], p. 26) or, more generally, between the physical and the psychical – an issue widely debated in the nineteenth century and which has in Gustav Fechner's psychophysics one of its main points of reference.[24]

Indeed, Mach's investigations presuppose Fechner's results, which Mach developed into a neutral monistic view, thus providing an anti-metaphysical solution to the mind-body problem.[25] Lange also relies on Fechner in his attack on the limitations of the explanations of the body/soul relation provided both by the materialism and the physiology of sense organs typical of psychology. In Lange's time, psychology was still engaged in seeking a substantial basis for its main object of study and, for that reason, remained in a "pre-scientific" stage of research. No wonder, then, that both Lange and Mach, taking a hint from Franz Brentano, raised the possibility of establishing a "psychology without a soul" and tried to show, in particular, that that position could be defended without resort to paradoxical formulations. Thus, they became spokesmen for a goal of considerable philosophical significance, that is, the fact that contemporary psychology no longer needed to refer to a substantial ground of psychic functions (without at the same time seeing its object of investigation vanish) is what brought about its liberation from the old scholastic metaphysics.[26]

The correspondence between Nietzsche's observation on the fictional character of the I and the outcomes of a scientific psychology which, at that time, demanded

---

[23] Nietzsche probably bought Mach's *Beiträge zur Analyse der Empfindungen* the year it has been published. For an account of Nietzsche's interest in Mach and on the similarities between their epistemological views, see Gori 2009 and 2014. For a comparison between Mach and Nietzsche in psychological matters and their criticism of the notion of "I", cf. instead Gori 2011a and 2015b.
[24] On this, see Guzzardi 2010 and Martinelli 1999.
[25] This interpretation of Mach's view of subjectivity has been defended by Bertrand Russell. See on this Banks 2014.
[26] A thorough account of all this is provided in Gori 2015b.

to be defined on a new basis, freeing itself from the remnants of an age-old metaphysics that surreptitiously attempted to introduce something that it could not specify, much less quantify or measure, should not surprise. Both these positions in fact arise from the same general context, namely the nineteenth-century scientific and philosophical debate where the seeds of Kantianism especially grew.[27] At that time, in particular, science engaged in freeing itself from animistic and mythological conceptions that had their origin in the worldview of common sense. More generally, during the nineteenth century, Western thought underwent a radical transformation, witnessing the collapse of the principles on which its knowledge was built. For those who are acquainted with Nietzsche, this can be easily understood by thinking of the "death of God": a formula with which he identifies the disorientation of his age, whose foundations lie beyond the religious and moral level.[28]

Metaphors aside, and remaining within the field of natural science, we may say that physical investigations at that time revealed a much less definite and unchangeable reality than what was believed. To these investigations were added mathematical studies, which in the nineteenth century undermined the foundations of Newtonian physics and reshaped the descriptive scope of the Euclidean system, on the basis of which the former stood. The emergence of Riemann's geometry, for example, made clear that the previously adopted model was not as "truthful" as it was previously believed. In fact, it says nothing about reality, merely describing it by means of a scientifically fruitful and "economic" system. A thorough treatment of this topic would go beyond the aim and scope of the present research. However, it is worth stressing the sense of disorientation experienced by scientists of those times, and how they dealt with it in a positive manner. Rather than being stuck in a sterile nihilistic disorientation, modern scientists faced the problem of meaning and explanation the crisis of truth posed them, and on that basis re-configured their very research process. This led to Henri Poincaré's conventionalism, as well as to Mach's studies

---

[27] On how deeply the scientific debate inspired Nietzsche, see the seminal works of Alwin Mittasch (1950 and 1952) and the more recent studies published in the collective volumes Heit/Abel/Brusotti 2012 and Heit/Heller 2014.

[28] The "death of God" announced by Nietzsche can be compared with the "*Ignorabimus!*" pronounced by Emil Du Bois-Reymond in the same period. The two lectures that Du Bois-Reymond pronounced in 1872 and 1880 respectively (*The Limits of Our Knowledge of Nature* and *The Seven World Riddles*) aroused great interest at the time and stimulated a heated debate (see Bayertz/Gerhard/Jaeschke 2007). Du Bois-Reymond, in particular, remarked the explanatory difficulty of modern epistemology, manifesting a radical scepticism towards the very possibility of overcoming our cognitive boundaries and resolving fundamental questions on nature. The latter include the discourse concerning the knowledge of psychic phenomena, with particular regard for their relationship with the material dimension – in contemporary terms, we would define it the mind-body problem (Du Bois-Reymond 1884). It is worth noting that a copy of these conferences is collected in Nietzsche's private library (cf. Campioni et alia 2003, p. 201), and that they could have played an important role on his reflections. As has been recently argued (Marinucci/Crescenzi 2015), Nietzsche's 1881 notebook M III 1 (where one first encounters the idea of an eternal recurrence of time and space) is deeply inspired by Du Bois-Reymond's ideas.

on the economic character of scientific knowledge, which marked the beginning of twentieth-century research on matter and space.

For what concerns the studies in psychology, one of the elements that revealed their ontological inconsistency was in fact the soul or I, which nineteenth-century psychologists, as well as Nietzsche himself, ended up considering "unsavable" ("*Das Ich ist unrettbar*," argues Mach 1914 [1886], p. 24). At the same time, however, it should be noted that neither scientific psychology nor Nietzsche completely rejected that concept. In fact, while by "sounding out" (TI Preface; KSA 6, p. 58) the I one discovers its inconsistency on the ontological level, from a logical point of view it still proves its *practical utility* as "*regulative fiction*" (cf. NL 1885, KSA 11, 35[35], and Gori 2015b, § 6). In other words, once stripped from its metaphysical surface – and therefore understood as a function rather than as a substance – the I can still be adopted in psychological researches as much as in man's self-representation (see Gori 2015b, §§ 3 and 7).[29]

This digression is important because, as argued above, it helps to contextualize the brief remarks that Nietzsche writes in NL 1886–87, 7[60], and especially to shed light on the anti-positivist attitude expressed in that passage. I will further investigate the general context of Nietzsche's observations in the fifth paragraph of this chapter, after having dealt with a further element that he addresses in the posthumous note. As for now, I can only anticipate that this context outlines a well-defined epistemological position; a view that arose in the late nineteenth century and that is known (by the few people interested in that period of the history of the philosophy of science) as "phenomenalism." That position included Ernst Mach and Richard Avenarius as the most important upholders (see Halbfass 1989, p. 483 ff.), and can be described as a post-Kantian development of positivism aimed at re-conceiving its principles in an anti-metaphysical direction. In particular, according to the phenomenalist conception of knowledge, the common-sense distinction between "reality" and "appearance" must be rejected. As argued for example by Mach (1976 [1905], p. 7), insofar as the boundaries of our actual knowledge lie within the phenomenal realm, that dichotomy is in fact inconsistent.[30]

---

[29] Both William James's psychological studies and his pragmatism should be at least mentioned, for they are particularly consistent with what has been argued so far. The epistemological view that James presented in 1907, in fact, arises from the outcomes of the nineteenth-century researches in psychology, which determined that a material seat of our thoughts could not be encountered. James's *Principles of Psychology* in fact started from that hypothesis, and aimed to find that particular seat. But the inquiry produced a completely unexpected outcome, and James decided to re-formulate his arguments. The only possibility for him was to abandon the traditional metaphysical view and to conceive the subject, the self, as a pragmatically fruitful notion, that is, as a mere *useful fiction*. Deeply influenced by Mach's research, and adhering to his so-called neutral monism, in the 1912 *Essays in Radical Empiricism* James finally got rid of the presupposition of an actual existence of consciousness (see Banks 2014 and Gori 2015d).

[30] The affinities between phenomenalism, perspectivism and pragmatism will be further explored in chapters 4 and 5.

The phenomenalists' view on psychology is quite close to Nietzsche's. A couple of notes from the years 1885–86 and 1888 allow us to further outline that conception. The first one is a draft editorial plan for the fifth book of *The Gay Science*. In that fragment, Nietzsche criticizes the "erroneous starting point [of modern philosophy], as if there existed 'facts of consciousness' – and no phenomenalism in introspection." (NL 1885, KSA 12, 2[204]; my translation) The second passage also deals with phenomenalism: Nietzsche in fact observes that "nothing is more phenomenal (or, more clearly:) nothing is so much deception as this inner world which we observe with the famous 'inner sense'." (NL 1888, KSA 13, 14[152]; my translation) These two posthumous fragments fully refer to the main issue under discussion, namely Nietzsche's criticism of the subject as a "fact of consciousness," which he claims to belong to an "inner world" full of ghosts and fictitious entities. Rather than being an objective, i.e. indisputable, datum, the subject belongs to the phenomenal realm, the only dimension we can gain access to, as it represents the boundary of our "knowledge" of reality, which we cannot cross. The impossibility of going beyond the phenomenal dimension does not entail, however, that it would be possible to define "facts" *within* it – which, according to Nietzsche, is exactly what positivists do. On the contrary, the phenomenal one is the realm of interpretation, of the conditioned and mediated, and this cannot be neglected by a honest critical reflection. Therefore, it is necessary to *re-define* the very notion of "knowledge," trying to give new meaning to that concept within a context that leaves no space for any immutable and universally valid certainty.

## 2.4 Inasmuch as the word "knowledge" has any meaning at all, the world is knowable

The remark on subjectivity closes what could be seen as the first part of the posthumous fragment 1886–87, 7[60]. In these few lines, Nietzsche criticizes what he pretends to be the fundamental view defended by positivists, whose contents he explores in detail. The second part of the fragment is characterized by an apparently "constructive" character. In fact, Nietzsche outlines a conception that, with all likelihood, he imagined as capable of contrasting positivism. As known, he famously calls that view "perspectivism." That conception is based on a not-trivial epistemological consideration, which, as in the case of previously analysed observations, is the result of a complex and interesting reflection. That is why it needs to be thoroughly explored.

The idea that "inasmuch as the word 'knowledge' has any meaning at all, the world is knowable" may seem self-evident, at first. However, a closer inspection shows that it presupposes a radical epistemological position. In fact, Nietzsche's observation implicitly holds that the very concept of "knowledge" should be reconceived, and, consequently, the range of our actual "knowability" is to be re-defined. Needless to say, this means that the view of knowledge defended by the previous philosophical and scientific tradition should be put up to question.[31] As known, Nietzsche is particularly critical towards the ordinary view that conceives "knowledge" as a trustful access to reality, that is, a description of things as they are "in themselves." According to that view, knowledge could be understood as *adaequatio rei* or correspondence with the state of things, a conception that Nietzsche strongly criticizes on the basis of a series of reflections that he expressed since *On Truth and Lies in an Extra-Moral Sense*.[32] According to Nietzsche, a direct, immediate knowledge of the external world (*Außenwelt*) cannot be achieved, and this is so because of the unavoidable "*dual falsification*, by the senses and by the mind," (NL 1886–87, KSA 12, 7[54]) that occurs anytime we deal with the external world.[33] For that reason, as Nietzsche observes for example in a 1881 posthumous fragment, we have to re-think the whole issue, and consider firstly that

> our knowledge is not knowledge in itself, moreover it is not even knowledge, but rather a chain of deductions and spider's webs: it is the result of thousand-years of necessary optical errors – necessary, since we basically want to live –, errors, since any perspectival law is basically an error. [...] Science describes the power that man have exerted in the past time, and that she nowadays puts forth – our poetic-logical power of determining perspectives [*die Perspektiven festzustellen*] with respect to all kind of things, which is species-preserving. (NL 1881, KSA 9, 15[9]; my translation)

This fragment deals with the evolutionary conception of knowledge defended by Nietzsche and that has been explored in the previous chapter. According to that view, the way both the cognitive and the perceptual process work is the product of the evolutionary development of mankind, which selected the intellectual and sensorial structures that proved to be the fittest to their environment (cf. GS 110; KSA 3, p. 469–71). Contrary to what the upholders of an *evolutionary epistemology*

---

**31** Nietzsche reflected for a long time on the meaning of the term "knowledge," especially in the years 1885–87. For the purposes of the present research, it is worth reading an excerpt from the 1886–87 posthumous fragment 7[4] (one of the preparatory notes for the *Will to Power* that has been mentioned above), in which Nietzsche calls into question Kant's critical project. Nietzsche argues that "what he wants is naive: *the knowledge of knowledge!*" And it is so because "if I do not already 'know,' if there is a thing such as knowledge, I cannot even reasonably formulate the question 'what is knowledge'." (NL 1886–87, KSA 12, 7[4]) Notably, in this note Nietzsche sees knowledge as one of those immutable certainties that should be critically analysed – that is, one of the "facts" discussed so far. According to him, the fundamental question is therefore: "How is it possible the fact of knowledge [*die Thatsache der Erkenntnis*]? Is it knowledge a fact [*Thatsache*], actually? What is knowledge? If we do not *know* [*wissen*], what is knowledge, we cannot ask the very question, if there is knowledge." (NL 1886–87, KSA 12, 7[4])
**32** Nietzsche's criticism of the ordinary conception of truth has been discussed in the previous chapter, section 4. As will be argued in the final chapter of this volume, Nietzsche shares the rejection of the correspondence conception of truth with Jamesian pragmatist epistemology.
**33** See also NL 1885, KSA 11, 34[54]: "The 'external world' affects us: the effect is telegraphed into our brain, there arranged, given shape and traced back to its cause: then the cause is *projected*, and *only then* does the fact [*Factum*] enter our consciousness."

holds, however, Nietzsche thinks that this process has nothing to do with the ability of these structures to reproduce an "adequate" image of the original datum. At least, he claims that it is not possible to us to have a final word on that issue (see above, chapter 1.1). According to Nietzsche, we can rather deal with the operational, "poetic-logical" character pertaining to our knowledge of the world. That is, we can reflect on the way both our senses and our intellect intervene on the external data, modifying them according to their basic structures. This given, it is quite unlikely that our cognitive and perceptual processes would be neutral, and that they would reproduce reality adequately. This is why, once rejected the ordinary notion of "truth" – already in *Human, All Too Human* – Nietzsche prefers to speak of "errors" and "falsifications," and argues that the very meaning of the traditional notion of "knowledge" should be re-defined.

Another issue mentioned, although *in nuce*, in the above-quoted 1881 fragment is perspectivism. The fragment is in fact antecedent to Nietzsche's elaboration of Gustav Teichmüller's terminology,[34] but the activity of the human cognitive apparatus is already described in terms of a determination of "perspectives." This is no surprise if, once again on the basis of what has been argued in the previous chapter, one considers that the perspectival epistemology and axiology developed by Nietzsche follows from the evolutionary conception he upholds. It is precisely that conception that determines Nietzsche's criticism towards the meaning of "truth" and, furthermore, the *value* that we ordinarily attribute to that notion. This is particularly well-expressed in *Beyond Good and Evil* § 34, an aphorism in which, after having reaffirmed his idea that it is not possible for us to go beyond the phenomenal dimension – the "apparent world" that Western metaphysics defines in opposition to the "true world" of fixed and absolute forms – Nietzsche argues that

> it is no more than a moral prejudice that the truth is worth more than appearance; in fact, it is the world's most poorly proven assumption. Let us admit this much: that life could not exist except on the basis of perspectival valuations and appearances; and if, with the virtuous enthusiasm and inanity of many philosophers, someone wanted to completely abolish the "world of appearances," – well, assuming *you* could do that, – at least there would not be any of your "truth" left either! Actually, why do we even assume that "true" and "false" are intrinsically opposed? Isn't it enough to assume that there are levels of appearance and, as it were, lighter and darker shades and tones of appearance – different *valeurs*, to use the language of painters? Why shouldn't the world that is relevant to us – be a fiction? (BGE 34; KSA 5, p. 53–4)

The fundamental problem that Nietzsche addresses here is the assumption that a "knowledge in itself" is possible, that is, that we can directly accede to reality. The contraposition between "truth" and "falsity" must be understood within that framework. We ordinarily attribute greater value to truth, because we believe that those concepts reflect two physiologically and ontologically different world-descriptions. Rather, according to Nietzsche, that distinction is merely logical, and when we

---

34 Cf. Dellinger 2012 and below, section 5.

speak of "truth" and "falsity" we are referring to the same process involving the active intervention of our perceptual and cognitive organs. Therefore, as argued above, the realm of our knowledge is a purely phenomenal one. Accordingly, any distinction between "true" and "false" can only be a pragmatic evaluation of "levels of appearance," on the basis of the *fruitfulness* and *operational efficacy* of particular interpretations of the external data (for example, in terms of utility for the preservation of the species, cf. GS 110; KSA 3, 469–71, and NL 1888, KSA 13, 14[153]). When the illusory character of the "fact" of knowledge is revealed (NL 1886–87, KSA 12, 7[4]) – that is, when we see that it is nothing but "a chain of deductions and spider's webs" (NL 1881, KSA 9, 15[9]) – then the dichotomy between truth and appearance is dissolved, as much as the belief that substance-concepts can be encountered (the "things in themselves" that traditional philosophy aimed to reach, cf. NL 1886–87, KSA 12, 5[14]).[35]

Thus, we encounter once more the problem of the *unconditioned* that have been briefly explored above, in § 2, and Nietzsche's related critique of a theory of knowledge claiming the existence of substance-concepts. According to that epistemological conception, the meaning of logical constructs would be based on the ontological dimension they refer to, and it would therefore possible to say something about a given object once it has been isolated from all its characters ("as if a world would still remain over after one deducted the perspective!" NL 1888, KSA 13, 14[184]; my translation). It is precisely from this criticism that Nietzsche develops his own new defi-

---

[35] On that issue, Mattia Riccardi's observations on the distinction between "true" and "apparent" world in Nietzsche are particularly interesting (2009, p. 207 ff.). Riccardi focuses on Nietzsche's reading of the works of M. Drossbach (*Über die scheinbaren und die wirklichen Ursachen des Geschehens in der Welt*) and G. Teichmüller (*Die wirkliche und die scheinbare Welt*), and stresses that both these authors distinguish between *apparent* (*Scheinbare*) and *real* (*Wirkliche*) world, whereas Nietzsche talks of a *true* world (*Wahre Welt*). This can be explained by making reference to the metaphysical view of the first two authors, that is, to their idea that human knowledge, being purely phenomenal, is no access to reality. Therefore, she must be devaluated, and we can call "apparent" the realm of our knowledge in contraposition to the world as it is *in itself*. Nietzsche's case is completely different. According to him, the "apparent" world is the (only possible) product of our human cognitive – perspectival – activity, and we should therefore evaluate it positively (Riccardi 2009, p. 216 ff.). Thus, that dimension must be contrasted to the "true" world, a purely logical construction that does not reproduce the "self-subsistent," "real" dimension at all (cf. HH I 11; KSA 2, p. 30–1). On the contrary, as we read for example in the posthumous fragment 1885, 40[53], Nietzsche considers "real" only the dimension of appearances: "N. B. *Appearance*, as I conceive it, is the real and only reality of things [*Schein wie ich es verstehe, ist die wirkliche und einzige Realität der Dinge*], to which only pertain all the existing attributes, and that can be relatively well described with attributes of any kind, even if contrasting. Nevertheless, that term means only what is *inaccessible* to logical procedures and distinctions: therefore 'apparent' compared to 'logical truth' – which is itself only possible in an imaginary world [*imaginären Welt*]. Thus, I do not see 'appearance' and 'reality' as contraposed, but rather conceive the appearance as reality, which herself contrasts the transformation in an imaginary 'world of truths.' A proper name for that reality could be 'will to power,' but only if we describe it from the inside, and not by making reference to her elusive and fluid protean nature." (NL 1885, KSA 11, 40[53]; my translation. On this, see also Figl 1982, p. 113.)

nition of "knowledge." According to him, that term cannot refer to something that does not depend on the active, interpretative character of both the sense organs and the intellect.³⁶ The *entire* range of what is "knowable" to us falls within the context of what is "conditioned," and it is not possible to speak of anything which is not filtered by our perceptual and cognitive apparatus. For that reason, on the one hand it is possible (indeed, necessary, according to that model) to admit the existence of an "external world" (*Außenwelt*) grounding any cognitive process (cf. NL 1886–87, KSA 12, 7[54]); but, on the other hand, any reference to a Kantian "thing in itself" must be rejected. According to Nietzsche, the thing in itself is quite different from the *Außenwelt*. The former is in fact the empty hypostatization of the product of a categorial activity, and therefore it is not possible to attribute to it an existence of any sort on the ontological level. The radicality of Nietzsche's critique of the "thing in itself" can be assessed by considering that, in his view, it rests out of the very *range* of "knowledge." Consequently, even to speak of it is meaningless. As stated above, by arguing that "inasmuch as the word 'knowledge' has any meaning at all," Nietzsche presupposes that we can only know what we shape (and therefore condition). Therefore, the very idea that something unconditioned (such as in principle every "thing in itself" should be, for it is precisely "in itself" and not "defined by anything else") may fall within the boundaries of the "knowable," is in fact a *contradictio in adjecto* (cf. BGE 16; KSA 5, p. 29, and NL 1885–86, KSA 12, 2[154]).³⁷

That view, which is consistent with the epistemological agnosticism that Nietzsche already defended in HH I 9, is well expressed in the important aphorism 354 published in the fifth book of *The Gay Science*, where Nietzsche explicitly

---

**36** This is well stated in GM III 12 (KSA 5, p. 363–5), a paragraph in which Nietzsche discusses some epistemological positions that he attributes to Kant. Nietzsche especially focuses on "the dangerous old conceptual fairy-tale which has set up a 'pure, will-less, painless, timeless, subject of knowledge', let us be wary of the tentacles of such contradictory concepts as 'pure reason', 'absolute spirituality', 'knowledge as such': – here we are asked to think an eye which cannot be thought at all, an eye turned in no direction at all, an eye where the active and interpretative powers are to be suppressed, absent, but through which seeing still becomes a seeing-something, so it is an absurdity and nonconcept of eye that is demanded. There is *only* a perspectival seeing, *only* a perspectival 'knowing'."
**37** The idea that, in principle, we cannot even speak of a "thing in itself," means that we cannot neither attribute or deny an existence to it. The very notion of "existence" has a meaning only within our cognitive dimension, in the context of a world-description that *translates* a datum into something that is understandable to us. For that reason, Nietzsche's criticism of the "thing in itself" must be understood first of all on the epistemological level, that is, by making reference to his reflection on the concept of "knowledge." The notion of "thing in itself" for Nietzsche is contradictory, *unthinkable*, something that simply "is not given" (as much as the notion of "absolute knowledge," which is related with the former. Cf. NL 1885, KSA 11, 34[120]). To say something about a "thing in itself" would mean to get it into the sphere of the conditioned, thus attributing to it features that pertain only to the "apparent" world – which is as contradictory as that of the absolute forms, for it arises from the contraposition with a presumed realm of substance-entities (NL 1884, KSA 11, 26[413]. Cf. Figl 1982, p. 113). As a result, we would alter the original purity and absoluteness which is essential to that notion.

addresses the question of perspectivism. After a long reflection on consciousness and language, Nietzsche observes:

> As one might guess, it is not the opposition between subject and object which concerns me here; I leave that distinction to those epistemologists who have got tangled up in the snares of grammar (or folk metaphysics). Even less I am concerned with the opposition between "thing in itself" and appearance: for we "know" far too little to even be entitled to *make* that distinction. We simply have no organ for *knowing*, for "truth." (GS 354; KSA 3, p. 593)

In this passage, Nietzsche develops the brief remark on the knowability of the world written in NL 1886–87, 7[60]. In GS 354, too, the word *knowledge* appears within quotation marks, as to express that is should be re-defined, that the meaning acquired by this notion during the history of Western philosophy as much as in the ordinary conception must be put up to question. What should be rejected firstly, in Nietzsche's view, is the very possibility of any knowledge leading to "truth." In fact, according to what has been shown above, he believes that a notion of this kind does not agree with the way our perceptual and cognitive organs are structured. According to what Nietzsche observes a few lines above in the same aphorism, perspectivism is the view that "due to the nature of *animal consciousness*, the world of which we can become conscious is merely a surface- and sign-world, a world turned into generalities [...]. All becoming conscious involves a vast and thorough corruption, falsification, superficialization, and generalization." (GS 354; KSA 3, p. 593) That falsificationist epistemology makes it impossible to conceive of a knowledge that directly relates us with reality. We have absolutely no access to that dimension, for everything which is "knowable" is filtered by our consciousness, thus becoming superficial and general.

The idea that anything that falls within the realm of the *unconditioned* is cognitively inaccessible for us, is consistent with that view. But the idea that it is not even possible to *think* of such an unconditioned and, therefore, that we are not even allowed to *make* the distinction between an apparent or phenomenal world and the dimension of hypothetical substance-notions (the "things in themselves"), arises from another reflection. Nietzsche developed that reflection in 1886, while he was writing the fifth book of *The Gay Science* (which has been published only the following year). In a posthumous fragment from that period, we find it well-expressed:

> [To make] the distinction between an "essence of things" and a world of appearances [...] one would have to conceive of our intellect as afflicted with a contradictory character: on the one hand adapted to a perspectival way of seeing, as precisely creatures of our species must be to preserve their existence; on the other, capable of grasping this perspectival seeing as perspectival, the appearance as appearance. In other words, equipped with a belief in "reality" as if it were the only one, and yet also with knowledge about this belief, the knowledge that it's only a perspectival restriction with respect to a true reality. Yet a belief looked at with this knowledge ceases to be belief, is dissolved as belief. In short, we must not conceive of our intellect as being so contradictory that it is simultaneously both a belief and a knowledge of that belief as

belief. Let's abolish the "thing-in-itself" and with it one of the least clear concepts, that of "appearance"! (NL 1886–87, KSA 12, 6[23])

In this fragment Nietzsche focuses on a problem that, elsewhere, he addresses to Kant, namely how an organ – and particularly reason – would be capable of criticizing itself? Isn't that critique pursued according to the same mechanisms that one aims to analyse – possibly in an objective way, and therefore from an external viewpoint? Nietzsche's reflections especially concern the perspectival feature of human cognitive activity, a feature that our intellect cannot "critically" investigate, for that would require us to leave aside something that physiologically belongs to it. In showing that even conceiving of that possibility is contradictory, Nietzsche invites us to abandon the fundamental distinction presupposed by Western metaphysics, namely the dichotomy between the realm of the illusory "things in themselves" and that of the equally illusory "appearances." According to Nietzsche, only by admitting the fundamental perspectival character of our knowledge it will be possible to realize an actual development, thus determining a new kind of culture – and, consequently, a new type of man.[38]

The same consideration expressed in the above quoted 1886–87 note 6[23] can be found in an important aphorism published in the fifth book of *The Gay Science*. In GS 374, titled *Our new "infinite,"* Nietzsche in fact writes:

> How far the perspectival character of existence extends, or indeed whether it has any other character, whether an existence without interpretation, without "sense"; whether, on the other hand, all existence isn't essentially an *interpreting* existence – that cannot, as would be fair, be decided even by the most industrious and extremely conscientious analysis and self-examination of the intellect; for in the course of this analysis, the human intellect cannot avoid seeing itself under its perspectival forms, and *solely* in these. (GS 374; KSA 3, p. 626)

But Nietzsche's argument goes further. Not only does he hold to be impossible for our intellect to reflect objectively and critically on itself, that is, to gain access to a *nonperspectival* level of reality; he also thinks that "it is a hopeless curiosity to want to know what other kinds of intellects and perspectives there *might* be." (GS 374; KSA 3, p. 626) The idea that "we cannot look around our corner" is thus for Nietzsche the principle of an intellectual modesty that he hopes future philosophers will embrace. That would imply the rejection of the prejudice according to which "in the categories of reason [one possesses] the criterion of truth or *reality*" (NL 1888, KSA 13, 14[153]), and rather to admit that our can be only one of the many possible ways of looking at

---

[38] Nietzsche's interest in the development of a higher *Typus Mensch*, and the possible connections of his mature thought with the aims of philosophical anthropology, have been explored in Schacht 2006 and 2015, and in Gori 2017c.

the world.[39] Moreover, in GS 374 Nietzsche expresses his belief in the fact that "today we are at least far away from the ridiculous immodesty of decreeing from our angle that perspectives are *permitted* only from this angle," and finally argues: "Rather, the world has once again become infinite to us: insofar as we cannot reject the possibility *that it includes infinite interpretations.*" (GS 374; KSA 3, p. 627)

The idea that there could be infinite interpretations, whose awareness is accompanied by a "great shudder" (GS 374; KSA 3, p. 627), is one of the most important outcomes of Nietzsche's mature philosophy.[40] In fact, it represents the core of a thought that invites men to bear the weight of the "death of God," and to experience that event as the final liberation from the old metaphysics. In Nietzsche's view, who would be capable of facing "the greatest recent event [which] is already starting to cast its first shadow over Europe," would also find an "open sea" full of possibilities in front of him, a clear horizon he would look to with optimism and "cheerfulness." (GS 343; KSA 3, p. 574)[41] I cannot thoroughly deal with this topic here. I will only show that the possibility of infinite interpretations can be also found *in nuce* in the posthumous note 1886–87, 7[60]. In that fragment, after having observed that "inasmuch as the word 'knowledge' has any meaning at all, the world is knowable," Nietzsche in fact argues that "it is variously interpretable; it has no meaning behind it, but countless meanings." The dichotomy that appears at the beginning of the posthumous note is further stated, here: the "fact" of knowledge, which Nietzsche puts up to question, is contrasted with the indefinite multiplicity of possible "interpretations." In so doing, Nietzsche outlines a new philosophical practice, which starts where modern critical thought stops. While the latter, after having dismantled the old metaphysical system, is not capable of building a new one, Nietzsche's future philosophy can rather achieve that goal. To put it differently, one could say that, for Nietzsche, questioning "facts" is not an ending point, but rather the foundation of a brand-new way of thinking. Of course, that will disorient, initially, given that the traditional reference points will disappear and, consequently, one could be worried for not knowing how to manage the multiplicity of possible interpretations. But this phase will pass, and to a properly educated man that chaos will soon appear as the fertile ground for the creation of new forms – none of which, of course, will ever exhaust its potentialities.

That philosophical practice follows from Nietzsche's reflections on "perspectivism," a notion which in NL 1886–87, 7[60] he introduces immediately after the remarks on "knowledge." That will therefore be addressed, but only after having com-

---

[39] Of course, this also involves the practical level. Even if Nietzsche's discourse arises from an epistemological question, intellectual modesty also concerns the assessment of moral values. Incidentally, the notion of "perspectivism" includes both these planes.
[40] This is especially explored in Figl 1982.
[41] For a discussion of the notion of "cheerfulness" (*Heiterkeit*) in Nietzsche, cf. Stegmaier 2012, p. 95, and Gori/Piazzesi 2012, p. 125, and Sommer 2012, p. 214.

pleted the contextualization of that fragment, for which we still need one last, fundamental element.

## 2.5 Against positivism

In the previous sections I have not considered an observation that Nietzsche writes at the very beginning of the 1886–87 note 7[69], which is fundamental in order to contextualize that fragment. The critical remark on the dichotomy between "facts" and "interpretations" is in fact addressed to the defenders of positivism, a philosophical position that Nietzsche explicitly faces, here. Interpreters have always stressed Nietzsche's generic anti-positivist orientation, describing him as an anti-scientist thinker as much as a strong critic of any rational description of the world, which, in his view, would be not capable of grasping the nuances and deeper meaning of reality. Indeed, the contraposition between "facts" and "interpretations" is consistent with the considerations that Nietzsche writes for example in GS 373, and it would therefore possible to see it as the supreme synthesis of a philosophy aimed at showing that any attempt to deal with the world by reducing it to logical formulas is destined to fail. However, this is not entirely true, as the content of the 1886–87 fragment so far analysed shows. In fact, that content refers to a quite specific epistemological position, within which Nietzsche's critique of positivism must be contextualized and, consequently, in the light of which it can be interpreted: "phenomenalism."[42]

The term "phenomenalism" appears in the works of several authors active during the second half of the nineteenth century (many of whom were known to Nietzsche).[43] It has been used to define a philosophical movement that occurred at the turn of the century and which has been programmatically described by Hans Kleinpeter in his *Der Phänomenalismus. Eine naturwissenschaftliche Weltanschauung* (1913).[44] As argued above, from a general point of view, phenomenalism can be seen

---

[42] For a brief examination of that concept and the philosophical movement related to it, cf. Halbfass 1989.
[43] Nietzsche knew for sure the works of maybe the most important upholders of phenomenalism, namely Richard Avenarius and Ernst Mach (see Gori 2009). Among the other authors known by Nietzsche, E. von Hartmann, F. Ueberweg and J. E. Erdmann referred to phenomenalism. As remarked by Werner Stegmaier (2012, p. 280 fn.), however, there is no evidence that Nietzsche read the works in which these authors dealt with that topic. Finally, another author who may have more directly influenced Nietzsche on phenomenalism (even though he talks about it more as a human cognitive dimension than as a philosophical position) is Otto Liebmann (see on this Riccardi 2014, p. 248f.).
[44] I deal with Kleinpeter's work in chapter 4 of this volume. What is worth mentioning, here, is that he includes Nietzsche among the forerunners of phenomenalism, claiming that Nietzsche shared Mach's epistemological views (Kleinpeter 2013, p. 27, 143, 174, 208, 226). On this, see also Gori 2012a. On the historical-cultural context of Mach's epistemology and his phenomenalism see Blackmore *et alia* 2001.

as a development of positivism in an anti-metaphysical direction. Phenomenalism started from the philosophy of Kant and its problematic approach to the "thing in itself," a fundamental question of modern epistemology that has been debated by many thinkers that inspired Nietzsche (e.g. F. Lange, A. Spir, and G. Teichmüller).[45] Phenomenalism is agnostic about that issue: according to that view, the problem of the "thing in itself" cannot even be posed, for it rests beyond the physiological limits of human knowledge.[46] Moreover, phenomenalist thinkers argue that it is not possible to reach an adequate knowledge of the world; therefore, the traditional notion of "truth" as "agreement of an idea with reality" must be abandoned, and the notion of truth has to be re-defined in instrumental and pragmatic terms.[47] But the theory of knowledge is not the only issue that phenomenalism shares with the view explored in the previous sections. Another issue is that of subjectivity, which phenomenalism, on the basis of the outcomes of the nineteenth-century scientific psychology, addresses critically, firmly contesting the existence of a substantial entity called "I" or "soul."[48] Contrarily to what is ordinarily assumed, the object of psychological studies would be only a fiction, a purely logical entity that cannot be encountered out of the field of theoretical studies. Psychology (cognitive science) traditionally aims to grasp that object, but in fact she cannot find anything *real* under the models and functions she develops.[49]

For the purposes of this chapter, the relationship between phenomenalism and positivism deserves to be further explored. All the elements that have been considered so far, in fact, define a philosophical position that, instead of being opposed to the positivists' view, is a critical development of the epistemology defended by them. Roughly speaking, we could conceive of it as a self-re-assessment of the scientific enterprise. What is especially disputed by authors such as E. Mach – which shares the general anti-metaphysical attitude of late-nineteenth-century thinkers – is the fact that natural sciences presuppose a substance-metaphysics which is inconsistent with the outcomes of scientific research. Subjectivity is an example from the field of psychology, but the same situation can be encountered in physics (just think, for example, at the debate on the atomic model that occurred at the beginning of the

---

[45] The literature on this is extensive. See, among others, Stack 1983; Salaquarda 1978; Green 2002; D'Iorio 1993; and Orsucci 1997.
[46] As argued in the previous section, Nietzsche defends this view in GS 354. On this, see also Stegmaier 2012, p. 281.
[47] Phenomenalism was immediately compared with pragmatism (see Kleinpeter 1912a and Berthelot 1911, chapter 3). Indeed, James's pragmatist conception of truth was inspired by Mach's epistemology, as James explicitly admitted (see James 1907, e.g. p. 57 and 190). I will deal with it more thoroughly in the fifth chapter of this volume.
[48] On this, the observations of both Lange and Mach (whose studies in psychology were grounded on J. Müller's physiology as much as on G. Fechner's psychophysics) are particularly important to understand Nietzsche's view on subjectivity. See above, § 3 and, for a more detailed study of this topic, Gori 2015b.
[49] On this, see Lange 1882 II/3, chapter 2; Mach 1914 [1886], chapter 1, and 1976 [1905], chapter 1.

twentieth century). More generally, the discussion involved the mechanistic paradigm as a whole, a view that was widely accepted ever since Newton and whose principles were undisputed (see Gori 2014). It is therefore necessary to better contextualize the issue, in order to understand what phenomenalism actually was: namely, a research program sharing with positivism several principles, but which can be distinguished from that view insofar as the former rejects the metaphysical features of positivism. That is why, for example in the case of Mach, it is possible to talk of *post-positivism*. Thus doing, one makes sense of the continuity relating Comte to twentieth-century logical positivists, so as of the fact that the latter have been deeply inspired by Mach's *anti-metaphysical* conception (on this, see Stadler 1982 and 2015).

With all likelihood, Nietzsche was aware, if not of phenomenalism as a philosophical movement (for it was still arising, at his time), at least of the reflections carried out by its most important representatives.[50] Above in this chapter (§ 2.2) I argued that in the 1888 fragment where the dichotomy between "facts" and "interpretations" reappears, Nietzsche explicitly refers to the mechanistic view. In that posthumous annotation, Nietzsche writes, in particular, that "all the presuppositions of mechanistic language – matter, atom, pressure and impact, gravity – are not 'facts-in-themselves' but interpretations aided by *psychological* fictions" (NL 1888, KSA 13, 14[82]), thus arguing that to deal with the inner senses within that theoretical framework is at least naïve as much as fruitless. As it has been shown, that reference is already a hint on the way Nietzsche's dichotomy between "facts" and "interpretations" should be contextualized, for it invites us to consider that observation within the post-positivistic view of phenomenalism. This is not enough to demonstrate that Nietzsche's critique of positivism in fact arises from that particular epistemology, of course. Further support can be however funded in two posthumous fragments where several of the elements considered so far can be encountered.

The first of them (NL 1885–86, KSA 12, 2[131]) is a draft index, probably for *The Will to Power*. In that fragment, Nietzsche refers to phenomenalism as the view affirming that "there are no facts" (*gibt es keine Tatsachen*). The second one (NL 1885–86, KSA 12, 2[184]) is a much shorter annotation, where Nietzsche briefly outlines determinism and phenomenalism, and attributes to the latter the idea that "we do know nothing of a 'thing in itself'." From what has been shown above, it can be easily seen that both these elements belong to the posthumous fragment 1886–85, 7[60]. In that note, Nietzsche in fact criticizes the idea of a knowledge ca-

---

[50] George Stack (1980, p. 37), deals with the type of phenomenalism proposed by Lange, who, according to Stack, "offers a psychologistic account of Kant's theory of knowledge that certainly had considerable influences on Nietzsche's epistemic reflections." Moreover, Stack argues that "in this regard, it is certainly true that Nietzsche himself did want to be a phenomenalist." (In support of this thesis, Stack refers to Hollingdale 1973, p. 138) Furthermore, Stack observes that "ironically, neither Lange nor Nietzsche seem to have known that Kant continued to wrestle with his notion of *Ding an sich* in his *Opus postumum*, reaching conclusions that, in some respects, anticipate Nietzsche's fictionalist interpretation of the idea." (Stack 1980, p. 39)

pable of reaching the noumenal plane of reality (the realm of "facts 'in themselves'") and, starting from the idea that "inasmuch as the word 'knowledge' has any meaning at all, the world is knowable," he invites us to conceive of an epistemology confined to the phenomenal dimension and which would not aim to trespass that limit. Moreover, and maybe most importantly, such an epistemology would admit that human knowledge has nothing to do with absolute "truths" or universal "facts." Therefore, it would affirm the illusory and hypothetical character of the phenomenal dimension. That involves everything that falls within the traditional (metaphysical) world-description, starting from the subject as "immediate certainty" and, from a broader point of view, the "internal facts" we ordinarily (and erroneously) pretend to refer to. To admit that viewpoint in fact means to de-construct all those conceptions and, consequently, to dismantle the whole metaphysical system of old Western philosophy.

That critical attitude has been explored above (§ 3), but it is worth dealing with it again, in order to stress that also on this point it is possible to find important connections with Nietzsche's thought. Indeed, his view of the phenomenal character of our world-description (both internal and external) seems to be inspired by the principles of the late-nineteenth-century epistemology. In NL 1888, KSA 13, 14[152], in fact, we read that "one must not look for phenomenalism in the wrong place: nothing is as phenomenal (or better) nothing is as *illusory [Täuschung]* as this inner world that we observe through the well-known 'inner sense'" (my translation). This remark can be also found in a later note, in which Nietzsche focuses on the "phenomenalism of the 'inner world'," which interferes with the way we conceive the relationship of cause and effect (NL 1888, KSA 13, 15[90]).

The semantic consistency between NL 1886–87, 7[60] and the passages where Nietzsche speaks of phenomenalism allow us to conclude that, with all likelihood, the dichotomy between facts and interpretations that he contrasts with the positivistic conception can be adequately contextualized (and therefore understood) only by referring to the scientific world-conception of his time. From what has been shown above, in fact, Nietzsche explicitly ascribes to phenomenalism a set of assumptions that he himself embraces in that posthumous note, and that epistemological view can be also found at the basis of some considerations he further develops. This cannot be neglected, if one aims to analyse Nietzsche's terminology and to understand the actual meaning of one of his most famous and controversial remarks. Thus, one must refer to phenomenalism in order to properly pursue the dichotomy between "facts" and "interpretations." Furthermore, that view can also shed light on the important notion of "perspectivism" that Nietzsche first mentions in the 1886–87 note, and which will be investigated in the following section. As for Nietzsche's criticism towards positivism (in the explored fragment as much as in his late period), the contextual reading provides relevant elements on the way he approaches that issues.

Rather than as a generic anti-scientist attitude, Nietzsche's criticism can in fact be seen as a post-positivistic one.[51]

## 2.6 "Perspectivism"

The last aspect that the present research must deal with is maybe one of the most famous and studied topics of Nietzsche's thought: "perspectivism." As known, this "visual metaphor" (Anderson 1998, p. 2) – that in Nietzsche has an original epistemological meaning, but whose consequences on the hermeneutical plane in general and morality in particular must not be neglected[52] – has often been seen by the interpreters as one of the "fundamental ideas" of Nietzsche's philosophy. Despite Nietzsche only develops that idea in his late period, and the references to "perspectivism" are but a few (in the published texts),[53] that notion in fact introduces a particularly interesting, multifaceted, and philosophically relevant thematic field.[54] In what follows, attention will be paid mainly to the contextualization of Nietzsche's concept of "perspectivism" in NL 1886–87, 7[60], but some observations on the value and scope of the philosophical position related to that notion will also be provided.

The noun "perspectivism" (*Perspektivismus*) has been coined by Nietzsche,[55] even though the idea of a "perspectival seeing" was already present in Gustav Teichmüller's *Die wirkliche und die scheinbare Welt* (1882), although in different terms.[56] With all likelihood, Nietzsche has been influenced by that book, which he read in 1883.[57] In that work, Teichmüller critically deals with Kantianism, and de-

---

[51] See on this the discussion between Hussain 2004a and Clark/Dudrick 2004.
[52] Cf. Gori 2011b and chapter 3 of this volume.
[53] Nietzsche especially speaks of "perspectivism" and "perspectival seeing" (in a philosophical and non-literal sense of the term) in *Beyond Good and Evil* (Preface, §§ 11 and 34; KSA 5, p. 24–6 and 52–4), in the *Genealogy of Morality* (GM III 12; KSA 5, p. 363–5) and in the fifth book of *The Gay Science* (GS 354 and GS 374; KSA 3, p. 590–3 and 626–7). Other references to that concept can be found in the prefaces added to the second editions of the *Birth of Tragedy* (Attempt at Self-Criticism 5; KSA 1, p. 17–9) and *Human, All Too Human* (Preface 6; KSA 2, p. 20–1), both written in 1886. The issue of perspectivism is more extensively mentioned in the unpublished writings, a fact that allow us to argue that Nietzsche was actually working on that topic. See on this Dellinger 2012.
[54] The richness of that notion can be judged from the interpretive work that has been developed in the past decades. See e.g. Leiter 1994; Clark 1990; Kaulbach 1990; Gerhardt 1989; and Stack 1981b.
[55] The word *Perspektivismus* appears four times in Nietzsche's writings, and only one of these occurrences can be found in a printed work. Moreover, only in GS 354 and in NL 1886–87, 7[60] the term identifies a philosophical position rather than a particular viewpoint that cannot be ignored (see e.g. NL 1888, 14[186]).
[56] Cf. Dellinger 2012; Small 2001; and Nohl 1913.
[57] Cf. Brobjer 2008, p. 52. Dellinger (2012, p. 133–4) observes that Teichmüller uses the concept of "perspectival" in two works, *Darwinismus und Philosophie* (1877) and *Über das Wesen der Liebe* (1879), which Nietzsche probably never read. However, continues Dellinger, in Otto Caspari's *Der Zu-*

scribes past philosophical systems as "purely perspectival images," since they project metaphysical forms or concepts onto reality (Teichmüller 1882, p. XVI). Moreover, Teichmüller contrasts the apparent (*scheinbar*) or perspectival (*perspektivistisch*) world with the real (*wirklich*) one, as Nietzsche, inspired by him, will do some years later (speaking of *Wahrheit* instead of *Wirklichkeit*). Indeed, while Nietzsche fully admits the idea that the realm of "appearances" is in fact the dimension of "perspectival" forms, he rejects the very possibility of stating *another* epistemic plane. Therefore, the existence of a non-perspectival reality that cannot be inferred rationally cannot even be posed (see Dellinger 2012, p. 135; Riccardi 2009, p. 216 ff.; and above, footnote 35).

Nietzsche disagrees with Teichmüller on the contraposition between the planes of reality, but he rather accepts other important ideas published in *Die wirkliche und die scheinbare Welt*, as one can infer especially from some passages published in *Beyond Good and Evil* (see Orsucci 2001, p. 215 ff., and Orsucci 1997). For example, Teichmüller is one of the "skeptical anti-realists and epistemo-microscopists" that Nietzsche describes in BGE 10 while rejecting the celebrated positivist philosophical view. Apparently, in Teichmüller's work Nietzsche found several examples of a reflection on language revealing the substance-metaphysics involved in the logico-syntactic forms we daily use. In his late writings, Nietzsche talks repeatedly of the "seduction of words" (BGE 16; KSA 5, p. 29), the "common philosophy of grammar" created by the "the spell of particular grammatical functions" (BGE 20; KSA 5, p. 34), and our being caught up in "the snares of grammar" (GS 354; KSA 3, p. 593); and he does so in the context of a criticism of "folk metaphysics" (GS 354; KSA 3, p. 593), that he blames to believe in substance-atoms and immortal souls (BGE 12 and BGE 54; KSA 5, p. 26–7 and 73).[58] Indeed, Nietzsche's dealing with the problem of subjectivity was also inspired by Teichmüller, albeit the latter is criticized because he admits the existence of a substance-subject creating the metaphysical, merely ideal, notions

---

*sammenhang der Dinge* (1881, p. 141–84) Nietzsche encountered a detailed (critical) analysis of Teichmüller's view. Nietzsche could have approached that topic for the first time in that occasion, before the actual reading of Teichmüller's 1882 book that inspired his late thought.

**58** More on this can be found in BGE 16 and BGE 281 (KSA 5, p. 29–30 and 230), where Nietzsche reflects on the "seduction of words," as much as in BGE 34, where he warns us about the excessive "belief in grammar" that we ordinarily show. See also GM I 13; KSA g, p. 279–80: "All our science, in spite of its coolness and freedom from emotion, still stands exposed to the seduction of language and has not rid itself of the changelings foisted upon it, the 'subjects' (the atom is, for example, just such a changeling, likewise the Kantian 'thing-in-itself')." These observations are further developed in TI, "Reason" in Philosophy 5, where Nietzsche criticizes precisely the metaphysics of language for conveying the idea of an I as a substance endowed with causal efficacy. Nietzsche conclusively remarks: "I am afraid that we have not got rid of God because we still have faith in grammar." (TI, "Reason" in Philosophy 5; KSA 6, p. 78) In general, it must be said that several references to Teichmüller can be encountered in the whole section *"Reason" in philosophy* (cf. Gori/Piazzesi 2012, p. 168, and Sommer 2012, p. 285 ff.).

that we "project" onto reality (on this, see Dellinger 2012, p. 134, and Loukidelis 2014, p. 227 ff.).

Therefore, although Teichmüller's ontological view proves to be deeply metaphysical, Nietzsche nevertheless shares (and consequently adopts) some of his epistemological observations related to the "perspectival" plane. On this, the posthumous fragment 1885, KSA 11, 40[23], where Nietzsche invites us to be "more cautious than Descartes, who was caught by the words's trap," is of some interest. That note deals with the problem of the *I think* that Nietzsche develops in BGE 16 and BGE 17, strongly rejecting Descartes's view according to which that notion is an "immediate certainty." As past researches have shown, that passage is in fact particularly consistent with some observations contained in Teichmüller's 1882 work. In that book, Teichmüller especially claims that metaphysicians always neglected the problem of "being" because ordinary language makes us believe that notion to be "something certain and self-evident." (Teichmüller 1882, p. 3 and 24 ff. See also Orsucci 2001, p. 216, and Loukidelis 2013.) Moreover, Teichmüller describes natural science as a mere "semiotic" and a "sign-system"; that is, an inquiry which is not capable to grasp even the surface of reality (Teichmüller 1882, p. 275).

It is not necessary to further explore that issue, to see how this conception could have influenced Nietzsche. Nietzsche's argument against modern physics, based on the idea that it is "only an interpretation and arrangement of the world [...] and *not* an explanation of the world." (BGE 14; KSA 5, p. 28. See also BGE 21 and 22; KSA 5, p. 35–7, and, more generally, GS 373; KSA 3, p. 624–6)[59] is in fact well known (and, unfortunately, most of the times misinterpreted as a general as much as superficial anti-scientific stance). Teichmüller's view of that topic is grounded on a broader epistemological reflection, namely on the idea that any knowledge we may have – with the only exception of the knowledge of the existence of an I as substance! – falls within the range of the mentioned semiotic. Therefore, our knowledge is nothing but a superficial and schematic representation of reality (cf. Small 2001, p. 44). This view is consistent with the principles of Nietzsche's epistemology explored above – of course, if we exclude the observations on the "real" world, a dimension that in Nietzsche's ontology cannot exist, and which he therefore substitutes with the *unreal* "true" world of the hypostatized logical forms. However, it is worth remembering that the idea that "there is *only* a perspectival seeing, *only* a perspectival 'knowing'" (GM III 12; KSA 5, p. 365) is grounded on an epistemology that already permeates Nietzsche's early writings (those written before 1883). Therefore, it cannot have been inspired by Teichmüller's work – at least not exclusively. The only influence one

---

[59] Orsucci (2001, p. 218) focuses on what Nietzsche argues in BGE 14; KSA 5, p. 28. In that aphorisms, Nietzsche deals with "our belief in the senses" and the "evidence" of "our eyes and fingers" as the foundation of the mechanistic view in physics. Moreover, Orsucci stresses Nietzsche's interest on atomism, that arose in the early years to be further developed only after 1884 and finally summed up in BGE 12; KSA 5, p. 26–7. All these topics directly lead to Teichmüller's *Die wirkliche und die scheinbare Welt*.

can attribute to that text concerns the terminology which Nietzsche adopted, with some modifications, in order to give a proper name to the multifaceted and original philosophical position he was elaborating.

Teichmüller's post-Kantian conception thus provides us with a first contextualization of the notion of "perspectivism," which is consistent with the content of the fragment 1886–87, 7[60]. However, from what has been argued above, it is possible to say that, although Nietzsche does not explicitly mention it, phenomenalism is the actual fundamental premise of the philosophical view that he outlines in that note. In fact, all the elements which Nietzsche deals with in the first part of that fragment – namely, the negation of the existence of "facts in themselves"; the deconstruction of the subject as a "fact"; and the affirmation of the interpretative character of "knowledge" – belong to the epistemology that arose from the development of Kantianism and that was widely debated during the second half of the nineteenth century. This hypothesis is supported by the important aphorism 354 of *The Gay Science*, the only published text in which Nietzsche not only uses the noun "perspectivism," but also provides us with a clear definition of that concept. Incidentally, this notion is closely linked to that of "phenomenalism," as if the two terms were synonyms:

> This is what *I* consider to be the true phenomenalism and perspectivism: that due to the nature of *animal consciousness*, the world of which we can become conscious is merely a surface- and sign-world, a world turned into generalities and thereby debased to its lowest common denominator, – [...] that all becoming conscious involves a vast and thorough corruption, falsification, superficialization, and generalization. (GS 354; KSA 3, p. 593)

Nietzsche's definition confirms that perspectivism is grounded on a theory of knowledge according to which our consciousness intervenes on the data we receive from the external world, and falsifies – that is, modifies – them, thus determining the fundamental phenomenal character of human knowledge. The way consciousness processes our knowledge has been considered while exploring the problem of the "immediate facts" and self-observation. In that occasion, it has been already remarked the pivotal role that issue plays in Nietzsche's posthumous fragment 1886–87, 7[60]. The connection of Nietzsche's view of consciousness with both the notions of phenomenalism and perspectivism is further stressed in two notes that can be encountered in the same 1886–87 notebook, among the preparatory material for *The Will to Power*. In the first of them (7[1]), Nietzsche rhetorically asks: "Are all the phenomena of consciousness not merely final phenomena, last links in a chain which, however, give the appearance of conditioning each other in their succession on a single plane of consciousness?" That description, according to Nietzsche, "could be an illusion." Consequently, it would be better to put up to question our belief in self-observation, and argue that we are most likely not capable to observe the alleged "facts of consciousness." Nietzsche further develops his reflection and, a few lines below, outlines an actual theory of knowledge that, given the language he uses, one can call "phenomenalistic" rather than "perspectivistic":

It is *not* the case that the world is thus and thus, and living beings see it as it appears to them. Instead: the world consists of such living beings, and for each of them there is a particular little angle from which it measures, notices, sees and does not see. There is *no* "essence": what "becomes", the "phenomenal", is the only kind of being. (NL 1886–87, KSA 12, 7[1])

The second note, number 7[9], deals with the same topic, but in a different way. In fact, Nietzsche focuses on the "value of *inner* and *external phenomenology* [*der Werth der inneren und der äußeren Phänomenologie*]" and, this time adopting a terminology more adherent to his reflections on perspectivism, observes that "inner phenomena are difficult to grasp, and the closest to error." (NL 1886–87, KSA 12, 7[9]; my translation) Furthermore, Nietzsche remarks that "inner processes essentially *imply errors*, for life is only possible on the basis of these narrowing and perspective-creating [*perspective-schaffender*] powers." What is mostly interesting in this posthumous fragment, however, is the premise of the whole reasoning, which is quite similar to the "definition" of perspectivism and phenomenalism that one encounters in GS 354. In the 1886–87 notebook, Nietzsche writes that "the development of *consciousness* occurred lately and miserably, pursuing external purposes and exposed to the greatest errors; she is *in her very core* something that falsifies, coarsens, summarizes." (NL 1886–87, KSA 12, 7[9]; my translation) These excerpts are not conclusive, if isolated from the general argument that Nietzsche develops throughout the years. But they support the idea that NL 1886–87, 7[60] contains all the necessary elements to outline Nietzsche's late "perspectivism," and that this position can in fact be contextualized properly within the phenomenalist conception. Indeed, that fragment is consistent with the definition that Nietzsche provides in GS 354, for in that aphorism the idea that consciousness has a falsifying nature is followed by considerations reaffirming Nietzsche's view that there are no "facts in themselves," that the notion of "subject" is but the product of a "false self-observation" and, in general, that our concept of knowledge must be re-defined in order to account for its merely interpretative value.

If this is true, and therefore perspectivism finds its definition within a *post-positivistic* anti-metaphysical context, it must be said that this context does not exhaust the complexity and actual meaning of the philosophical position that Nietzsche develops with reference to that notion. In the light of the reflections – both published and unpublished – on the perspectival feature of human knowledge and on the interpretative character of our *existence* (i.e., not only of our knowledge! Cf. GS 374, KSA 3, p. 626–7) that Nietzsche expresses before and after 1887, it is possible to argue that the considerations that one encounters in the posthumous fragment 1886–87, 7[60] are only the foundation of a more elaborate thought.

That issue exceeds the goal I aimed to achieve in the present chapter.[60] However, it is worth considering just one detail following from the definition of "phenomen-

---

[60] For a broader reflection on the philosophy of perspectivism and interpretation, see, among others, Kaulbach 1990; Simon 1986; and Figl 1982.

alism and perspectivism" published in GS 354. In the part omitted from the above quoted excerpt, Nietzsche writes that "everything which enters consciousness thereby *becomes* shallow, thin, relatively stupid, general, a sign, *a herd-mark*." (GS 354; KSA 3, p. 593; my emphasis) This reference to the herd is quite important, for it leads us to the philosophically-relevant issue of European culture and its (Christian) morality, an issue which Nietzsche is especially concerned with in his late period.[61] This should not surprise, all the more so in the light of what has been shown above (§ 2.1). If, in fact, we presuppose that perspectivism is related to the dichotomy between "facts" and "interpretations," and that the latter can be seen as an actual definition of the former, we should remember that in the published works that dichotomy is always applied to morality (BGE 108; KSA 5, p. 92, and TI, "Improving" Humanity 1; KSA 6, p. 98). In so doing, not only is Nietzsche extremely coherent, but he also allows us to see that, in his view, the epistemological framework is only the starting point of further reflections aimed at going far beyond the merely theoretical plane.

The contextual reading of NL 1886–87, 7[60] thus outlines both the scope and the thematic framework of the view that Nietzsche will develop in his late years, and that in the pages of that notebook was still to be defined. That fragment, therefore, can be the starting point of an investigation aimed at assessing the actual philosophical value of perspectivism. One can already guess which is the value that can be attributed to this new philosophical conception, given that Nietzschean perspectivism arises from a modern anti-metaphysical world-conception as much as from a problematization of the ordinary notion of truth which permeated European culture. That investigation could start precisely from the final remarks of the 1886–87 posthumous fragment, that is, by reflecting on which are the "subjects" of the individual perspectives that "interpret the world" (*if* any subject can be found), and which is their mutual relationship.[62] In the next chapter, I will try to say something more about that.

---

[61] For more on this, see e.g. Stegmaier 2012. That issue will be further explored in the next chapter.
[62] On the "subjects" of perspectivism, see Cox 1997 and 1999, § 3.3). On the possible individualism that would follow from Nietzschean perspectivism, see Gori/Stellino 2018.

# 3 Perspectivism and Herd Morality

What is the subject of the perspectives Nietzsche talks about? And, primarily, does Nietzsche actually identify *any* subject in particular? On these questions, Nietzsche has always been vague.[1] Whenever he speaks of a perspectival seeing, Nietzsche refers to viewpoints of various kinds. The scholars who dealt with that issue usually selected among the possible subjects, choosing the one which – according to *their own* interpretation of perspectivism – they believed to be the actual object of Nietzsche's reflections. Such a difficult choice, for it obliges one to determine a hierarchy among Nietzsche's texts (both published and unpublished), according to which some of them are less important than others; such an unnecessary choice, given that it can be argued that the views on perspectivism expressed by Nietzsche throughout his writings are connected to each other in a coherent and absolutely non-mutually-exclusive way, insofar as they arise from a general conception of natural dynamics. As will be clearer when those views are explored, Nietzsche's reflections on perspectivism follow from his observations on the nature of reality, that is, on the relationship between *power-quanta* (*Macht-* or *Kraft-Quanta*) outlined in the 1880s notebooks and that Nietzsche describes through the problematic notion of "will to power."[2] As will be shown, starting from this viewpoint it is possible to argue that the perspectival model fits different situations, and it can be applied to subjects of various kinds and complexity, depending on the single case. Anyhow, no one of these subjects can be considered as privileged, *a priori*.

If this is true, it is also true that in GS 354 Nietzsche identifies a subject that deserves special attention: the *herd*. Besides the fact that it is mentioned in the only passage of the published texts where Nietzsche provides us with a proper definition of "perspectivism"[3] (he writes emphatically "this is what *I* consider to be *true* [...] *perspectivism*," my emphasis), the herd also plays a quite important role in Nietzsche's dealing with European culture and morality – an issue that permeates Nietzsche's entire philosophical activity and which in *The Gay Science* is particularly explored. A thorough reading of GS 354 will therefore allow us to develop some considerations on the relationship between perspectivism and herd morality, thus providing some remarks on the role this topic – which interpreters ordinarily restrict to the theoretical sphere – plays in Nietzsche's mature thought.

---

[1] The question of "*who* or *what* is it that *has* perspectives and interpretations" has been posed by Cristoph Cox (1997 and 1999: § 3.3). In the present section, I will refer to his position.
[2] On the relationship between the *Wille zur Macht* and the *Kraft-quanta* natural dynamics, see Abel 1998 and Gori 2007, chapter 3.
[3] See above, chapter 2.

## 3.1 The "subjects" of perspectivism

If one explores the aphorisms and notebook entries where Nietzsche deals with perspectivism, one encounters several different subjects, the broader one being the *animal species*. Nietzsche in fact refers many times to a biological collective subject, observing that, throughout its evolution, each species developed a peculiar psycho-physiological structure that made it better fit to the environment. Although each member of the species experiences the world from its particular viewpoint (e.g. from its own spatial position, which is of course always different from that of the other members of its biological group), it nevertheless shares the general perspective on reality which is determined by the perceptual mechanisms and cognitive apparatus pertaining to the whole species.[4] This consideration, which bares the imprint of Kant's reflections on human knowledge (although mediated through neo-Kantian thinkers such as Friedrich Lange), is the basis of Nietzsche's epistemological conception. He refers to it, for example, in GS 110, when he talks of the fundamental intellectual processes of humankind (an issue that he further explores in his notebooks, e.g. in NL 1885, KSA 11, 43[1] and 5[36]; and NL 1886, KSA 12, 7[2]). Moreover, in an 1882–83 posthumous fragment one reads: "It is not *our* perspective, that through which we see things; it is rather the perspective of a being [*Wesen*] of our kind, although *bigger*." (NL 1882–83, KSA 10, 4[172]; my translation)

A special case within this generalization is, of course, the human subject, who is often mentioned by Nietzsche, for example in *Beyond Good and Evil* (in particular §§ 11 and 34). In the notebooks from that period one encounters several references to the human dimension as the viewpoint on the world shared by the individual members of our biological group. In 1886, for example, Nietzsche speaks of "qualities" as "our insurmountable barriers [...], our real human idiosyncrasy." (NL 1886, KSA 12, 6[14]) One year before, he considered the possibility that "other interpretations than merely human ones" might exist, which would imply a whole hermeneutic horizon separated from our own, and consequently unknown to us. In that occasion, Nietzsche in particular re-affirms that "perspectival appraisals" are useful for the preservation of life (NL 1885–86, KSA 12, 2[108]). This is further stated in GS 374, where Nietzsche observes how difficult, indeed purely illusory, it is "to want to know what other kinds of intellects and perspectives there *might* be; e.g. whether other beings might be able to experience time backwards, or alternatively forwards and backwards (which would involve another direction of life and different conception of cause and effect)." (GS 374; KSA 3, p. 626) In this passage, too, Nietzsche seems to refer primarily to the only type of subjectivity that we can experience – namely, the human one – and to focus on the cognitive and perceptual features shared by the members of our species. At the same time, however, he considers

---

[4] George Stack especially defends this view in his studies on the relationship between Nietzsche and Lange. See for example Stack 1991 and 1992. See also Cox 1997, p. 274–5.

that subjects of other kinds can be encountered, animals who look at the world through different interpretive perspectives. Thus, while privileging – necessarily, one could say – the viewpoint of the human species, Nietzsche relativizes its epistemic value, for in principle it is only one of several possible world-descriptions.

Nietzsche's speaking of shared world-interpretations, be they human or not, is not reduced to the mere epistemological plane only. On the biological level, a shared perspective is an intellectual process belonging to a particular animal species; but it is also possible to refer to the *social* level and consider the assessment of common values (a practice pertaining especially to human communities) as another kind of shared view. Therefore, it can be argued that the interpretations Nietzsche deals with in his notebooks, in fact, have a wider scope: instead of being exclusively theoretical considerations, they also involve moral evaluations. In the posthumous fragment 1886–87, 6[14] quoted above, for example, Nietzsche speaks of "human interpretations and values" that we ordinarily claim to be "universal and perhaps constitutive values" due to "the hereditary insanit[y] of human pride, which still has its safest seat in religion." In an earlier notebook, he argues that "the good or evil action is to be called good or evil not in itself but only from the perspective of what favours self-preservation among particular kinds of human community." (NL 1885–86, KSA 12, 2[206]) Finally, in an 1888 entry – where Nietzsche still reflects on perspectivism as a specific feature of life, but now within the thematic context of the projected *Attempt at a Revaluation of All Values* – one reads that "in all the correlations of Yes and No, of preferring and refusing, loving and hating, all that's expressed is a perspective, an interest of particular types of life."[5] (NL 1888, KSA 13, 14[31]) The most important passage where Nietzsche refers to a social collectivity as the subject of perspectivism is, however, *Gay Science, § 354*, which I will explore in the following paragraphs. As will be shown, in that aphorism Nietzsche focuses on the necessity of communication for the creation of a social community, and the way consciousness developed in compliance with the herd-perspective is especially stressed.[6] The herd would therefore be the subject of a viewpoint within which each individuality is annihilated, in order to make it possible for the human community to arise.

A further possibility, for what concerns the question of what subject (if any) ought to be attributed to Nietzsche's perspectivism, is the individual human being.

---

[5] The notion of "human type" (*Typus Mensch*) is particularly important for the late Nietzsche, and its meaning goes far beyond the strictly biological dimension. The human type that Nietzsche aims to educate, thus developing a new humanity (e.g. "future philosophers"), should be considered both on the theoretical and the practical plane. That kind of man would bear a new way of thinking, a perspective on the world capable of determining also a new kind of action, thus *creating new values*, as Nietzsche repeatedly argues. On this see e.g. Schank 2000.

[6] "Our thoughts themselves – argues Nietzsche – are continually as it were *outvoted* and translated back into the herd perspective." (GS 354; KSA 3, p. 592) For more on this, see below. See also Ibbeken 2008, p. 75, and NL 1887–88, KSA 12, 11[120].

The latter would in fact be considered as the referent of a singular perspective determined not only by its space-time perception, but also by its specific interests and needs.[7] On this level, one finds a multiplicity of singular perspectives pertaining to individual subjects whose fundamental tendency, according to Nietzsche, is to affirm their own worldview (their own "taste") over those of the other subjects. Therefore, this picture can lead to the dangerous idea that Nietzsche is a supporter of a radical form of normative ethical egoism, for given this conflictive picture, moral agents could seem to be justified in doing what is their own self-interest, even if this means to act in detriment of others' interest.[8] Without denying that, in Nietzsche's view, individual perspectives conflict with each other and often tend to overmaster different or opposite perspectives, it should be pointed out that this interpretation suffers one serious flaw: it overlooks the constitutive character that *relationalism* plays in Nietzsche's perspectivism. Indeed, it can be argued that Nietzsche considers the individual as always making part of a species or a social collectivity. Within both of them, the individual is not like a monad, but is rather situated in a net of dynamic and interpersonal relations. Moreover, even when emphasis is put on the individual, it should not be forgotten that Nietzsche conceives the individual itself in terms of a plural multiplicity, a collectivity.[9] This is evident, for instance, in *Beyond Good and Evil*, where Nietzsche's criticism towards the traditional view of the "subject" as a substance-concept makes reference to "social structures" like the *soul*, "a society constructed out of drives and affects" (BGE 12; KSA 5, p. 27), or the body, made of many souls from which the action that *we call* "individual" arises (BGE 19; KSA 5).[10] Thus, behind individualities, as well as behind the species and the social collectivity, lies a network of relations between singularities, singularities that we ignore in favour of a more unitary and inclusive perspective. Within this picture, the *I* (or the subject) is a non-substance entity, a logical notion whose ontological ground is only that of the pure activity that we attribute to it.[11]

---

**7** The idea that perspectivism is limited to the description of human knowledge has been supported in particular by Maudemarie Clark 1990 and Brian Leiter 1994, and subsequently discussed by Cox (1997, p. 276 f.). Also Grimm, in his seminal work on Nietzsche's epistemology, considers as privileged subject of perspectivism the individual knower (Grimm 1977, p. 68). On this, see also Gerhardt 1989.
**8** On the problem of ethical individualism in relation to Nietzsche's perspectivism, cf. Gori/Stellino 2018.
**9** Cox builds on this point his argument against Clark and Leiter. The question is further and more extensively developed in Cox 1999, p. 122 ff.
**10** Nietzsche made a similar point in NL 1880, KSA 9, 6[70], where he describes the I or *ego* as "a plurality of forces," that alternatively arise over the others. Moreover, in that fragment Nietzsche argues that we project the dynamic of "social relationships" onto the way we describe our own individuality.
**11** See also BGE 16, 17, 19 and 21. This topic has been variously explored in the last decades and is still investigated, due to its correlation with some issues related to contemporary philosophy of mind. For a further examination, cf. Lupo 2006, Gori 2011a and 2015b.

Therefore, the idea that Nietzsche is an individualist seems to be debatable. At least, it cannot be defended if one assumes "individuality" in the ordinary sense, that is, by making reference to the traditional conception of subjectivity. As known, Nietzsche de-constructs the very notion of subject, focusing on the level of human instincts, on the complexes of drives acting "unconsciously." (NL 1885, KSA 11, 40[42])[12] For Nietzsche, the I is "a perspectival illusion – the illusory unity in which, as in a horizon, everything converges." (NL 1885–86, KSA 12, 2[91]) It is nothing but an intellectual notion that helps us orienting within that dynamics between drives, each of which is also the origin of a specific perspective, of an hermeneutic relationship with the external world. This view is expressed, for example, in the posthumous fragment 1886–87, 7[60] that has been explored in the previous chapter. In that text, Nietzsche rejects the positivistic idea that behind our world-description an actual subject can be encountered, and rather argues that "the 'subject' is not something given but a fiction added on." On the contrary, Nietzsche argues that "it is our needs *which interpret the world:* our drives and their for and against. Every drive is a kind of lust for domination, each has its perspective, which it would like to impose as a norm on all the other drives." (NL 1886–87, KSA 12, 7[60])

For Nietzsche, the idea of a "single subject" is therefore "unnecessary" and must be discarded, in favour of a more detailed conception holding that a multiplicity of "subjects" works at the unconscious level (NL 1885, KSA 11, 40[42]). Nevertheless, a usefulness of some sort can be attributed to the ordinary concept of subjectivity, given that, like other substance-notions, it proved its operational efficacy and fruitfulness in a pragmatic sense.[13] With no reference to an individual subject, our practical activity is in fact inconceivable.[14] Therefore, at least at this level it should be permitted to speak of perspectival viewpoints originating from each person. However, that does not allow us to consider the individual human being as the proper subject of the interpretation Nietzsche talks of, thus conceiving of him as the privileged reference of a hermeneutical enterprise. What emerges from this picture is a plural conception of the human being: on the one side, we find a supra-individual (biological and/or social) perspective that includes the individual one; on the other side, there is the plane of the single entities that constitute the human being and which are (merely logically, i.e. illusorily) unified into him.[15]

---

**12** As is now well-known, Nietzsche's idea that the organism hosts an inner dynamic of drives and instincts has been inspired by the work of W. Roux (1881). On this, see Müller-Lauter 1978.
**13** On the practical value of substantial entities in Nietzsche, cf. Gori 2009b.
**14** According to what Nietzsche writes for example in BGE 12, it is possible to answer negatively to the question whether, along with the I of psychology and philosophy (i.e. the cause of thought), the soul (i.e. the principle of the practical self-awareness of mankind) also disappears. As can be argued, Nietzsche's critique of the I is quite radical, but it does not prohibit the human being from referring to its own subjectivity – provided, however, that the latter is conceived of in a different way, that is, stripped from its metaphysical surface. On this, see Gori 2015b, § 7.
**15** Cf. Cox 1997, p. 290: "The subject does not *have* these various perspectives and interpretations; rather, they are what the subject *is*. According to Nietzsche, the subject is nothing over and above

The reflection on the subject thus leads us to a further option: namely the fact that, when dealing with perspectivism, Nietzsche has in mind an even more restricted and fundamental dimension of being. The viewpoints of the single individual subject, society or even the species would be only special cases of that dimension, which would therefore lay at the very basis of any form of interpretation. In his late annotations, Nietzsche apparently leads perspectivism to the extreme, considering that the plane of interpretation coincides with that of being, that is, with the dimension of pure and necessary relationship among the different viewpoint-holders, which can be defined only from within their mutual relation. Furthermore, it can be observed that the level Nietzsche refers to in these posthumous fragments lies below the very determination of an "interpretation" and a "perspectival knowledge," for it focuses on the natural dynamics that is only subsequently described in terms of human actions. The last subject that it is possible to find in Nietzsche's writings is in fact the *single centre of force (Kraftcentrum)* involved in that natural dynamics. In an 1888 posthumous fragment devoted to the problem of appearance vs. the "true" world, Nietzsche observes that the apparent world is "a world viewed according to values [...], in this case according to the viewpoint of utility in regard to the preservation and enhancement of the power of a certain species of animal. The *perspective* therefore decides the character of the 'appearance'!" (NL 1888, KSA 13, 14[184]) Continues Nietzsche:

> As if a world would still remain over after one deducted the perspective! By doing that one would deduct relativity! Every center of force adopts a perspective toward the entire remainder, i.e., its own particular valuation, mode of action, and mode of resistance. The "apparent world," therefore, is reduced to a specific mode of action on the world, emanating from a center. Now there is no other mode of action whatever; and the "world" is only a word for the totality of these actions. Reality consists precisely in this particular action and reaction of every individual part toward the whole. (NL 1888, KSA 13, 14[184]; my translation)

The idea that the *Kraftcentrum* is the fundamental subject of perspectivism is further stated in the same notebook. In NL 1888, KSA 13, 14[184], Nietzsche focuses on the scientific world-description, and pays particular attention to the concept of atom of modern physicists. For Nietzsche, "the atom they posit is inferred according to the logic of the perspectivism of consciousness – and is therefore itself a subjective fiction." What physicists do not realize, and therefore neglect in their world-description, is the "necessary perspectivism by virtue of which every center of force – and not only man – construes all the rest of the world from its own viewpoint, i.e., measures, feels, forms, according to its own force."

In Nietzsche's late reflections, the subjects originating the hermeneutical process are indefinitely multiplied, and Nietzsche leads us far beyond the plane of human

---

the various physical/spiritual affective perspectives and interpretations that compose it, and the relationships between these perspectives and interpretations."

beings. However, this should not disorientate, but only stress which are the actual dynamics that Nietzsche has in mind whenever he talks of "perspectivism" or of a "perspectival seeing." The different interpretations of the world (be they of either theoretical or moral nature) are all expression of that dynamics, on the basis of which the internal articulation of the most complex structures existing in the world is grounded. Everything is based on a non-teleological and necessary, but constitutively unstable action-reaction process. Value judgements can be defined only by reference to that relationship, where, at the micro-level, a "quantum of force" (GS 360; KSA 3, p. 608) gains power only insofar as it exchanges energy with other quanta. The kind of mastery grounded on this relationship is therefore not fixed and immutable. On the contrary, once the power of a centre of force is exhausted, the equilibrium of the total mass of energy changes and another centre becomes "master" for a limited period of time.[16]

Finally, for what concerns the "subject" of perspectivism, it must be said that, although Nietzsche offers a multiplicity of options, his view seems not to be incoherent. If one considers that the various options pertain to different levels of complexity, all replicating the same dynamics, that view gains consistency. Any level would depend on the scope of the investigation – or on the *perspective* of the *interpreting* observer – and the process would involve "individual" subjects that are not substance-entities but rather only functional unities. The society, the individual, even the single centre of force – they are all a *product* of a dynamics that involves, respectively, a group of people, of impulses, of energy. The "reality" of these entities is therefore as fictitious as impermanent. At least, this is what emerges from the observations that Nietzsche presents both in his notebooks and in the published works, and from which it can be argued that, in his view, anything we identify as origin of the perspectives has only a descriptive and practical semantic value.[17] Everything is grounded on the same relational mechanism, and the developmental process of that mechanism can be encountered in all living beings. Whether we talk of the categorization of the world, of the relationship between individuals, or of wider collective forms, we always deal with power relationships destined to never find balance. The problem of how to define the actual origin of the various perspectival views must therefore be considered from a pragmatic point of view, that is, by defining the context within which it is possible to talk of a "subject," thus avoiding the risk of falling into a bad metaphysics.

---

**16** Elsewhere (Gori/Stellino 2018, p. 166) has been argued that the reference to this dynamic relationship avoids the risk of interpreting Nietzsche's moral perspectivism as leading to a form of autarchic individualism. But the affirmation of perspectival knowledge does not imply a strong relativism either. Rather, the *dynamic* relationship established between power relations can be the metaphysical basis of a democratic ethics arising from the comparison between different interpretations. The interpretations provided by Hatab (1995) and Abel (2010), discussed e.g. in Gori 2011b, support this view. Finally, Kaulbach (1980 and 1990) defines the free spirit as the human type that accepts the limitation of his interpretation and embraces a new model of social relation.
**17** On this, cf. NL 1885–86, KSA 12, 2[87] and Luca Lupo's observations in Lupo 2006, p. 179 f.

## 3.2 Tones of appearance

What has been argued so far aimed to shed light on Nietzsche's reflection on perspectivism. As I tried to show, it is not possible to find a privileged viewpoint that, for Nietzsche, would represent the perspective *"par excellence."* Moreover, the metaphysical picture of an unceasing relational dynamics that can be found behind Nietzsche's perspectivism leads us to a potential absolute relativism, given that within that picture there is no space for fixed reference points. However, as I tried to argue, our need to find our way in the world can be satisfied, if we consider that matter from a pragmatic point of view. In fact, although no proper privileged subject can be encountered, we can deal with Nietzsche's perspectivism in a "perspectival" way, thus considering several different levels, within each of which it would be possible to identify reference points. The biological and the political or cultural dimensions are an example of this. They are in fact realms of meaning within which the very notion of "perspectival seeing" has two different senses and, furthermore, within which there is no doubt on what is the subject originating the shared viewpoint (in this particular case, the species and societies respectively).

An important passage to reflect on this and, consequently, to say something on the philosophical meaning and value of Nietzschean perspectivism, is the long aphorism 354 published in the fifth book of *The Gay Science*. Its relevance for the issue I am exploring is especially clear for, as I already pointed out, in that passage Nietzsche provides us with the only proper *definition* of the notion he developed during his late years, showing us what *he* "consider[s] to be true phenomenalism and perspectivism." This way of presenting his views is not new to Nietzsche, and anyone accustomed with his style knows that he mostly uses such emphatic expressions when he aims to introduce something new or to differentiate his view from established traditions. As will be shown, with all likelihood the view against which Nietzsche argues in GS 354 is that of Gustav Teichmüller, whose main work, *Die wirkliche und die scheinbare Welt* – which describes the phenomenal dimension, the "apparent" world, as "perspectival" – has been read by Nietzsche in 1883.[18] In what follows, I will try to explain wherein lies the originality of Nietzsche's standpoint on that particular issue.

The definition that Nietzsche presents in the final part of GS 354 is this one:

> This is what *I* consider to be true phenomenalism and perspectivism: that due to the nature of *animal consciousness*, the world of which we can become conscious is merely a surface- and sign-world, a world turned into generalities and thereby debased to its lowest common denominator, – that everything which enters consciousness thereby *becomes* shallow, thin, relatively stupid, general, a sign, a herd-mark; that all becoming conscious involves a vast and thorough corruption, falsification, superficialization, and generalization. (GS 354; KSA 3, p. 593)

---

[18] On Nietzsche's reading of Teichmüller cf. Nohl 1913; Dickopp 1970; Orsucci 1997; Small 2001, chapter 3; Riccardi 2009b; and Dellinger 2012.

In order to understand this definition – and before addressing the specific issue of the *herd* as the collective subject that Nietzsche, in this passage, attributes to perspectivism – one must explore the whole content of GS 354.[19] Firstly, the aphorism must be contextualized, not so much and not only within Nietzsche's writings, but rather thematically in a broader sense. The aphorism belongs to the fifth book of *The Gay Science*, composed immediately after *Beyond Good and Evil* and published in 1887. In that text, Nietzsche develops some ideas he presented in BGE and which represent the core of his late thought and philosophical attitude. After the failure of *Thus Spoke Zarathustra* as both an editorial and a philosophical project, Nietzsche re-worked on his previous writings and published a second edition of most of them (e.g. *The Birth of Tragedy; Human, All Too Human;* and of course *The Gay Science*), with the addition of a preface aimed at interpreting these books in the light of his mature thought. This allowed him to reconsider and further develop some issues he dealt with in his early years.[20]

All this can be encountered in GS 354. In that aphorism, Nietzsche addresses some questions he explored in previous writings (namely, how does consciousness work and what is the "herd instinct" of modern Europeans) and, inspired by some readings he did meanwhile, connects them in an original way. Moreover, the observations on knowledge that one finds at the end of GS 354 and, of course, Nietzsche's dealing with perspectivism (which, in the fifth book of *The Gay Science*, is explored also in GS 374), directly relates this aphorism with *Beyond Good and Evil*. In fact, in the first paragraphs of the 1886 book, Nietzsche is concerned with problems arising from the outcomes of modern epistemology and the scientific world-description (of which Nietzsche mainly criticizes the mechanistic viewpoint). Most importantly, in the *Preface* to *Beyond Good and Evil* he describes *"perspectivism"* as the "fundamental condition of all life." (BGE Preface; KSA 5, p. 13)[21] In dealing with these issues, Nietzsche develops some views that he already defended in his early years, e.g. the idea that our relationship with the outer world has to be expressed in terms of

---

**19** For a contextual interpretation of GS 354, see Stegmaier 2012, p. 262ff.
**20** As an example of this, see the fundamental problem of the "death of God," that Nietzsche addresses in the very opening of the fifth book of the *Gay Science*, titled "We fearless ones." That problem was famously introduced in GS 125 as maybe the most important event of European cultural history, that at the end of the modern age experiences a crisis following from the collapse of its epistemic and axiological principles. While in GS 125 (*The Madman*) that event is accompanied by disorientation and bafflement, in GS 343 (*How to understand our cheerfulness*) the fundamental feeling is *Heiterkeit* ("cheerfulness"). That is, humanity is not disoriented by the death of God, but rather reacts to is positively, with courage, and interprets that event as unfolding new possibilities for the cultural development of humankind. On this, see Stegmaier 2012, p. 95ff., and Gori/Piazzesi 2012, p. 125.
**21** It is worth noting that in this passage Nietzsche does not use the name "Perspektivismus," which appears only twice in his writings (in NL 1886–87, 7[60] and GS 354); rather, he speaks of a "perspectival character of life." The original German text is in fact: "Es hiess allerdings die Wahrheit auf den Kopf stellen und das *Perspektivische*, die Grundbedingung alles Lebens, selber verleugnen, so vom Geiste und vom Guten zu reden, wie Plato gethan hat."

a *falsification* and *simplification*, for it is mediated by both our sensorial apparatus and our intellect, whose activity has played a fundamental role in the development and preservation of the human species.[22] This implies that, in principle, it would be quite difficult to support a "correspondence theory" of knowledge.[23] Consequently, a reconsideration of the ordinary notions of "truth" and "falsehood" is required.

Nietzsche already considers this in the first edition of *The Gay Science*. In GS 110, for example, he defends an evolutionary (biological) conception of knowledge, and observes that, throughout its development, the intellect produced a series of "errors" that "turned out to be useful and species-preserving," "erroneous articles of faith" mostly concerning the substantial nature and materiality of things (GS 110; KSA 3, p. 469). Starting from these premises, Nietzsche conclusively remarks that "the *strength* of knowledge lies not in its degree of truth, but in its age, its embeddedness, its character as a condition of life." (GS 110; KSA 3, p. 469) That view is further considered in GS 121, where Nietzsche reflects on the value and function of the substance-concepts as means for our orientation: "Without these articles of faith no one could endure living! But that does not prove them." (GS 121; KSA 3, p. 478) For Nietzsche, we are not allowed to attribute any truth-value to these concepts on the basis of their biological usefulness. But this must be understood in the light of the traditional notion of truth, that is, the notion of truth as correspondence with reality – as will be further stressed below. In other words, in GS 121 Nietzsche claims that, the fact that substance-concepts proved to be conditions of life does not entail their being an *adequate representation* of the world. That is, their value as means for the preservation is no warrant of their epistemic validity. As it will be argued, I believe that Nietzsche's further remarks that "life is not an argument," and that "the conditions of life might include error" (GS 121; KSA 3, p. 477–8) can be properly understood only with that specification in mind. "Erroneous" is in fact any reproduction of the external world involving an active intervention of our sense organs or of our intellect. Both of them modify the original datum, according to their categories and physiological mechanisms. As a result, we know something that is not *unbedingt*; rather, it is a creation of our mind and senses, a production whose actual correspondence with reality one can hardly evaluate. The question therefore arises: what is the epistemic value of those "article of faith," given that they definitely do not provide us with an adequate description of reality? To what extent, and in which sense, is our knowledge "truth"?

---

[22] On Nietzsche's evolutionary conception of knowledge, see the first chapter of this volume. On Nietzsche's "falsificationism," cf. Riccardi 2011. Nietzsche's idea that our knowledge of reality is mediated by the sense organs and the intellect has been inspired first and foremost from F. Lange's *History of Materialism* (1882 [1875]). On this, see Stack 1983.

[23] The literature on Nietzsche's position on the "correspondence theory" of truth is extensive. See for example Danto 1965, p. 54 ff.; Grimm 1977; Figl 1982, p. 181 ff.; Wilcox 1986; Simon 1989, p. 244 ff.; Clark 1990, chapters 2 and 4; Gemes 1992; Cox 1999, p. 28 ff.; and Stack 1981a.

## 3.2 Tones of appearance — 87

It is not my aim to deal with a topic that has been extensively explored in the Nietzsche scholarship. I would only stress that the observations that Nietzsche publishes in the first edition of *The Gay Science* are the starting point of the further reflections on knowledge and truth that he develops in *Beyond Good and Evil*. The first section of the 1886 book is especially related with the ideas expressed in GS 121. In the opening paragraph, Nietzsche introduces the notion of "will to truth" and the "problem of the value of truth" (a problem that, for Nietzsche, "has never been raised until now"; BGE 1; KSA 5, p. 15) precisely on the basis of his previous epistemological considerations. Subsequently, in BGE 4 Nietzsche argues that we need to re-define the very principles of our way of judging, due to the fact that "the falsity of a judgment is itself no objection to a judgment," and that "the question is how far the judgment promotes and preserves life, how well it preserves, and perhaps even cultivates, the type." (BGE 4; KSA 5, p. 18) Furthermore, according to Nietzsche "we are fundamentally inclined to claim that the falsest judgements (which include synthetic judgements *a priori*) are the most indispensable to us," for the role they played for the preservation of the species and its further development (BGE 4; KSA 5, p. 18). Precisely with reference to our *faith* in synthetic a priori judgements, in BGE 11 Nietzsche speaks of "the perspectival optics of life" which involves the necessary belief in the truthfulness of these judgements (BGE 11; KSA 5, p. 26). The new terminology that Nietzsche uses here, in dealing with a topic that he also explored earlier, is the most interesting aspect for the aim of the present research. In fact, it shows that Nietzsche's late epistemological investigations have been influenced, among other thinkers, by Gustav Teichmüller. Moreover, this allows us to directly connect *Beyond Good and Evil* to GS 354. Not only the imagine of a "perspectival" relationship with reality, but also the idea that concepts are "signs"[24] and that, in general, we can ascribe a merely superficial character to our consciousness – all ideas that we find stated at the end of GS 354 – are either directly or indirectly references to Teichmüller's *Die wirkliche und die scheinbare Welt*, which can also be encountered in *Beyond Good and Evil*.[25]

---

[24] In particular, Teichmüller (1882, p. 275) describes modern physics as a "sign-system," a "semiotic" within which "a sign is explained on the basis of another, and it is [...] reduced to movements and spatial relations, without ever reach the inner essence of things."

[25] In BGE 10, for example, the title of Teichmüller's work is almost literally reproduced, when Nietzsche writes that "all over Europe these days, the problem 'of the real and the apparent world' gets taken up so eagerly and with such acuity [...] that you really start to think and listen." (BGE 10; KSA 5, p. 23–4) Another clear reference to that work is the critique of Descartes's "I think" expressed in BGE 16 and BGE 17, and further stated in BGE 54; in fact, that question was also addressed by Teichmüller (see Loukidelis 2013). Finally, one should consider the less explicit BGE 2 (KSA 5), where Nietzsche writes that "the fundamental belief of metaphysicians is the *belief in oppositions of values*," and that "we can doubt, first, whether opposites even exist and, second, whether the popular valuations and value oppositions that have earned the metaphysicians' seal of approval might not only be foreground appraisals. Perhaps they are merely provisional perspectives." According to Andrea Orsucci (2001, p. 212), Nietzsche's letter to Overbeck written on July

A passage where Teichmüller's influence can be especially evaluated, and that allow us to further support what has been argued so far, is BGE 34. In that aphorism, Nietzsche claims that "the *erroneousness* of the world we think we live in is the most certain and solid fact that our eyes can still grab hold of," and then observes:

> It is no more than a moral prejudice that the truth is worth more than appearance; in fact, it is the world's most poorly proven assumption. Let us admit this much: that life could not exist except on the basis of perspectival valuations and appearances; and if, with the virtuous enthusiasm and inanity of many philosophers, someone wanted to completely abolish the "world of appearances," – well, assuming *you* could do that, – at least there would not be any of your "truth" left either! Actually, why do we even assume that "true" and "false" are intrinsically opposed? Isn't it enough to assume that there are levels of appearance and, as it were, lighter and darker shades and tones of appearance? (BGE 34; KSA 5, p. 53–4)

In this passage Nietzsche reflects on the distinction between "true" and "apparent" world, and uses Teichmüller's terminology to deal with a fundamental question discussed within the post- and neo-Kantian debate.[26] Nietzsche seems not to be interested in the origin of that distinction (a fictitious distinction destined to be abandoned, as he argues for example in TI, How the "True World" Finally Became a Fable); what is worth exploring, for him, are rather the consequences it entails. According to Nietzsche, the categories of "true" and "false" belong to the "moral prejudice" that characterizes the ordinary metaphysical conception pretending that an adequate knowledge of reality can be provided. This "will to truth" determines a devaluation of the phenomenal dimension (i.e. the "apparent world"), whereas, in Nietzsche's view, this is in fact the only realm which we can gain access to. The idea that a "perspectival valuation" could be a viable alternative to the dualism between "truth" and "falsehood" involves that the ordinary truth-value of our knowledge must be put up to question, thus proving the importance of that valuation for Nietzsche's late thought – whose main aim is precisely to deal with the question of the value of truth.[27]

In GS 354, these issues are further addressed, for example when Nietzsche speaks of a "true phenomenalism and perspectivism" and insists that the only dimension accessible to our consciousness is the product of a fundamental "falsification, superficialization, and generalization." Moreover, in the closing remarks of that aphorism Nietzsche especially deals with the epistemological principles of phenomenalism, and rejects the very "opposition between 'thing in itself' and appearance: for we 'know' far too little to even be entitled to *make* that distinction." (GS 354;

---

23, 1884, where Nietzsche talks of his own new "doctrine, according to which the world of good and bad is only an apparent and perspectival world" (KGB III/1, Bf. 521), would reveal Teichmüller as the hidden reference of the passage quoted from BGE 2.

[26] For a consideration of the Nietzschean distinction between "true" and "apparent" world, with reference to Teichmüller (who contrasts the "apparent" with the "real" world), see Riccardi 2009, p. 207 ff. I briefly dealt with it in the previous chapter, section 4, fn. 35.

[27] On this see e.g. Gori 2015c.

KSA 3, p. 593)[28] For Nietzsche, this is in fact a pseudo-problem that pays attention to an issue which is of scarce interest for a proper philosopher. As a matter of fact, since Plato that pseudo-problem has been extensively addressed, and it is possible to say that the whole of European culture is grounded on that issue (cf. BGE Preface). This is what Nietzsche presupposes in GS 354 – an aphorism that appears in the fifth book of *The Gay Science*, a section especially devoted to the consequences of the crisis of that culture that Nietzsche diagnoses in his late writings. In his view, during the nineteenth-century, Europe (a cultural space, not just a political one)[29] reached the final stage of its development, and she is about to collapse due to the effects of one of its principles, namely "the concept of truthfulness that was taken ever more rigorously." (GS 357; KSA 3, p. 600; and GM III 27; KSA 5, p. 410) The problem of both the "will to truth" and the "value of truth" (cf. e.g. GM III 24 and GM III 27), which is closely related to Nietzschean perspectivism, is therefore to be tackled in order to make the further step towards "that great drama in a hundred acts reserved for Europe in the next two centuries, the most terrible, most questionable drama but perhaps also the one most rich in hope…" (GM III 27; KSA 5, p. 410–1)

But this critical attitude is as powerful as dangerous, for it leaves us with no reference points either on the epistemological or on the axiological plane, thus leading to a potential disorientation. That disorientation is of course frightening for whoever – contrary to the "fearless ones" mentioned in the title of the fifth book of GS, among whom Nietzsche includes also himself (the title in fact is "*We* fearless ones") – did not embrace Zarathustra's doctrine, and therefore do not experience the death of God with a cheerful attitude. Who still experiences the world according to the viewpoint of Western metaphysics, is destined to react with terror to "the greatest recent event [which] is already starting to cast its first shadow over Europe." (GS 343; KSA 3, p. 573) After all, in *The Gay Science* Nietzsche repeatedly stresses that the metaphysical viewpoint and the value system arising from it are grounded on *fear*, a feeling that belongs to the very essence of humankind. For Nietzsche, fear is the actual origin of morality, the latter being an attempt to satisfy our fundamental need for orientation. Our need of communication is related to that feeling, too. Allowing people to gather in society, and therefore to protect each other, communication is a fundamental instrument against fear. Nietzsche connects morality and communication in GS 354, which is especially devoted to the problem of consciousness and its relation to the herd.

---

**28** In this passage Nietzsche refers polemically to the "epistemologists" who insist in distinguishing subject and object on the ontological plane, thus constantly falling back into "folk metaphysics"; in doing that, Nietzsche remarks, they "have got tangled up in the snares of grammar." (GS 354; KSA 3, p. 593) This metaphor, which is quite known in the Nietzsche-scholarship, is originally Teichmüller's.
**29** On Nietzsche's view of Europe as a cultural and/or spiritual dimension, instead of a purely political space, see Witzler 2001 and Gentili 2014.

## 3.3 Consciousness and language

In the previous section I briefly outlined the thematic context of GS 354. Let's now address the main issue, namely the definition of "true perspectivism" that Nietzsche presents in that aphorism. As said, in order to define that notion, Nietzsche deals with two topics that he explored earlier, especially after 1880: human consciousness and the herd. The original way in which Nietzsche connects these topics in GS 354 is particularly interesting, and helps us to better understand his view on perspectivism.

The "problem of consciousness (or rather, of becoming conscious of something)" is the main issue GS 354 is devoted to. The examination that Nietzsche provides in that aphorism (the most extensive that can be encountered in his published works) is the final stage of a reflection on consciousness and human thought that Nietzsche developed throughout many years, whose originality and importance attracted several scholars involved in the contemporary debate on the philosophy of mind. The value of this reflection also depends on the role it plays in Nietzsche's general approach to Western culture, basically aimed at dismantling ordinary metaphysical concepts. Among them, the notion of consciousness – or subject, or soul – is of course fundamental, and that is why Nietzsche is so interested in dealing with it critically.[30] In particular, Nietzsche re-defines the traditional notion of consciousness in two steps: firstly, he understands it as an evolutionary and biological phenomenon; secondly (but, as we shall see, this passage is linked to the first one) he attributes to consciousness a merely practical function, interpreting it as a linguistic and communicative phenomenon. It is not my intention to deal thoroughly with an issue that has already been exhaustively discussed by other scholars.[31] I will rather focus on the conclusions that Nietzsche draws in GS 354, in order to shed light on the definition of "perspectivism" that he provides in the final part of that aphorism. Two related aspects must thus be considered. Firstly, Nietzsche claims consciousness to be basically "superfluous," and describes it as a "superficial" phenomenon; secondly, he holds that consciousness has arisen, and therefore has value only, as a "communication tool."[32]

In GS 354, Nietzsche first deals with the possibility that consciousness has a purely *epiphenomenal* function, that is, as Leiter (2002, p. 92) observes, that it

---

[30] One of the most important aspects on which Nietzsche focuses is that the concept of soul, understood as the independent and voluntary cause of actions, lies at the basis of the Cristian notion of responsibility. Cf. BGE 54; KSA 5, p. 73; and TI, The Four Great Errors 3; KSA 6. For more on this, see also Gori 2015a and 2015b.

[31] The most detailed examination of Nietzsche's reflections on consciousness can be found in Lupo 2006 (I will further refer to this text in this section). Lupo pays special attention to the "substratum of the aphorism 354 of *The Gay Science*" in the third chapter of his book (pp. 178 ff.). For other studies on Nietzsche's view of consciousness, cf. Leiter 2002; Katsafanas 2005; Constâncio 2011; Riccardi 2015 and 2018. The first four of these articles discuss especially whether Nietzsche defended a strong epiphenomenalism or not. I will say something more on this in what follows.

[32] Riccardi 2018 deals thoroughly with both these aspects.

does not have a causal power. In other words, according to Nietzsche, it can be argued that consciousness is nothing but a superficial effect of the activity of the drives that constitute the inner dynamics of the organism. "We could think, feel, will, remember, and also 'act' in every sense of the term, and yet none of all this would have to 'enter our consciousness' (as one says figuratively). All of life would be possible without, as it were, seeing itself in the mirror." (GS 354; KSA 3, p. 590)[33] As Lupo (2006, p. 191) rightly observes, Nietzsche conceives consciousness as two-fold:

> There is a first level, that Nietzsche calls the intelligence of the body (*Klugheit des Leibes*). This includes physiological processes and instinctual interactions [...]. Then, one finds a second level, that of consciousness as it is ordinarily conceived. Here one finds the cognitive abilities which we are aware of, the self-awareness and, more generally, self-consciousness.

Lupo calls these two levels "primary" and "secondary" consciousness. According to his interpretation, secondary consciousness is "an activity of sign-production [...] only apparently independent and separated from the activity of primary consciousness. In fact, the activity of the secondary consciousness is nothing but the result of the activity of primary consciousness, the latter emerging to an actual conscious level." (Lupo 2006, p. 193) Therefore, human consciousness, with its characteristic self-reflective power, is a secondary event, for Nietzsche. It is in fact the result of the physiological activity of the organism. The secondary consciousness would then share various functional aspects with the primary one, since both are responsible for the assimilation and selection of what they engage with. According to this distinction, the second level is nothing but "a variation or development of the first one" (Lupo 2006, p. 193), a product of the primary consciousness that, for Nietzsche, seems not to be necessary – at least on a biological level.

Based on these considerations, Nietzsche therefore wonders "*to what end*" consciousness "exist[s] at all when it is basically *superfluous*." (GS 354; KSA 3, p. 590) In dealing with this question, Nietzsche shifts from the biological to the social level, and especially focuses on the idea that the "strength of consciousness is always related to a person's (or animal's) *ability to communicate*; and the ability to communicate, in turn, to the *need to communicate*."[34] (GS 354; KSA 3, p. 590) The fundamental

---

[33] In GS 354 Nietzsche attributes this position to Leibniz, while hermetically referring to a "precocious suspicion" dawned in the mind of that thinker. This is further addressed in GS 357; KSA 3, p. 598, where Nietzsche admires "Leibniz's incomparable insight [...] that consciousness is merely an *accidens* of the power of representation and *not* its necessary and essential attribute; so that what we call consciousness constitutes only one state of our spiritual and psychic world [...] and *by no means the whole of it*." Riccardi (2018: § 2) observes that Nietzsche found this idea in Otto Liebmann's *Zur Analysis der Wirklichkeit* (cf. also Loukidelis 2006).
[34] The relationship between the development of human consciousness and its communication ability has been explored by several authors, at Nietzsche's time, especially within the Pragmatist and neo-Kantian framework. Among the pragmatists, for example, George Herbert Mead in his book *Mind, Self, and Society* (1934) defends a position which can be compared to Nietzsche's (see Fabbri-

idea is that the human being (the human animal) was originally in a state of danger, from which he could not have come out except through the help of his fellows. This fundamental necessity stimulated his ability to communicate, "forcing him" to elaborate a sign-system that would allow him to express his own feelings.³⁵ As Nietzsche clearly argues in GS 354, the main function of consciousness is to express (partially) an animal's inner dimension, in order to communicate it to the other members of the species or social group:

> I may go on to conjecture that *consciousness in general has developed only under the pressure of the need to communicate*; that at the outset, consciousness was necessary, was useful, only between persons [...]; and that it has developed only in proportion to that usefulness. Consciousness is really just a net connecting one person with another – only in this capacity did it have to develop; the solitary and predatory person would not have needed it. That our actions, thoughts, feelings, and movements – at least some of them – ever enter into consciousness is the result of a terrible 'must' which has ruled over man for a long time; as the most endangered animal, he *needed* help and protection, he needed his equals; he had to express his neediness and be able to make himself understood – and to do so, he first needed "consciousness", i.e. even to "know" what distressed him, to "know" how he felt, to "know" what he thought. For, once again: man, like every living creature, is constantly thinking but does not know it; the thinking which becomes *conscious* is only the smallest part of it, let's say the shallowest, worst part – for only that conscious thinking *takes place in words, that is, in communication symbols*; and this fact discloses the origin of consciousness. (GS 354; KSA 3, p. 591–2)

Nietzsche abandons the idea of consciousness as a separate faculty, thus rejecting the metaphysical value that was traditionally attributed to it. In the light of what has been argued above, it is possible to say that Nietzsche holds that consciousness is for us only a secondary phenomenon, which allows the human animal to become aware of the mere result of an inner process which is destined to remain largely unknown to him.³⁶ For Nietzsche, consciousness developed together with language. The latter especially produces a sign-system, that makes possible the actual expression of the inner feelings which one becomes conscious of. As has been mentioned above, Nietzsche's speaking of "signs" is another important reference to Teichmüller, who also inspired an aphorism published in *Beyond Good and Evil* where Nietzsche explores the relationship between experience and language. The content of this aphor-

---

chesi 2012 and 2015). On the other hand, Hans Vaihinger, in his main work based on the same developments of Kantianism that influenced Nietzsche, speaks of intellectual "fictions" that our thought produces for "practical and communicative purposes," and observes that consciousness is only a "secondary and accessory" phenomenon of our intellectual life (cf. Vaihinger 1925, p. 168 ff.).

**35** Of course, this is nothing more than a biological "duty," a necessity that influences the development of an organism in an unconscious and involuntary way.

**36** On this point, it is worth considering Nietzsche's reflections on thought in the posthumous fragments NL 1884, KSA 11, 26[94] and NL 1885, KSA 11, 38[1]. Given that these notes are quite elaborated, one can infer that Nietzsche originally intended to include them in a published writing, with all likelihood *Beyond Good and Evil*.

ism helps us to better understand Nietzsche's view of consciousness (incidentally, let me stress once more how strictly BGE and the fifth book of GS are related):

> Words are acoustic signs for concepts; concepts, though, are more or less determinate pictorial signs for sensations that occur together and recur frequently, for groups of sensations. Using the same words is not enough to get people to understand each other: they have to use the same words for the same species of inner experiences too; ultimately, people have to have the same experience *base*. This is why a people in a community will understand each other better than they understand people belonging to other groups, even when they all use the same language. Or rather, when individuals have lived together for a long time under similar conditions (of climate, soil, danger, necessities, work), there *arises* something that "understands itself" – a people. In all souls, an equal number of frequently recurring experiences have gained an upper hand over ones that occur less frequently: understanding takes place faster and faster on this basis (the history of language is the history of a process of abbreviation); and people join closer and closer together on the basis of this understanding. The greater the danger, the greater the need to agree quickly and easily about necessities. (BGE 268; KSA 5, p. 221)[37]

In this passage one finds some ideas later reaffirmed in GS 354. In particular, Nietzsche holds that language is a mechanism of abbreviation arisen from a fundamental human need to become understandable, a need stimulated by the "condition of danger" determined by the state of nature. Moreover, in BGE 268 Nietzsche stresses that it is not enough that people use the same linguistic signs, in order for them to understand each other. What is most important is that the language adopted refers to the "same species of inner experiences," thus expressing shared feelings. It is precisely this type of communicative relationship that makes it possible to create a social community. Finally, in BGE 268 Nietzsche argues that this relationship arises from the "fear of the 'eternal misunderstanding';" the very same feeling that in GS 354 Nietzsche calls the "genius of the species." As Lupo observes, it is possible to argue that this "benevolent genius" is not

> the primitive reproductive impulse, the manifestation of the Schopenhauerian metaphysical will, but rather a need for an unambiguous communicative interaction between members of the same species. [...] The "genius of the species" should therefore be understood as a language shared by individuals with the same psycho-physiological nature. (Lupo 2006, p. 190)

These considerations help us to understand the idea that Nietzsche expresses in GS 354, when he presents the definition of "true perspectivism"; that is, the fact that, in the passage from the "first" to the "second" level of consciousness, the drives

---

[37] Riccardi (2014, p. 252–3) observes that the idea that concepts are abbreviations for "groups of sensations" that occur together and recur frequently can be found in Teichmüller (1882, p. 132). See also Small 2001, p. 43. Moreover, Lupo (2006, p. 196 fn.) shows that NL 1884–85, KSA 11, 30[10] is the actual link between BGE 268 and GS 354. In that fragment, Nietzsche in fact argues that the "necessity of consciousness" arose when animals first related, thus needing to mutually understand one another.

and instincts are processed according to a shared viewpoint. Consequently, what should be the higher expression of our individuality, becomes rather "stupid, general, a sign, a herd-mark." Shortly before these conclusive remarks, Nietzsche declares:

> My idea is clearly that consciousness actually belongs not to man's existence as an individual, but rather to the community- and herd-aspects of his nature; that accordingly, it is finely developed only in relation to its usefulness to community or herd; and that consequently each of us, even with the best will in the world to *understand* ourselves as individually as possible, "to know ourselves", will always bring to consciousness precisely that in ourselves which is "non-individual", that which is "average"; that due to the nature of consciousness – to the "genius of the species" governing it – our thoughts themselves are continually as it were *outvoted* and translated back into the herd perspective. (GS 354; KSA 3, p. 592)

These observations are most likely Nietzsche's most original contribution to the problem of consciousness, and it is interesting the way he links this notion with that of herd.[38] The latter, in fact, outlines a far narrower field than the social one: namely, Christian morality – which especially interests Nietzsche. Moreover, it is possible to say that Nietzsche uses the word "herd" with a well-specific semantic value; a fact which is worth exploring in order to shed further light on Nietzsche's dealing with perspectivism in GS 354. Indeed, if the herd is our actual shared perspective on the world, then our consciousness is filtered through the value-system of our collectivity – it is value-laden. The translation of our inner physiological states into signs and communication formulas would therefore be influenced by the shared morality, and the produced language would bear the traces of that influence.

---

**38** Nietzsche's idea that consciousness is a product of social interaction probably has been inspired by some readings from the early 1880s. Based on a series of posthumous fragments that Nietzsche wrote between 1880 and 1881, Lupo (2006, p. 178 ff.) focuses on the work of W. Roux, arguing that he would have suggested to Nietzsche the idea of finding connections and analogies between biology and physiology on the one hand and sociology on the other. Orsucci (2001, p. 106 ff.), instead, stressed the influenced that A. Espinas's *Des sociétés animales* (1879) played on Nietzsche. According to Orsucci (2001, p. 107), Espinas could have shown to Nietzsche that, "at different levels of the evolutionary scale, 'consciousness' is always, to a certain extent, something 'artificial,' imposed by the needs and obligations of the interaction. 'Naturality' is thus nothing more than 'convention'." Espinas is also mentioned by Fornari (2009), in relation to the importance of H. Spencer in the development of Nietzsche's reflection on consciousness. Fornari also focuses on another important source of Nietzsche's view on that issue, namely A. Fouillée's *La science sociale contemporaine*. In discussing the development of national instincts and popular tendencies from an evolutionary (generically Lamarckian, Darwinian and Spencerian) viewpoint Fouillée critically remarks that "one could defend the radical opinion according to which the individual, while believing to be self-conscious, is in fact only conscious of the society. And, indeed, what do we have which is our own, coming from ourselves? Nothing, or almost nothing. Our language comes from society, our education comes from society, our instinctive tendencies, our supposed personal character are inherited from society [...]. In short, it is society that *works* and *breathes* in a human community [...]. Our own consciousness cannot be but the social consciousness in one of its forms." (Fouillée 1880, p. 241 f. The underscores correspond to those that can be found in Nietzsche's personal copy of that book. See on this Fornari 2009, p. 149 fn.) Further reflections on the topic can be found in Emden 2014.

## 3.4 The herd instinct

Thus, the falsification and alteration operated by our consciousness is not a mere theoretical issue. On the contrary, it involves our evaluation activity, this including our view of our own cognitive relationship with the world, which plays a pivotal role in Nietzsche's late thought – namely, the problem of the "value of truth."

## 3.4 The herd instinct

Nietzsche started working on the notion of "herd" in the early 1880s,[39] as we can see from its presence in several published works of that period. That zoological metaphor – which seems to be a clear reference to one of the most iconic images of Christianity, that of the priest as shepherd of souls – is the name that Nietzsche gave to "the instinct that pertains to the formation of modern morality and to the choice of its value system: [...] 'the herd instinct' (*Heerdeninstinkt*)." (Fornari 2009, p. 126) To put it briefly, it can be said that the herd is for Nietzsche a community of individuals sharing the same values. Moreover, Nietzsche has a quite specific morality in mind – that belonging to European culture, which he critically explores throughout his entire philosophical activity. Given that the herd can be seen as a possible collective subject of Nietzsche's perspectivism, an analysis of its most important features can help to shed further light on the latter notion, and especially to stress its relationship with morality.

In the fifth book of *The Gay Science*, Nietzsche deals repeatedly with European morality and her value. In GS 352, in particular, this value is assessed on the base of the masking function that morality provides to mankind. For Nietzsche, morality is in fact a disguise, a mask that man wears when entering society (GS 365), thus hiding his actual essence. Contrary to what one might think, Nietzsche remarks, what is considered to be hidden is not our evil or savage nature, but rather "the herd animal with its deep mediocrity, fear, and boredom with itself." (GS 352; KSA 3, p. 589) Within the herd, humankind has become a sick and crippled animal, "almost a monstrosity, something half, weak, awkward," which therefore should be "tamed." (GS 352; KSA 3, p. 588)[40] Precisely this petty nature must be hidden. But the most important aspect, for the purposes of the present research, is that a distinctive feature of the herd animal is its mediocrity, it's being similar to the other members of the community it belongs to. That feature, for Nietzsche, is the result of a degenerative education,

---

[39] According to Fornari (2009, p. 127) "the characterization of man as a 'herd animal' – which would become a central topic of Nietzsche's reflections, starting from *The Gay Science* – first appears in an 1873 fragment (29[149]), but subsequently it cannot be encountered until the spring of 1881, with the only exclusion of an aphorism published in *Assorted Opinions and Maxims* [AOM 233; KSA 2, p. 485]." Furthermore, Fornari observes that Nietzsche's use of this metaphor was fostered by a controversy with Herbert Spencer (Fornari 2009, p. 127).

[40] Cf. TI, Morality as Anti-nature and "Improving" Humanity, KSA 6. On this, see also Schank 2000.

which discourages the affirmation of individuality up to its complete annihilation, privileging a shared and common view.

These observations can be already found in GS 116, where Nietzsche especially deals with the notion of herd (in fact, the aphorism is titled *Herd instinct*). In this passage, Nietzsche defines that instinct as the assimilation of the normativity which satisfies the needs of the community the individual belongs to, and to which he surrenders, sacrificing his own needs.

> Wherever we encounter a morality, we find an evaluation and ranking of human drives and actions. These evaluations and rankings are always the expression of the needs of a community and herd: that which benefits *it* the most – and second most, and third most – is also the highest standard of value for all individuals. With morality the individual is instructed to be a function of the herd and to ascribe value to himself only as a function. [...] Morality is herd-instinct in the individual. (GS 116; KSA 3, p. 474–5)

In the early 1880s, Nietzsche reflected on the idea that, in order to live in society, the individual must abandon his own idiosyncrasies, adapting himself to the viewpoint and value-system of the majority. This view can be found in several fragments of the period, where Nietzsche deals with the State, community and society, mostly stressing their anti-individualistic feature.[41] Moreover, Nietzsche talks about it in an aphorism of *Beyond Good and Evil*, where he sums up his previous observations on the herd and further explores that notion. Similarly to what we read in GS 116, in BGE 201 Nietzsche argues that "herd utility [*Heerden-Nützlichkeit*] is the only utility governing moral value judgments, [and] the preservation of the community is the only thing in view and questions concerning immorality are limited to those things that seem to threaten the survival of the community." (BGE 201; KSA 5, p. 121) This is the premise of Nietzsche's argument. Subsequently, Nietzsche criticizes Herbert Spencer's view, according to which the development of humankind would lead to a form of adaptation to the environment, both on the physical and on the moral

---

[41] Among these, the posthumous fragment 1881, KSA 9, 11[156] (written in the same period as *The Gay Science*) is especially interesting. Here, Nietzsche observes that society, religion and science all seek "the uniformity of sensation," and push the individual to give up his "idiosyncratic taste – [they] work against individualization, taste, which is a condition of life for the single individual." Lupo (2006, p. 182) also refers to that fragment in dealing with the thematic framework of GS 354. Lupo especially shows that, after having read Wilhelm Roux's work, Nietzsche stresses some similarities between biology, physiology and sociology. As for the relationship between the individual and the community, it is also worth considering NL 1881, KSA 9, 11[182], which belongs to the same notebook as the aforementioned note. The concept of "taste" (*Geschmack*) that Nietzsche uses in NL 1881, KSA 9, 11[156] plays an important role in his whole philosophy (in fact, it can be found in several works as much as in unpublished writings). With that notion, Nietzsche defines the deepest individual perspective, the idiosyncrasy of the individual in his relationship with both the world and himself. More precisely, the taste is the expression of all the processes working at the affective, sensible, and pre-rational level: namely at the level grounding the evaluative activity of each life-form. Therefore, the taste is what best characterizes the individual, as much as a community and/or a culture.

level. Spencer's optimistic evolutionary conception thus explains the developments of ideals such as those of freedom, equality and peace, which in his view are supported by harmonious cooperation between the whole members of society.[42] With this in mind, in BGE 201 Nietzsche focuses on the features that can be attributed to the herd, and especially stresses the mediocrity which, for him, distinguishes it. Within the herd-community, there is no space for "vigorous and dangerous" instincts; rather, the opposite inclinations, which do not jeopardize the status quo, are appreciated and well-esteemed. More precisely, Nietzsche argues that

> When the highest and strongest drives erupt in passion, driving the individual up and out and far above the average, over the depths of the herd conscience, the self-esteem of the community is destroyed – its faith in itself, its backbone, as it were, is broken: as a result, these are the very drives that will be denounced and slandered the most. A high, independent spiritedness, a will to stand alone, even an excellent faculty of reason, will be perceived as a threat. Everything that raises the individual over the herd and frightens the neighbour will henceforth be called *evil*; the proper, modest, unobtrusive, equalizing attitude and the *mediocrity* of desires acquire moral names and honors. (BGE 201; KSA 5, p. 122–3)

The very possibility that an individual would rise above others and affirm his own "idiosyncratic taste" (NL 1881, KSA 9, 11[156]) is experienced with fear by a herd-community, whose strength lies in its members being confined within a shared viewpoint and value-system. This observation is quite important, in the light of GS 354. Nietzsche, in fact, introduces the notion of fear as origin of both the herd-instinct and the need of men to organize themselves in social groups. In BGE 201, Nietzsche argues that morality favours those instincts according to which an individual adapts to the community and abandons any tendency to affirm his own view over the others. On the contrary, anything that "frightens the neighbour" is banned as "bad." This is clearly stated in the opening lines of that passage. As Nietzsche argues, the first example of esteem, from the community viewpoint, is the reward of whatever favours its defence. At the initial stages of formation of any society – Nietzsche's example are the great civilizations of the Renaissance, e.g. Rome – what is most important is to preserve it; therefore, there is no space for *moral* evaluation of the kind of "drives that would later come to be called by the honourable name of 'virtues' (and, in the end, basically coincide with the concept of 'morality')." (BGE 201; KSA 5,

---

42 Cf. on this Moore 2002, p. 64 and 71. Nietzsche especially rejects Spencer's altruistic model, which he considers as an obstacle to the development of a higher type of man. Humankind's adaptation to the environment *á la* Spencer produces a weak subject – the herd animal – thus limiting the tendency towards expansion and self-overcoming which, according to Nietzsche, is a fundamental feature of all living beings. Cf. GS 373; KSA 3, p. 625: "What makes, for instance, the pedantic Englishman Herbert Spencer rave in his own way and makes him draw a line of hope, a horizon which defines what is desirable; that definitive reconciliation of 'egoism and altruism' about which he spins fables – this almost nauseates the likes of us: a human race that adopts as its ultimate perspective such a Spencerian perspective would strike us a deserving of contempt, of annihilation!" For more on this, see Fornari 2009.

p. 121) That evaluation arises subsequently, "after the structure of society seems on the whole to be established and secured against external dangers," and for Nietzsche "it is this fear of the neighbour that again creates new perspectives of moral valuation." (BGE 201; KSA 5, p. 122) As he conclusively remarks, what matters for the community is what is useful, what helps preserving herself, and "fear is once again the mother of morality." (BGE 201; KSA 5, p. 123)

One last feature of herd morality that deserves to be explored, before turning back to perspectivism, is found in BGE 202. When Nietzsche reflects on the integration of an individual into a society, and on fear as the origin of moral evaluation, most of the times he develops generic observations (this can be said especially of the unpublished notes from 1880–81, where Nietzsche deals with these issue for the first time). In GS 116, too, Nietzsche speaks of herd, community, State and society without making a clear distinction within these notions. In BGE 202 the herd metaphor is rather applied to a well-specific community: that of modern Europe. The herd morality is therefore the peculiar value-system grounded on the metaphysical worldview first outlined by Plato and then popularized by Christianity (cf. BGE Preface). For Nietzsche, that morality dominated the European culture, although

> it is only one type of human morality beside which, before which, and after which many other (and especially *higher*) moralities are or should be possible. But this morality fights tooth and nail against such a "possibility" and such a "should": it stubbornly and ruthlessly declares "I am morality itself and nothing else is moral!". (BGE 202; KSA 5, p. 124)

These reflections should be considered, if one wants to better understand GS 354. In that aphorism, Nietzsche seems to defend the idea that the herd is the subject of perspectivism. If this is so, then perspectivism is placed within a well-defined context, and its fundamental epistemological framework is thus expanded. Perspectivism would in fact be no more a pure question of knowledge; on the contrary, its scope would involve value judgements and especially *moral* judgements. This will be discussed just after a short digression.

From what has been shown above, the way consciousness and herd-morality work can be compared. As Nietzsche describes these processes, in fact, from a general viewpoint is it possible to say that both consciousness and morality enable societies to be established and developed. Therefore, they are means for the creation of a network connecting individuals, this being the context within which an individual can recognize himself as a community-member. Moreover, both consciousness and morality arise from the feeling of fear, and they both work by devaluating the single human being, that is, by making the individual "shallow, thin, relatively stupid, general." (GS 354; KSA 3, p. 593) Thus, it is no coincidence that Nietzsche connects them in GS 354. Given their operational similarity, Nietzsche can easily reflect on their mutual influence. One of the most interesting features that consciousness and herd morality share is probably their "falsifying" reality, that is, the fact that they both *translate* what is known or assessed according to a shared view – thus enabling communication and the actual establishment of a social community. The process that Nietzsche identifies as the fundamental mechanism of consciousness (that is, the way she works on the purely theoretical level), would therefore be applicable to morality, and it would explain how a single, shared value system has been developed.

The connection between the epistemological and the axiological dimensions determines a conception according to which the selection occurring at a physiological level is influenced by the needs of the herd community, by the herd-instinct (which, as such, belongs to the biological dimension of humankind). As a result, it can be argued that a selective apparatus pertains to us, which modifies our inner states and drives according to a well-defined filter – namely, *herd morality*. Therefore, our interpretation of those inner states, and their subsequent expression in linguistic signs, reflect a particular society and culture, actually translating what happens at the organic (unconscious) level in terms of the morality belonging to that social community.

This would be the "true" perspectivism, then. A view that arises from purely theoretical reflections, but that also involves other issues, as one can argue from Nietzsche's remarks on the interpretative privilege of the herd. His observation that "everything which enters consciousness thereby becomes [...] a herd-mark" (GS 354) in fact presupposes the idea that our worldview is mediated by a well-specific value-system, and that it is not possible to get rid of that viewpoint. Moreover, given that, as I tried to show, Nietzsche argues that the herd is the expression of a well-specific morality, the value-system which he refers to in GS 354 must be that of modern Europe – that is, Christianity (and, broadly speaking, Western metaphysics).

As a conclusion, it is possible to say that the philosophical value of Nietzsche's perspectivism can be assessed properly only with reference to his late criticism towards European morality and his reflection on the degenerative anthropology she produced (on this, see Gori 2015c). Contrary to ordinary interpretations,[43] in fact, Nietzschean perspectivism is not limited to theoretical issues, but plays an important role in Nietzsche's diagnosis of modern culture. The observations on the problem of "knowledge" published in GS 354, can also be read accordingly. In arguing that "we have no organ for *knowing*, for 'truth'," and that "we 'know' (or believe or imagine) exactly as much as is *useful* to the human herd" (GS 354; KSA 3, p. 593), Nietzsche reaffirms his critical remarks on the type of morality to which pertains a fundamental "will to truth." Nietzsche's perspectival thought contrasts that view. His investigation of the human intellectual processes allows him to conclude that our world-description is "phenomenal" at her very core; that is, it is no "true" picture of reality. From this epistemological remark follows that it is *nonsensical*, for a "knowing" subject, to even "*make* [the] distinction [...] between 'thing in itself' and appearance." (GS 354; KSA 3, p. 593) But this has important consequences on the cultural and social plane.

---

[43] On this, see Gemes 2013.

If we *believe* that this opposition can be affirmed, and therefore explored and, perhaps, even explained, this is so due to the fact that our relationship with the world is *conditioned* by herd morality, which actually claims that an adequate knowledge of reality can be achieved. This is one of the fundamental "prejudices of philosophers" Nietzsche deals with in the first section of *Beyond Good and Evil* (whose first aphorism, it is worth stressing, is devoted to the "will to truth"). This is in fact the idea which lies at the origin of Western culture (cf. BGE Preface; KSA 5). As Nietzsche claims in GM III 27, the time has now come to put up to question the *value* of truth and face – cheerfully – the consequences of that critique. If Nietzsche is right, that will determine the final collapse of Christian morality, and the possibility for a new, re-valuated and higher type of man to arise.[44]

---

[44] According to Nietzsche, that collapse is in fact a self-destruction or, as he calls it, a "self-overcoming." The critique of the value of truth is indeed the final step of the development of Western metaphysics herself, that is, of "the concept of truthfulness which was taken more and more seriously," until "it will finally draw the *strongest conclusion*, that *against* itself; this will, however, happen when it asks itself, '*What does all will to truth mean?*'." (GM III 27; KSA 5, p. 410) On the anthropological consequences of Christian morality, see Schacht 2006.

# 4 Many Names for the Same Way of Thinking

Arthur Danto's famous text that aims to introduce Nietzsche to analytic philosophers, includes a chapter devoted to the fundamental notion of perspectivism. In that chapter, Danto deals especially with Nietzsche's view by comparing it with the correspondence conception of truth, and focuses on some problems arising from that contraposition (Danto 1965, p. 54 ff.). In exploring Nietzsche's theory of knowledge and his epistemology, Danto declares that Nietzsche "advanced a pragmatic criterion of truth: $p$ is true and $q$ is false if $p$ works and $q$ does not." This consideration leads to a complicated issue, which concerns the similarity between Nietzsche's attitude towards the problem of truth – and, more specifically, his late notion of "perspectivism" – and that which can be encountered in the works of classic American pragmatists.[1] This question can be tackled on two distinct but intertwined levels. The first one is purely theoretical, and involves the comparison between Nietzsche's conception of truth and the view that William James presents in the seminal essays collected in *Pragmatism* (1907) and *The Meaning of Truth* (1909) – a view that, at Danto's time, was quite popular among Anglo-American analytical thinkers. On the other hand, the second level leads to a historico-philosophical research: an investigation that pays attention to the way in which both Nietzsche's thought and American pragmatism historically arose.

As known, Danto focuses on the first of these levels, for his audience included primary his colleagues, who defended an analytic approach to philosophy. In so doing, Danto expresses Nietzsche's epistemological view through a quite simple logical formula, which only partially represents the far more complex pragmatist position. It is not my intention to criticize Danto's choice, given that his attempt to shed new light on Nietzsche and make it dialogue with the non-continental contemporary philosophical tradition deserves great respect. However, some remarks can be expressed, to warn those who still take his interpretation of Nietzsche's epistemological view as referential. In fact, as I will try to show, in dealing with Nietzsche's theory of knowledge and his perspectivism, Danto neglected some aspects of primary importance. Most importantly, Danto's oversimplification of both Nietzschean perspectivism and (basically Jamesian) pragmatism does not stimulate further investigations of these conceptions, whose ideal relationship is in fact as multifaceted as fertile from an historico-philosophical viewpoint. If one observes pragmatism and perspectivism from a broader standpoint, it is possible to see both of them as attempts to

---

[1] Studies on this have been carried out by Kai-Michael Hingst (1998 and 2000) and Rossella Fabbrichesi (2009). From a different viewpoint, a comparison between Nietzsche and James has been recently provided by Tahir Karakaş (2013). The final chapter of this volume is devoted to Nietzsche's and James's views of truth. In that section, I shall develop some reflections in addition to the picture that will be outlined in the following paragraphs. As regards Danto's view of Nietzsche's conception of truth, discussions on it can be found in Stack 1981 and, more extensively, Wilcox 1986.

deal with some important philosophical problems which arose from the cultural context that influenced both Nietzsche and James. A well-defined context, actually, which can shed light on the proper aim and scope of their philosophical attitudes.

As the title of James's work shows, he conceived of pragmatism as *A New Name for Old Ways of Thinking*. Therefore, James presents his view as the elaboration of issues already discussed within the philosophical and scientific debate of his time, in a way that can be compared with other approaches developed during the nineteenth century. Among the several common features that one can encounter, the conception of knowledge influenced by Darwinian evolutionism and some modern development of Kantianism is maybe the most important.[2] Within this context, pragmatism proves to be more articulated than what is commonly held. Furthermore, it can be argued that its philosophical relevance lies in the *premises* of the conception of truth to which that movement is often reduced. Pragmatism is not a mere formula to assess the truth-value of a sentence (or idea, or theory). Rather, it is primarily a *reaction* to a given conception of truth whose reliability is finally questioned, a *strategy* for dealing with an epistemological problem. This is what can be actually compared of James's and Nietzsche's views. As has been widely demonstrated in the Nietzsche-scholarship, both evolutionism and Kantianism were in fact two important roots of Nietzsche's thought.[3] In particular, they constitute the principles of the theory of knowledge that Nietzsche defended throughout his life, and which played a fundamental role in the development of his mature view on the "will to truth" that, for Nietzsche, has to be blamed for the nihilistic degeneration of modern Europeans (cf. Gori 2015c and 2017c). As much as pragmatism, also Nietzschean perspectivism must not be reduced to a mere epistemological conception. On the contrary (as I tried

---

[2] On the relationship between pragmatism and evolutionism, see the seminal study Wiener 1944, which is still worth reading, and Franzese 2009. The relationship between pragmatism, Kantianism and neo-Kantianism is scarcely explored by the secondary literature. On this, see for example Murphey 1968, and Ferrari 2010 and 2015. For a broader account of the issue, see also Rorty 1991a.
[3] See, for example, Himmelmann 2005; Gentili 2015; Fazio 1991; Gerhard/Reschke 2010; Fornari 2006; and Stegmaier 1987. In the context of this research, it is worth pointing out that the Kantian root of Nietzschean thought had been identified at the beginning of the twentieth century by Hans Vaihinger, an author who will be considered in the second paragraph of the current chapter. At the beginning of the section dedicated to Nietzsche, which Vaihinger included within the "historical confirmations" of his *Philosophy of "As-If"* (1925, p. 342), one reads that "as a matter of fact there is a great deal of Kant in Nietzsche; not, it is true, of Kant in the form in which he is found in the textbooks (and in which he will probably remain for all eternity), but of the spirit of Kant, of the real Kant who understood the nature of appearance through and through, but who, despite having seen through it, also consciously saw and recognized its usefulness and necessity." Carlo Gentili (2015, p. 154) commented this passage in the light of the fundamental interpretations developed by Josef Simon (1989) and Friedrich Kaulbach (1980). He especially argued that "Nietzsche's perspectivism [develops] the perspectivism *ante litteram* which follows from the Kantian Copernican turn, whose proper meaning is that 'the subject freely chooses his own position towards the essential world [*Wesen*].' (Kaulbach 1980, p. 60) Therefore, truth is perspectival for it gives meaning [...] to the actual choice between perspectives that a living and knowing subject constantly makes."

to show in the previous chapters) "perspectivism" can be seen as a philosophical-anthropological project for the humanity to come – that is, as a *strategy* to face the crisis of modern European culture, which is about to collapse.

In what follows, I will defend the idea that Nietzsche's perspectivism can be seen as one of those "old ways of thinking" that James collects under the label "pragmatism," with no aim of reducing them to his own research program. In fact, several *forms* of pragmatism can be found. Several views sharing their basic principles with Jamesian pragmatism, but which nevertheless do not give up their originality. These views acknowledged the epistemic and ontological void pertaining to the traditional notion of truth, and tackled it by admitting "that from the positive practical implications of certain ideas, the value of these ideas may be determined, such implications being conceived in terms of operational convenience and of fruitfulness." (Bouriau 2009, p. 248) However, these positions also differ due to the variety of goals their upholders aimed to achieve through them. Therefore, in the case of perspectivism and pragmatism, it would not be correct to completely reduce the first one to the latter. Nietzsche's view is of course original, and differs from the ideas defended by Peirce, James and Dewey in several respects. Nevertheless, perspectivism can be considered as a *form* of pragmatism, for it shares with this American philosophical movement both a diagnosis of modern culture (and anthropology), and an attitude towards the assessment of truth and values.[4]

The similarity between Nietzsche's thought and classical pragmatism in relation to truth can be especially studied through the work of some scholars who lived at the beginning of the twentieth century. These thinkers were familiar with classic American pragmatism, its epistemological foundations, and its early reception in Europe. But they also witnessed the way Nietzsche's thought spread throughout Europe, and paid particular attention to some of his less-noticed ideas. These authors – namely, Hans Kleinpeter, Hans Vaihinger and René Berthelot – published almost at the same time works which outlined an image of Nietzsche quite different from that ordinarily conceived in that period. Nietzsche's though was especially read by them in the light of the ongoing scientific debate inspired by post- and neo-Kantianism as much as by evolutionism; a framework within which also Kleinpeter, Vaihinger and Berthelot were involved, and which can be related with pragmatism in many respects.

## 4.1 Nietzsche as phenomenalist and/or pragmatist

What should be first explored is "phenomenalism," the post-Kantian world-conception that we already encountered intertwined with Nietzsche's remarks on perspecti-

---

[4] As Jennifer Ratner-Rosenhagen pointed out (2012, p. 287), for Richard Rorty "the similarities between Nietzsche's and American Pragmatist's epistemology were similar enough to justify defining them as part of a coherent philosophical movement."

vism, especially in GS 354 and NL 1886–87, 7[60]. This view has been thoroughly outlined by Hans Kleinpeter, an Austrian scholar mostly known for his popularization of Ernst Mach's epistemology, who published a book titled *Der Phänomenalismus. Eine naturwissenschaftliche Weltanschauung* (1913). In that volume, Kleinpeter described a new worldview grounded on the ideas of Mach, which throughout the nineteenth century has been developed by other authors who played an important role in the history of the philosophy of science, such as Johann W. Goethe, Richard Avenarius, William Clifford, Karl Pearson, John Stallo – and Friedrich Nietzsche. The idea that Nietzsche defended that position was ground-breaking at Kleinpeter's time, that is, at the early stage of Nietzsche's reception. Indeed, Kleinpeter himself did not expect that Nietzsche was in fact a "pure phenomenalist," as we read in a letter that Kleinpeter sent to Elisabeth Förster-Nietzsche on November 9, 1912.[5] But when he first read some passages from his unpublished writings, Kleinpeter immediately convinced himself that "Mach and Nietzsche were both phenomenalists," and that "they shared the same epistemological principles." (Kleinpeter 1913, p. 143)

Kleinpeter was primarily interested in Nietzsche's conception of knowledge, which seemed to him to be so close to Mach's. This was a bit surprising, given that at the beginning of the twentieth-century Nietzsche was mostly known as the author of works such as *The Birth of Tragedy* and *Thus Spoke Zarathustra*, and the very idea that he developed views comparable with modern epistemology would have contrasted his popular image. But Kleinpeter was quite convinced of his intuition, and in 1911 he started working on Nietzsche's writings, paying special attention to his *Nachlass*. Between 1912 and 1913, Kleinpeter published the outcomes of his research in a series of articles and, later, in the volume on *Phenomenalism*. In these articles, Kleinpeter aims to describe a "new" Nietzsche, namely a thinker quite different than the one he himself most likely had in mind before reading his less-known writings. For Kleinpeter, Nietzsche was not a traditional philosopher, but rather the forerunner of a brand-new worldview out of which would have arisen a "scientific philosophy" destined to play an important role in the further twentieth-century debate.[6] Kleinpeter especially compares Mach's and Nietzsche's epistemological views, and aims to show to his contemporaries that Nietzsche was "a phenomenalist as much as Mach." (Kleinpeter 1912c)

If one wants to understand what led Kleinpeter to defend that idea, one must consider what he meant by "phenomenalism." For Kleinpeter, the new world-description was grounded on a theory of knowledge contrasting the mechanistic conception which can be encountered at the basis of Newtonian physics (Kleinpeter 1913, p. 5–6). Moreover, that epistemology arose from a particular interpretation of Kant's philosophy, aimed at dealing with – and possibly solving – the problems concerning

---

5 Cf. Gori 2011c. The four letters that Kleinpeter sent to Elisabeth Förster-Nietzsche are collected at the *Goethe-Schiller Archiv* in Weimar.
6 On this, see especially Reichenbach 1951; Frank 1949; Stadler 1982, 1993 and 2015.

the notion of "thing in itself." In short, it can be said that phenomenalists defended two main ideas:
a) Sensations are the origin of our knowledge;
b) Scientific concepts (but this can be extended to concepts of all kinds) are only labels or symbols; consequently, every "truth" has only a relative value.[7]

In the 1913 book, Kleinpeter writes that the phenomenalist conception of knowledge is based on the certainty of immediate experience (*unmittelbare Erfahrung*) and quotes a sentence by Goethe that he finds particularly consistent with both Mach's and Nietzsche's ideas: "The senses do not deceive." (Kleinpeter 1913, p. 68–9)[8] For Kleinpeter, phenomenalists think that all our knowledge is based on sensual experience; given that any logical conceptual construction involves a creative action of the intellect, which modifies the original, "pure" datum, sensual experience seems to be a more "honest" – that is, direct – relationship with reality. According to this view, the words that we ordinarily use (and the scientific concepts, too) are mere labels and symbols that our intellect elaborates to detect only relatively stable complexes of sensations.[9] This is consistent with the principle of the economy of thought formulated by Mach (see e.g. Mach 1895; 1896, chapter 26; and 1991 [1910]), who especially focuses on the instrumental role of scientific concepts and theories, which helps us to manage and share our knowledge. What is worth stressing, for Kleinpeter, is the fact that "the principles of the phenomenalist world-conception imply that a purely logical deduction of both the world and our experiences cannot be even conceived." (Kleinpeter 1913, p. 193) Let's leave aside the question of whether Kleinpeter defends a radical form of empiricism, here, for that would lead us far from the subject of the

---

7 These ideas can be properly understood only in the light of Mach's epistemology. Out of that context, in fact, one could misinterpret the phenomenalist view as a form of empiricist sensualism. However, the very notion of "sensation" is itself highly problematic, in Mach, for it is not clear whether it has a pure empirical or rather idealistic character (on this, see Banks 2003). A digression on these topics would exceed the scope of the present research. In what follows, I will focus on Kleinpeter's view only, leaving a discussion of the basic principles of phenomenalism to further studies.
8 Most probably, Kleinpeter has in mind TI, "Reason" in Philosophy 2, where Nietzsche observes that "the senses do not lie [*lügen*]." This remark actually led some interpreters to argue that Nietzsche defended a form of direct sensualism (see e.g. Small 1999 and Riccardi 2013). It is worth noting that this position might have deep Kantian roots. In the transcendental dialectics of the *Critique of Pure Reason* (KrV A 293 / B 350), Kant indeed argued that "the senses do not err [*irren*]; yet not because they always judge correctly, but because they do not judge at all." Kant later reaffirmed that view, in his *Anthropology from a Pragmatic Point of View*. In that work, for example, he argues that "the senses do not confuse [*verwirren*]" and that "the senses do not deceive [*betrügen*]." (Kant 2007 [1798], §§ 9 and 11) See on this Caygill 2003 and Gori 2015a, § II.C.
9 In the previous chapter (section 3), the first part of BGE 268 has been quoted. In that aphorism, Nietzsche writes that "words are acoustic signs for concepts; concepts, though, are more or less determinate pictorial signs for sensations that occur together and recur frequently, for groups of sensations." As has been shown (and as we also read in Riccardi 2014, p. 252–3), this position has been inspired by the post-Kantian Gustav Teichmüller (1882, p. 132).

present research. Rather, his criticism of logicism – that is, the view that pays attention to the logical dimension as more important and truthful than the empirical one – must be stressed. According to Kleinpeter (and for Mach, too), the logical dimension is the realm of intellectual creations whose value is limited to their practical fruitfulness. On this, the phenomenalist conception of knowledge seems to be quite close to that defended by pragmatist thinkers, as Kleinpeter observed in 1912:

> Kant was the first to consider all human sciences as a product of the relationship between Intellect and Reason; in so doing, however, he made a terrible mistake, since he attributed an absolute value to the results of intellectual activity, while he should have recognized that it is experience which is crucial, in fact. This has been especially stressed by Ernst Mach, in his works devoted to the natural sciences and to a critical inquiry into human knowledge. Moreover, in Nietzsche's posthumous writings, it is possible to find outlined the same epistemological conception. The fundamental idea of this biological theory of knowledge – which has been discussed within natural scientists since long time, as well as among the upholders of the new philosophical movement called pragmatism – consists in rejecting the idea that science is a collection of norms whose validity lies in themselves, and to hold instead that the concepts she uses are nothing but a fundamental tool for our intellectual activity. (Kleinpeter 1912b, p. 101)

In this passage, Kleinpeter briefly summarizes the historical development of the new epistemology he is referring to. In his view, Mach, Nietzsche and the pragmatists overcome Kant's view that human concepts are endowed with an absolute value. Contrary to this view, they developed a biological and instrumental conception of knowledge: that is, the idea that human knowledge is nothing but a means which helps us to orient ourselves in the world and is therefore useful for the preservation of our species.[10] The role of our intellect, within this picture, is to shape a content which is essentially *neutral* – namely the sensations – according to cognitive schemes developed during the evolutionary history of man, and naturally selected due to their adaptive efficacy.[11] This conception of the value of "truths" is thus connected to the first thesis of phenomenalism: the idea that our knowledge arise from sensations. Sensations "do not deceive" for they have no truth-value *in themselves*, which could be assessed independently from the categorial activity of the intellect. But, precisely for it is not possible to deal with them directly, given that we can only be aware of them through our intellect, any form of knowledge will only have

---

[10] On Mach's idea that the main aim of science is to help us finding our way in the world, see e.g. Mach 1914 [1886], p. 37, and Gori 2018b.
[11] Cf. for example Mach 1895, p. 163 ff.; Čapek 1968; Gori 2009, p. 64 ff. Kleinpeter (1912a and 1912c) especially focuses on the biological conception of knowledge, in stressing the similarities between Nietzsche and Mach. On Mach's evolutionary conception of knowledge, and on the relationship between this position and modern evolutionary epistemology, see above, chapter 1.3.

an artificial and relative value, and its meaning will be limited within the boundaries of human rationality.[12]

In Nietzsche's both published and unpublished writings, Kleinpeter found several passages which show that the former defended this conception of truth. The metaphorical value of "truths" presented in *On Truth and Lies in an Extra-Moral Sense*; the ideas on language and knowledge published in the first volume of *Human, All Too Human* (in particular §§ 9, 11 and 16); the famous remarks expressed in the first edition of *The Gay Science* (§§ 110 – 12), and also stated in the posthumous fragments from the late 1880s – these are all examples of Nietzsche's criticism towards the value traditionally attributed to our intellectual and rational dimension, which support Kleinpeter's interpretation of Nietzsche as phenomenalist and (proto-)pragmatist. For Nietzsche, indeed, "logic falsifies reality, […] our cognitive activity 'logicizes' reality." Moreover, in agreement with Mach and the other forerunners and upholders of phenomenalism, Nietzsche also argued that "the concepts we elaborate do not exist in reality and do not correspond to any 'thing', but are only instruments that allow us to reproduce our experience with good approximation." (Kleinpeter 1913, p. 83 – 4. Cf. also Kleinpeter 1912c.) The rejection of a correspondence theory of truth and the defence of a relativist view of knowledge is of the greatest importance, for it leads precisely to the anti-metaphysical attitude that characterizes the phenomenalist world-conception. This conception in fact follows from the idea that man has no access to any reality independent from his own intellect and that, consequently, he cannot refer to anything permanent and immutable, both on the epistemological (concepts) and on the ontological plane (things). It is only our intellect that fixes what essentially becomes, as Nietzsche states repeatedly. According to him (TL), our ordinary language has a metaphorical value, for it constantly produces symbols, thus simplifying a complex, chaotic, and unceasingly becoming reality, and allowing us to manage it (see also HH I 11 and 16; and GS 110). Moreover, Nietzsche believed that the "truth"-value of these intellectual products is related with their "usefulness."[13]

Kleinpeter focuses on these epistemological remarks in order to argue that Nietzsche's and Mach's views are quite similar, and, furthermore, that Nietzsche actually forerun phenomenalism (Kleinpeter 1913, p. 27, and 1912c). The similarity between Nietzsche and Mach is also supported by the fact that they both defended a biological (evolutionary) conception of knowledge, as much as a pragmatist theory of truth. As Kleinpeter observes (1913, p. 209),

---

[12] As described by Mach, however, sensations are a mediated access to the "real," to the "external world," too. Like Nietzsche, Mach also argued that the external world is completely inaccessible to our actual "knowledge". For him, sensations are a sort of "limit" which cannot be trespassed. Therefore, the problem of the "thing in itself," which was so relevant to the whole Kantian tradition, is completely dismissed as nonsensical by Mach.

[13] On this, cf. NL 1888, KSA 13, 14[153], and below, chapter 5.

like Goethe and Darwin, Nietzsche also argued that man is an active being constantly struggling, that knowledge is a collection of man-made judgments, and that these judgements are tools for the struggle for life. [...] Nietzsche focused on the biological foundations of knowledge and developed a pragmatist conception of truth. These are the principles of the new instrumental theory of scientific knowledge.

In outlining Mach's epistemology and the phenomenalist theory of knowledge, Kleinpeter compares this new world-conception with the new-born American pragmatism (whose reception in the German-speaking world started at the beginning of the twentieth century. See Ferrari 2017). It can be argued that Kleinpeter conceived phenomenalism as one of the "old ways of thinking" that – as much as others which arose in the same period and from the same principles that inspired Mach – fall within the "new name" *pragmatism*, since phenomenalism embodied the same epistemological view defended by James.[14] This is particularly clear in an article where Kleinpeter, driven by the recent publication of the German translation of James's 1907 work, by Wilhelm Jerusalem,[15] compares the pragmatist conception of truth with Mach's epistemology. In this paper, too, Kleinpeter includes Nietzsche within the forerunners of the new philosophical conception, thus interpreting him as "the first prophet" of pragmatism (Kleinpeter 1912a). For Kleinpeter, the consistency between phenomenalism and pragmatism is quite strong. Both these views in fact overcome the old schools of thought, for they defended a non-metaphysical conception of truth and aimed to get rid of the absolute principles whose existence was traditionally inferred on pure logical basis. According to phenomenalism (and, apparently, according to pragmatism, too), a lack of consistency can be encountered in the old worldview. Its fundamental concepts are indeed alleged substance-concepts, whose ontological value cannot in fact be assessed. This is so because they are mere logical notions, that *we believe* to represent the real essence of reality, due to their usefulness as means for the orientation and preservation! – argues Mach. Kleinpeter deals with this in his 1912 paper, and outlines an historical development of the new world-conception:

> Locke, Berkeley, Hume, Kant, Schopenhauer, Nietzsche, and Mach stressed that there is no absolute and *a priori* truth. The old notion of truth, as it was discussed in Plato's *Theaetetus* and later presented by Kant in his *Critique* almost without questions, showed its total lack of content, since no unconditional truth can be taken as premise of any act of thought, and, on the other hand, we cannot gain such knowledge in any way. (Kleinpeter 1912a, p. 406)

Modern critical thinking is challenging, for it leaves a set of questions to be solved. Pragmatism tackles some of these questions, and especially develops a strategy for

---

[14] This is not surprising, if one considers that James elaborated his own position inspired by Mach and his school. On this, see Holton 1992; Ryan 1989.
[15] Jerusalem played an important role in the dissemination of pragmatism in Europe, and especially in Austria. On this, see Ferrari (2015 and 2017).

dealing with the problem of the value of truth. This strategy consists in considering that value as merely relative, thus endorsing instrumentalism vs. essentialism. For Kleinpeter, this is also true for phenomenalism. According to this view, scientific concepts (atom, energy, etc.) do not denote "real objects, which actually exist in the external word; on the contrary, they are but instruments created by our intellect in order to remember experiences which are not currently present." (Kleinpeter 1912a, p. 406) Similarly, pragmatist thinkers hold that "words, concepts and theories are nothing more than simple tools for our practical activity," or, as James observes (and as Kleinpeter quotes from the German translation of *Pragmatism*) "all our theories are instrumental." (Kleinpeter 1912a, p. 406)

If we accept that it is impossible to "achieve a 'complete' conceptual determination of truth" (Kleinpeter 1912a, p. 406) – both on the level of ordinary thought and on the higher, more refined one of scientific knowledge – then epistemological nihilism *stands at the door*, to use a famous Nietzschean expression. But it can be avoided, and this is possible precisely if we find new principles for evaluating our knowledge. This is exactly what pragmatism did. As Kleinpeter points out, pragmatists thinkers focused on the plane of human activity and judged the value of a theory or a concept "from its *practical consequences*." (Kleinpeter 1912a, p. 405) In so doing, they abandoned the sterile and interminable disputes on metaphysical issues, which characterized old philosophy, and rather focused on the actual relevance and influence of theories, ideas, concepts, etc. for our practical activity. On this, Kleinpeter develops some interesting remarks. He describes pragmatism in a way that differs from the purely theoretical image that has been popularized during the twentieth century. Once "empty words and purely conceptual disputes" have been put aside – argues Kleinpeter – pragmatism "invites us to focus on life itself," and confers "a crucial value [...] to our actions." (Kleinpeter 1912a, p. 406)[16] Moreover, Kleinpeter observes that "the actions which pragmatism talks do not necessary fall within the

---

[16] For Kleinpeter, a particularly relevant affinity between pragmatism and Nietzsche's thought can be found in their interest in the active and creative character of human life (Kleinpeter 1912a). It is worth noting that Kleinpeter's interpretation of pragmatism is consistent with the outline provided by A.C. Armstrong at the international congress of philosophy held in Heidelberg in 1908. Armstrong presented a paper called *The Evolution of Pragmatism*, which explores the principles of the new philosophical conception. He especially stresses that pragmatism "proposes primarily a method of thought and inquiry – a method inherent in all thinking, when this is rightly understood, one which has been victoriously followed by the natural sciences, and which is now introduced into philosophy for the latter's regeneration and revival. And the benefits of this method are held not to accrue to thought alone – it brings knowledge into touch with life and promotes action as well as cognitive work." (Armstrong 1909, p. 720–1) Rorty (1991b, p. 2) also considered that Nietzsche, James and Peirce can be compared for they "took care of the question 'what concrete difference will an idea's being true make in any one's actual life?'." (On Rorty's interpretation of Nietzsche as a "German pragmatist," see Ratner-Rosenhagen 2012, p. 285 ff.) In Gori 2017c, I defended the idea that the ethical and anthropological question permeates Nietzschean perspectivism as much as Jamesian pragmatism. Moreover, I believe that a philosophically relevant comparison between Nietzsche and James can be provided by looking at that issue.

field of the natural sciences; rather, even simple act of thoughts, in the light of well-defined experiences, can be useful or even crucial for the development of further thoughts." (Kleinpeter 1912a, p. 406)

This consideration allows us to develop some remarks on the possibility of interpreting Nietzsche as a pragmatist in a broader and more inclusive sense than that suggested by Danto. According to Kleinpeter, pragmatism is a philosophical position grounded on a well-defined conception of truth, but whose philosophical value exceeds the mere epistemological plane. The pragmatic method deals with concrete actions and human life; therefore, it can be interpreted as a strategy to tackle issues that pertain to both the theoretical and the ethical or moral plane, thus involving a multifaceted system of thought. That is why Kleinpeter considers pragmatism as a turning point in the history of thought and esteems phenomenalism so highly, given that this view shares with pragmatist the same epistemological principles and the new conception of truth.[17] As he conclusively remarks in 1912, "pragmatism and Mach's theory of knowledge are brand new viewpoints, grounded on solid basis and therefore well-established. For that reason, they can undermine the old schools of thought." (Kleinpeter 1912a, p. 407)

A few brief remarks would be sufficient to stress the value of these considerations for the aim of the present research. Firstly, Kleinpeter outlines a world-conception that arose independently from American pragmatism, but which is grounded on the same epistemological principles. Phenomenalism and pragmatism pursue different aims and scopes, but agree on a crucial element: the relative value of truth. For this reason, they can be considered as two different names for the same way of thinking. Secondly, Kleinpeter includes Nietzsche in this picture. As for him, Nietzsche is "the first true upholder of pragmatism" (Kleinpeter 1912a, p. 406) and "one of the most important phenomenalists" (Kleinpeter 1913, p. 27), for the roots of his main philosophical ideas lie in the same theory of knowledge defended by James and Mach. In fact, according to Kleinpeter, "in defining the concept of truth, [Nietzsche] falls completely within pragmatism" (Kleinpeter 1912c, p. 9) as much as within phenomenalism, since on that point these two views overlap.[18]

---

**17** Another author who dealt with the influence of Mach's ideas on twentieth-century philosophical and scientific thought was Philipp Frank. In his *Modern Science and its Philosophy* (1949), Frank also stresses the similarities between Mach's and James's criticism of the traditional concept of truth and, in agreement with Kleinpeter, also mentions Nietzsche as a forerunner of the kind of "enlightenment" that scientific philosophy aimed to achieve (Frank 1949, p. 77 ff. On this, see also Gori 2009a: XXXIX–XLIII).

**18** On December 22, 1911, Kleinpeter wrote a letter to Mach, presenting the outcomes of his inquiry on Nietzsche and phenomenalism (cf. Gori 2011c, p. 295–7). In that letter, Kleinpeter argues that Nietzsche shared Mach's conception of matter and sensations, as well as Mach's critical view of the "thing in itself" and his radical epistemological relativism. Moreover, Kleinpeter observes that "pragmatism is already fully endorsed by Nietzsche. In his writings, the truth-value of the categories of logic is determined by their efficacy in helping us to increase both our knowledge and our capacity

Even if it only addresses one aspect of Nietzsche's thought, Kleinpeter's view is worth to be included in the present historico-philosophical inquiry, for the way he related Nietzsche with two research projects sharing an anti-metaphysical world-conception is someway original. What must be especially stressed is that, to argue that Nietzsche's view falls within pragmatism, does not mean that his epistemological conception is in fact a "pragmatic criterion of truth." It only means that Nietzsche was concerned with the notion of truth, with the problem of her value, in a way quite similar to that expressed by classic American pragmatists as much as by other thinkers who attempted to avoid the epistemological nihilism arising from the outcomes of modern science. Therefore, Kleinpeter does not only (merely) describe Nietzsche as a pragmatism. Rather, he stresses the pragmatist feature of his thought, that is, the ideas that he shared with authors such as Peirce and James. These ideas do not exhaust the richness of his philosophy, even though they play an important role in its development, for they are but the basis of Nietzsche's *original* strategy for finding new principles of theoretical and practical orientation.

## 4.2 Fictionalism and critical thought

Another viewpoint to be considered is also introduced by Kleinpeter. In a 1912 article devoted to some of the issues explored in the papers considered above (*Die Erkenntnislehre Friedrich Nietzsches*), Kleinpeter especially focuses on Nietzsche's criticism towards the "old ideal of knowledge" and on the way he deconstructs the traditional notion of truth (Kleinpeter 1912c, p. 8). According to Kleinpeter, knowledge "must no longer be conceived from a purely logical perspective," and it is time to admit that "an absolute and unconditional truth is a chimera, in the same way as any 'thing in itself'." (Kleinpeter 1912c, p. 8) Kleinpeter concludes that

> if, therefore, one accepts that truth is unattainable, it is necessary to affirm that the human mind *must work*, and therefore *think, through fictions*. This conclusion has been presented in an exhaustive and praiseworthy manner in a book written by Vaihinger, *The Philosophy of As-if*, which has been recently published, although he started working on it several years ago. (Kleinpeter 1912c, p. 8)

Kleinpeter thus focuses on the *fictionalist* view developed by the neo-Kantian thinker Hans Vaihinger, who, in the final section of the aforementioned book (first published in 1911), deals with Nietzsche as forerunner and "historical confirmation" of his *System of the Theoretical, Practical and Religious Fictions of Mankind*. It is worth mentioning, for the purposes of the present investigation, that Vaihinger's view has

---

of action, in short, by their actual contribution to the development of the organism." (Gori 2011c, p. 296)

been recently compared with classic pragmatism; thus, it can be argued that this is also one of the "old ways of thinking" mentioned by James.[19]

In *The Philosophy of "As-if"*, Vaihinger presents an original philosophical perspective grounded on nineteenth-century neo-Kantian epistemology. The book is an in-depth and exhaustive investigation of the concept of "fiction," the basis of which Vaihinger programmatically aimed to lay out (see Neuber 2014). As summarized by Ceynowa (1993, p. 9), "*The Philosophy of 'As-if'* supports the thesis that we must not see scientific theories as representing outer reality, but only as instruments to manage it." This thesis is particularly "grounded on the idea that the human intellect has a fundamental practical function," since it creates a manageable world-image that helps human self-preservation (Ceynowa 1993, p. 9). Vaihinger (1925, p. 170) in fact states that "the logical function is an instrument for self-preservation," and that "knowledge is a secondary purpose, [...] the primary aim [of logical thinking] being the practical attainment of communication and action." This is better argued in the opening page of the first part of *The Philosophy of "As-if"*, where Vaihinger presents the basic principles of his view:

> The object of the world of ideas as a whole is not the portrayal of reality – this would be an utterly impossible task – but rather to provide us with *an instrument for finding our way about more easily in this world*. Subjective processes of thought [...] represent the highest and ultimate result of organic development, and the world of ideas is the fine flower of the whole cosmic process; but for that very reason it is not a *copy* of it in the ordinary sense. (Vaihinger 1925, p. 15)

It is easy to see that Vaihinger's fictionalism is first contrasted with a correspondence theory of truth – that is, the idea that our knowledge is a copy of outer reality. In his view, human knowledge is only the final product of a biological development and its value is merely *instrumental*.[20] This is perhaps the most interesting idea that Vaihinger defends in his book – especially if one aims to compare his fictionalism with both American pragmatism and Nietzsche's view of knowledge. Indeed, Vaihinger's critique of the common-sense correspondence conception of truth does not lead to an epistemological nihilism, for he holds that a value of some sort can be attributed to our intellectual products (due to their operational efficacy and fruitfulness). Thus, according to Vaihinger, we can keep on using ordinary concepts, but we must be

---

**19** Matthias Neuber remarks that the Kantian excerpts that Vaihinger includes in his book to demonstrate that Kant uphold the fictionalist viewpoint, are imbued of (proto)pragmatism. This given, it could be argued that "Kant – and Vaihinger! – were both forerunners of one of the movements that mostly influenced the twentieth- and twenty-first-century (although the latter has just begun)." (Neuber 1914, p. 13) For a comparison between fictionalism and pragmatism, see e.g. Ceynowa 1993 and Bouriau 2009.

**20** For Vaihinger (1925, p. 63), the logical functions are not "copies of events or processes. All these concepts are not pictures of events, but are themselves events. [...] The world as we conceive it is only a secondary or tertiary construction, arising in our heads through the play of the cosmic process and solely for the furtherance of this process. This conceptual world is not a *picture* of the actual world but an *instrument* for grasping and subjectively understanding that world".

*aware* of the fact that they are mere intellectual instruments. This is in fact a crucial point that Vaihinger stresses, for he believes that our whole world-conception would change if we hold that anti-realist stance, whose importance can be assessed on the practical plane primarily.[21]

I will deal with this detail of Vaihinger's system later in this chapter. As for now, further remarks are needed, in order to define his view more adequately. Vaihinger holds that our "mind is not merely appropriative," but rather "assimilative and constructive;" consequently, "logical thought is an active appropriation of the outer world, a useful organic elaboration of the material sensation." (Vaihinger 1925, p. 2)[22] Thus, according to him, the "psyche" (to be understood not as a substance, but rather as "the organic whole of all so-called 'mental' actions and reactions," Vaihinger 1925, p. 1) is an organic formative force, which independently changes what has been appropriated (Vaihinger 1925, p. 2). Finally, Vaihinger considers scientific thought as a function of the psyche and calls "fictions" the products of its activity: "The fictive activity of the mind is an expression of the fundamental psychical forces; fictions are mental structures." (Vaihinger 1925, p. 12)

It is worth noting that this view is strongly influenced by Lange's *History of Materialism*.[23] In that book, Vaihinger found an exposition of the most important topics debated by German neo-Kantian thinkers and scientists during the second half of the nineteenth century. In particular, Lange made reference to the studies of the German physiologist Johannes Müller and focused on the epistemological value of sense organs (cf. Ceynowa 1993, p. 134f.). As for Lange, "pure" knowledge is not possible; anything we know is first moulded by our sense organs, and therefore by our intellect and its logical structure. This is coherent with the development of Kant's epistemology that Lange aimed to provide and whose radicalization led to Vaihinger's philosophical position.[24] In Vaihinger's view, his own fictionalism – that is, the idea that "psychical constructs [...] are only fictions, i.e. conceptual and ideational aids," and "not hypotheses relating to the nature of reality" – is in fact a "'critical' standpoint." (Vaihinger 1925, p. 177)

The reference to neo-Kantianism is particularly important in order to understand Vaihinger's philosophical perspective, since it leads to the fundamental and widely debated question of the "thing in itself," and, consequently, to the problematic con-

---

21 The value of this intellectual turn can be evaluated if one considers some fictions that play an important role on the practical plane, such as the notion of *I* and that of *freedom*. On this, see Gori 2015a. Nietzsche is especially aware of this, as we can infer from BGE 16, 17 and 54. On this, cf. also above, chapter 2.3.
22 Michael Heidelberger (2014, p. 53) directly compared Vaihinger's view of human thought as a "biological function" with Ernst Mach's epistemology.
23 As we read in Vaihinger 1925, p. xxxv, in Lange he found "a master, a guide, an ideal teacher." Vaihinger particularly devotes to Lange's "Standpoint of the Ideal" one section of the third part (*Historical Confirmations*) of his *The Philosophy of "As-if."* On Lange's influence on Vaihinger, see Ceynowa 1993, chapter 3; and Heidelberger 2014.
24 On this, see Heidelberger 2014, p. 51; and Vaihinger 1925: xxxvi, fn. 1.

cept of "subject" or "soul." From what has been shown above, it follows that Vaihinger considers the scientific concepts as having a merely logical value. Vaihinger particularly stresses this point, and in a way comparable to Nietzsche's stating the four great errors of human reason, deplores the traditional "error" of "attributing to the means value which really belongs exclusively to what is achieved by the means." (Vaihinger 1925, p. 167) In other words, Vaihinger argues that, whereas "concept and proposition serve merely as a means for communication [...], the psyche believes that it has grasped something when it has merely applied its fictional categories to the sensation complex." (Vaihinger 1925, p. 169) The final result of this fundamental error is thus the creation of the concept of substance, which – to use Nietzsche's words (TI, "Reason" in Philosophy 5) – is "pushed under" the world of experience:

> We get the fiction of a substance, supposed to exist outside the realm of experienced objects, which then become mere *attributa* or *modi* of the substance. In the same way there arises the fiction of an absolute cause of which the world of experience is supposed to be the effect; [...] and finally we get the fiction of the "Thing in itself" which is supposed to be the essence of phenomena. All these are unjustified transference-fictions, since a relationship which only has a meaning within the sphere of experience is extended beyond this into the void. (Vaihinger 1925, p. 165–6)

That of "thing in itself" is maybe the most representative case of a fiction whose value has been misunderstood, as if it were not merely logical. In dealing with that concept, Vaihinger especially argues that

> only within the world of ideas are there things, things that are causes; in the real world these ideas are but empty echoes. The fiction of the *Ding an sich* would be the most brilliant of all conceptual instruments. Just as we introduce into mathematics and mechanics ideas which facilitate our task, so Kant introduces a device in the form of the concept *Ding an sich*, as an x to which a y, the ego, as our organization, corresponds. By this means the whole world of reality can be dealt with. Subsequently the "ego" and the *Ding an sich* are dropped, and only sensations remain as real. From our point of view the sequence of sensations constitutes ultimate reality, and two poles are mentally added, subject and object. (Vaihinger 1925, p. 75–6)

In complete agreement with Lange and other contemporary neo-Kantian thinkers (especially Mach, see e. g. 1914 [1886], chapter 1), Vaihinger argues that the "ultimate reality" is constituted by sensations. For him, the logical fictions are only means to make reality manageable, for example, by marking relatively stable complexes of sensations, or by introducing imaginary causes, thus giving direction and – particularly – *meaning* to the flux of sensations.[25]

---

[25] Vaihinger (1925, p. 169) defends this view by arguing that "this assumption of a Thing would never have been possible without the assistance of language, which provides us with a word for Thing and gives the attributes specific names. It is to the word that the illusion of the existence of a Thing enables the mistake to become fixed. The logical function selects a complex of sensations

## 4.2 Fictionalism and critical thought — 115

I believe that further remarks on Vaihinger's book and his dealing with nineteenth-century philosophical and scientific thought are not needed, in order to grasp what is interesting, for the aim of the present research. Completely adhering to the epistemological view of his time, Vaihinger acknowledged that an inquiry on human knowledge leads to great problems – problems that are theoretical at first, but that also involve further metaphysical questions. Because of their fruitfulness as means for the preservation of the species, our intellect ordinarily projects on the ontological plane the substance-concepts and universal notions *it processes*, as if they were more than mere logical entities. But this is a mistake as trivial as dangerous, which can be corrected only by critical thinking. This approach would in fact contrast the common-sense realism with a new conception which stresses both the metaphysical inconsistency of those entities and their practical usefulness, thus explaining why they can be used anyway.

Vaihinger's view can be compared with that of Nietzsche, as the former himself admitted.[26] Indeed, in the *Vorbemerkungen zur Einführung* published in the 1911 German edition of his book, Vaihinger declares: "When I read Nietzsche at the end of the 1890s [...] I have been pleased to notice a strong affinity between our views of both life and the world, which are partially inspired by the same sources: Schopenhauer and F. A. Lange." (Vaihinger 1911, p. xiv)[27] Furthermore, in the final section of *The Philosophy of 'As if'*, Nietzsche is included within the "historical confirmations" of Vaihinger's view (the other pretended forerunners of fictionalism discussed in that section are Kant, Forberg and Lange). For Vaihinger, Nietzsche's both published and posthumous writings allow us to argue that he defended the idea that the categories of reason only have a pure logical value; stressed the role of these categories as tools for the preservation of the species; finally, considered as a fundamental error of ordinary thought the idea that causes of some sort can be actually encountered within the dimension of empirical experiences. Vaihinger especially observes that Nietzsche "had realized the utility and necessity of fictions" (Vaihinger 1925, p. 358); that he recognized "that life and science are not possible without imaginary or false conceptions" and "that false ideas must be employed both in science and life by intellectually mature people and with the full realization of their falsity." (Vaihinger 1925, p. 341) Finally, Vaihinger argues that "it was Lange, in all likelihood,

---

from the general stream of sensations and events, and creates a thing to which these sensations, possessed by the psyche alone, are to adhere as attributes."

26 During the last decades, studies on his original development of Kantianism have been published and attention has been paid to the way Vaihinger addressed Nietzsche. On this, see e.g. Schmid 2005, Gentili 2013, and Ribeiro dos Santos 2015.

27 In this introductory section Vaihinger mentions four elements of philosophical inspiration that made him realize that the system he sketched as early as 1877 could be actually worth to be published. Nietzsche is the third of these elements, the other three being *Voluntarism* (Wundt, Rickert, Paulsen); Ernst Mach's *biological theory of knowledge*; and *Pragmatism* (Peirce and Ferdinand Schiller). Cf. Vaihinger 1911, pp. xiii-xv and, for some remarks on this, Gentili 2013 and Gabriel 2014.

who in this case served as his [Nietzsche's] guide." (Vaihinger 1925, p. 341)[28] This shared reference is an important as much as undisputable explanation of the similarity between Vaihinger's and Nietzsche's views on some issues. Both of them are in fact inspired by the same epistemological principles, that each of them developed in an original way, according to his own standpoint and aim. Nevertheless, these principles played a fundamental role in both Vaihinger and Nietzsche, and they imbue their most elaborated and philosophically relevant ideas.

If, on the one hand, it is possible to stress the similarity between Vaihinger and Nietzsche, on the other hand it is also possible to ascribe to Vaihinger a pragmatist conception – albeit with some necessary clarification and if pragmatism is not interpreted as a mere methodology for assessing truth-values. It is Vaihinger himself that gives us a hint in this sense. In the preface to the 1925 English translation of *The Philosophy of As-if*, he compares pragmatism and fictionalism, and expresses his personal remarks:

> "Pragmatism," so widespread throughout the English-speaking world, has done something to prepare the ground for Fictionalism, in spite of their fundamental difference. Fictionalism does not admit the principle of Pragmatism which runs: "An idea which is found to be useful in practice proves thereby that it is also true in theory, and the fruitful it thus always true." The principle of Fictionalism, on the other hand, or rather the outcome of Fictionalism, is as follows: "An idea whose theoretical untruth or incorrectness, and therewith its falsity, is admitted, is not for that reason practically valueless and useless; for such an idea, in spite of its theoretical nullity may have great practical importance." But though Fictionalism and Pragmatism are diametrically opposed in principle, in practice they may find much in common. Thus, both acknowledge the value of metaphysical ideas, though for very different reasons and with very different consequences. (Vaihinger 1925, p. viii)

These remarks help us to better understand not only which was Vaihinger's aim in developing his fictionalism, but also how he interpreted American pragmatism (and why he thought that his view was to be distinguished from this one). The correctness of Vaihinger's interpretation of pragmatism is an issue that can be addressed separately. For the aim of the present research, it is worth stressing that Vaihinger argues that the two positions have a common ground (albeit perhaps he admits so just as a strategy, for the purpose of having his work better received in the land of Peirce, James, Dewey, and Schiller). That common ground was the nineteenth-century scientific debate and its epistemological framework. A debate that especially discussed the traditional conception of truth and revealed the illusory and

---

**28** A few lines below, Vaihinger remarks that "Nietzsche, like Lange, emphasizes the great significance of 'appearances' in all the various fields of science and life and, like him, points out the fundamental and far-reaching function of 'invention' and 'falsification'." Therefore, Vaihinger claims that "this Kantian or, if you will, neo-Kantian origin of Nietzsche's doctrine has hitherto been completely ignored, because Nietzsche, as was to be expected from his temperament, has repeatedly and ferociously attacked Kant whom he quite misunderstood." (Vaihinger 1925, p. 341–2) On this see Gentili 2013 and 2015, and above, footnote 3.

changing nature of that notion, thus determining the necessity to develop alternative strategies in order to avoid the total collapse of the Western theoretical world-conception.

In the opening pages of his book (1925, p. 4), Vaihinger in fact holds that "from the standpoint of modern epistemology we can no longer talk about 'truth' at all, in the usual sense of the term" – a sense that refers to the same correspondence theory criticized by James (1907, chapter 1).[29] This given, Vaihinger does not aim to determine a new principle of "truthfulness," but he rather focuses only on how scientific research (and, broadly speaking, also our practical activity) can still be possible. He thus proposes a "practical test as to whether it is possible with the help of those logical products [whose correspondence with an assumed 'objective reality' cannot be judged] to *calculate events that occur without our intervention.*" (Vaihinger 1925, p. 3)[30] This "operational" conception is not so different from pragmatism, which can be seen as an epistemology endorsing the idea "that a logically irrelevant view, especially that of a completed infinite series, assumes some *practical* value insofar as it gives rise to a fruitful process." (Bouriau 2009, p. 227) Apparently, this interpretation contrast with Vaihinger's introductory remarks. In distinguishing his view from that defended by American pragmatism, Vaihinger seems not to notice that James's pragmatic method derived from the same neo-Kantian epistemology inspired by nineteenth-century evolutionism that also imbues Vaihinger's inquiry.[31] Indeed, James argued for the impossibility of achieving a "true" knowledge in the sense of the correspondence theory, too, and rejected the idea that our knowledge – a chiefly logical process – is capable of describing reality in a certain and adequate way. When James argues that the "truthfulness" of a given theory, idea or belief must be judged on the basis of its fruitfulness and operational efficacy, he therefore focuses on the practical value of a "logically irrelevant view," in a way which is quite similar to Vaihinger's. The only difference between their attempts, on this point, is basically that James holds that it is still possible to talk of "truth," albeit this term must be *understood in a completely new sense* (i.e. with a relative meaning), whereas Vaihinger argues that it would be more coherent to abandon the old terminology.[32] On this, contrary to Vaihinger's, Nietzsche's view seems to be consistent with James's idea that the meaning of fundamental concepts of ordinary language must be re-con-

---

[29] For a discussion on pragmatism and the correspondence theory of truth, see McDermid 2006.
[30] According to Bouriau (2009, p. 223), Vaihinger developed "a brand of pragmatism when illustrating the operational value of fictions [...] in science, a pragmatism distinct from that of both James and Peirce." Moreover, this allows us to compare Vaihinger's position with Poincaré's conventionalism.
[31] On this, see below, chapter 5.
[32] Bouriau (2009, p. 235) remarks that, in physics, Vaihinger "still thinks about truth in accordance with some order (the lawlike structure of nature) that ideas (differential equations) are supposed to express. Even if this order is still the order *as seen by human knowledge*, by way of its finite capabilities, it remains that some natural order (to which one has partial access) pre-exists the discovery one is making." With all likelihood, this is why Vaihinger did not accept James's methodological principle as a criterion of "truth" instead of or mere "fruitfulness" and "operational efficacy."

ceived (and not merely abandoned). The principles of James's pragmatic method could indeed be compared with Nietzsche's BGE 34 reflections: given the lack of truthfulness of human knowledge and the merely instrumental character of logical notions, James worked out a new practical and operational criterion of truth, which lead us to "assume that there are levels of appearance" or, in other words, to determine what we might call a "hierarchy of fictions."[33]

From what has been shown above, it is possible to argue that fictionalism is grounded on nineteenth-century epistemology, as much as other views of the same period, especially American pragmatism. That is why fictionalism can be included within the "old ways of thinking" James talks of – although it maintains its originality on some issues. Or, conversely, one can say that pragmatist epistemology – conceived in a broader sense as a view that acknowledges the inner problematic nature of the ordinary notion of truth, and aims to avoid epistemological nihilism by looking at the practical plane as origin of our evaluations – historically occurred in several forms and with several names. All of them are the product of a phase of transition for European culture, which is particularly important in the history of philosophy. The various issues these views deal with, each of them in an original way and with different aims, intersect in a single point: the problem of the value of truth, whose questioning is considered by Nietzsche as the task future philosophers would have to deal with.[34]

## 4.3 Artistic pragmatism and scientific pragmatism

A third author to be considered in this historico-philosophical investigation is René Berthelot. In 1911, Berthelot published an essay devoted to the pragmatist movement, entitled *Un Romantisme Utilitaire: Etude sur le Mouvement Pragmatiste*. The book is worth reading, for the aim of the present research, firstly for it provides an account of the historical realization of pragmatism in a series of different (but converging) research programs, and secondly for Berthelot deals with Nietzsche's perspectivism.[35]

---

[33] For more on this, see chapter 5 of this volume.
[34] On this, see Gori 2015c. Simon (1989, p. 255) also argues that "pragmatism tackles the problem that no concept can be considered as the final one – neither that of truth." In so doing, pragmatism is a typical product of contemporary thought, which is especially concerned with the crisis of old metaphysics (whose fundamental notion is in fact that of "truth"). However, Simon also maintains that the conception of truth that Nietzsche started developing in the *Second Untimely Meditation*, and whose final result is the rejection of the ordinary universal value of that notion, does not lead him to a "pragmatic belief." On the contrary, Simon argues that Nietzsche's late philosophy, focused on the perspectival character of life, is a form of critical thinking which includes itself within its objects (Simon 1989, p. 251 and 258–9).
[35] Karakaş 2013 also deals with Berthelot as forerunner of a comparison between Nietzsche and James.

Berthelot's main reference is James, who first developed systematically Peirce's seminal work. For James, the term "pragmatism" has three meanings, the most important of which – Berthelot argues – is that involving a conception of truth. As we read in Berthelot's 1911 book (p. 4),

> According to that theory, particular truth as much as the Truth in general are created for "action," for "practical activity," for "life," and we call truth precisely those beliefs which are most favourable to action, to practical activity or to life; that is, those which better satisfy all our needs.

Moreover, Berthelot observes that in Jamesian pragmatism

> the distinction between true and false is not removed, as if it were a merely sceptical view. On the contrary, that distinction loses its ordinary meaning: its value is no longer assessed on epistemological basis, but rather by making reference to action; our evaluation is not theoretically-grounded, but practically-grounded. (Berthelot 1911, p. 4)

These observations are consistent with what has been argued above. Berthelot also stresses that James aimed firstly to re-conceive the very notion of truth in a non-correspondentist sense, and that his pragmatism is an attempt to give a new meaning to ordinary terms which are metaphysically-problematic, without getting rid of them. This is further stated in the opening section of the 1911 work (p. 12), where Berthelot argues that James rejects the previous philosophical conception of knowledge, by claiming that there is no "necessary and impersonal truth, [no] truth to which pure intellect must adapt, and existing in itself." Moreover, pragmatism do not speak of truth, but rather of *several particular truths*, each of which is evaluated on the basis of its usefulness and practical fruitfulness (Berthelot 1911, p. 13).

As argued by other scholars of his time (especially Kleinpeter), Berthelot also admits that a form of pragmatism can be found in Nietzsche. In his view, Nietzsche was in fact "the boldest pragmatist" and even "the most rigorous upholder of that conception of truth." (Berthelot 1911, p. 5 and 29) According to Berthelot, Nietzsche defended a completely new theory of knowledge rooted in both British utilitarianism and biological evolutionism, whose main thesis is that our intellect is "an instrument that life develops in order to perform her activity more efficaciously, and [that] we call truth the mere beliefs which proved to be life-preserving." (Berthelot 1911, p. 8–9. On this, see also p. 78 and 141.) Furthermore, Berthelot argues that Nietzsche conceived the relationship between truth and error in a new way, namely as a contraposition between more or less fruitful beliefs. In so doing, he avoided falling into a sterile scepticism or epistemological nihilism. According to this interpretation, Nietzsche's "perspectivism" arises precisely from a pragmatist viewpoint and, consequently, it should not be reduced to a mere epistemological question, but rather proves to be relevant for the development of a "new view of morality." (Berthelot 1911, p. 9)

This is perhaps the most interesting feature of Berthelot's interpretation of Nietzsche's perspectivism, namely, the fact that he conceived of that notion as both epistemologically and morally relevant.[36] As shown by Berthelot, Nietzsche's rejection of the idea that an absolute, fixed and universal truth-value can be attributed to our knowledge, can be extended to moral judgements, for both in the case of theoretical assessments and in that of moral evaluations one deals with an unceasingly becoming content (Berthelot 1911, p. 167). Moreover, Berthelot holds that philosophy should acknowledge this critical conception of knowledge, but she must also stop trying to substitute old truths with new ones, of the same sort. Rather, philosophy should focus on her *creative artistic power* and develop a new kind of dynamic "truth." (Berthelot 1911, p. 57)[37] Nietzsche's pragmatism – an "artistic pragmatism," as Berthelot calls it – consists in fact in that rejection of the ordinary contraposition between true and false, and in the outlining of a new behaviour which tackles (cheerfully) the relativism implied in that rejection.

Berthelot's study is of some interest for the present research also because it provides us with some reflections on the historical and cultural contextualization of Nietzsche's view, paying special attention to the pragmatist movement. For Berthelot, Nietzsche's perspectivism arose from the "particular mood that influenced pragmatist ideas." (Berthelot 1911, p. 33) Nietzsche's thought would thus be the result of the encounter of ideas pertaining to romantic philosophical culture, utilitarian psychology and sociology, and Lamarckian as much as Darwinian biology (Berthelot 1911, p. 76). But the strongest influence, for Berthelot, came from Herbert Spencer, that Nietzsche knew thanks to his friend Paul Rée.[38] As he argues (Berthelot 1911, p. 78), it was the application of utilitarian principles to the problem of truth that allowed Nietzsche to overcome the common-sensical conception of truth vs. error. Therefore, we should give credit to Nietzsche for having drawn the consequences of both the utilitarian empiricism and the evolutionism debated at his time, and for having developed them into a philosophy which tackled the main questions left unanswered by the common-sense worldview. As stated above, Berthelot especially stresses that these observations concern the moral plane as much as the epistemological one (see e.g. Berthelot 1911, p. 171). "Nietzsche expresses old problems with a new language" (Berthelot 1911, p. 178) and, for example, develops some ideas and conclusions that was *in nuce* in Darwin and in empirical psychology. In so doing, Nietzsche's thought is especially consistent with that particular outcome of nineteenth-century romanticism and modern science which is American pragmatism.

---

**36** This view has been defended in the previous chapters.
**37** On the concept of truth as a process, cf. NL 1887, KSA 12, 9[91], and James (1907, p. 201 and 218). For more on this, see below, chapter 5.3.
**38** On Nietzsche's interest in Spencer, and on how deeply Spencer's ideas inspired him, see the thorough study Fornari 2009.

Berthelot supports what I am trying to argue in this chapter, namely that in the history of Western thought one can encounter several forms of pragmatism. In other words, I hold that the same epistemological conception, the same attitude towards knowledge and truth, imbues different position; therefore, there are in fact many names for the same way of thinking. "Perspectivism" can be one of these names, but this "artistic pragmatism" is of course not the only one, and other views consistent with Jamesian pragmatism can be found. In his 1911 book, Berthelot deals with Henri Poincaré's *conventionalism*, that he calls a "scientific pragmatism," which is worth considering for its relationship with both the phenomenalist Ernst Mach and the fictionalist Hans Vaihinger.[39]

Poincaré's epistemology is a complex position, and in order to discuss his view of the value of scientific hypotheses one must first distinguish between the field of geometry and that of physics. Berthelot focuses on the latter and argues that it is within this field that one finds the pragmatist feature of Poincaré's conventionalism. Indeed, Poincaré especially deals with the mechanist conception of physics, which in his view has a mere relative value. For him, the world-description provided by physics only aims to help us to manage reality; therefore it is not an adequate reproduction of it (Berthelot 1911, p. 270). This is crucial for Poincaré's evaluation of scientific theories. For him, they are only practical means to describe reality and to make it measurable; consequently, their value can be only judged by assessing their *usefulness* and *simplicity* (Berthelot 1911, p. 260 and 267). It is not necessary to explore in detail this complex subject to see why it can be argued that Poincaré defended a form of pragmatism. In fact, he rejected the idea that scientific theories have a descriptive and universal truth-value, claiming that we can rather only work with theories that are chosen *conventionally*, within a range of world-*interpretations*, on the basis of their (relatively) *greater usefulness* for calculus. This view arises from the same critique to the ordinary concept of truth defended by American pragmatists, and the strategy that Poincaré seems to adopt is coherent with the utilitarian principles that, for Berthelot, can be also found in James. As Berthelot conclusively observes, "Poincaré conceived the concept of convenience in a sense quite close to the meaning utilitarian associationism and Spencerian psychology gave to it." (Berthelot 1911, p. 276)

Once identified these principles, Berthelot can make an important connection. In fact, he argues that Mach's epistemology is grounded on the same assumptions as Poincaré's, and therefore can be compared to it. Furthermore, Berthelot thinks that Mach in some sense completes Poincaré's observations on the hypothetical value of scientific knowledge, his view being a more radical form of pragmatism. Mach also stresses the practical usefulness of scientific laws and concepts (in particular, of the laws of physics, see Berthelot 1911, p. 280), and outlines an *economic* con-

---

**39** As Murray G. Murphey remarks (Murphey 1968, p. 19ff.), Josiah Royce also noticed the similarity between Poincaré's thought and classic pragmatism.

ception of knowledge which arises from the modern studies in physiology and biology. As has been argued above, Mach developed a biologically- and evolutionary-oriented epistemology, paying particular attention to the adaptive role of knowledge and, consequently, to the mere instrumental value of science (see Berthelot 1911, p. 278–9). Mach's and Poincaré's views are of course different on several details, but it can be argued that they both share some principles that characterize also James's position – even though, Berthelot remarks, the form of pragmatism one can ascribe to them is not as radical as Nietzsche's.

Thus, Berthelot's outline of Poincaré's scientific pragmatism leads to Mach, the "father" of the phenomenalistic world-conception we dealt with above, and which Kleinpeter claims that Nietzsche forerun. What is worth noting – but Berthelot neglects it – is that James himself mentioned both Mach and Poincaré in his essays on *Pragmatism*. His view, the "new name" he gives to old ways of thinking, in fact has been developed from the fundamental epistemological conceptions of both these authors (see e.g. James 1907, p. 57 and 190). This given, to conceive of Mach's and Poincaré's epistemologies as a form of pragmatism seems to be not only a viable option, but also a well-funded one, despite Berthelot repeatedly holds that they defended only a "limited and mild type of pragmatism." (Berthelot 1911, p. 283)[40] Finally, it must be stressed that Poincaré has been recently compared to Vaihinger.[41] As Christophe Bouriau points out, in fact, it can be argued that Poincaré adhered to the form of pragmatism defended by Vaihinger, instead of to the Jamesian original one. "The characteristic feature of Vaihinger and Poincaré's 'pragmatism' [is] to justify the employment of views with no truth value, but which render scientific activity possible." (Bouriau 2009, p. 225) That means that they both believed "that from the positive practical implications of certain ideas, the value of these ideas may be determined, such implications being conceived in terms of operational convenience and of fruitfulness." (Bouriau 2009, p. 248) This is in fact a pragmatist attitude: metaphysical disputes are left aside, and the meaning or value of ideas, theories, etc. is judged on the basis of their actual outcomes. On the other hand, there is no reference to the notion of "truth," which is maybe the most problematic detail of James's view. In dealing with that notion and, more generally, in tackling the epistemological difficulties which arose from the outcomes of modern science, Poincaré attempted firstly to save the scientific enterprise by re-conceiving the value of her discoveries. In so doing, like Vaihinger and contrary to James, Poin-

---

[40] Frank (1949) repeatedly refers to Mach, James, and Poincaré as the authors who contributed to dismantle the "schools of traditional philosophy" in the age of modern science.

[41] Stack (1980, p. 53) also connects Vaihinger's fictionalism and Poincaré's conventionalism, remarking that Nietzsche anticipated both those views. Moreover, Stack stresses the "pragmatic value" of the substance-concepts which Nietzsche speaks of, that in his view are mere "regulative fictions" generated by language. Thus, their value is limited to their fruitfulness and we cannot claim them to be an adequate world-description, for they do not represent "existing" entities (Stack 1980, p. 46–7).

caré argues that the notion of truth is idle, that it cannot be re-defined, or at least one should try to avoid using it as much as possible. Once we reject the idea of truth as correspondence and argue that no adequate description of reality can be gained, to keep talking of "truth" is no further admitted. In fact, Poincaré ascribes to scientific theories only simplicity, fruitfulness, and "operational convenience." For him, these intellectual products have no (theoretical) truth-value, but we can only assess their efficacy on the practical plane.[42]

Poincaré helps us to complete a picture which is multifaceted but coherent. It consists of several different epistemological views that arose from the same cultural framework, within which modern science plays an important role. Given this shared framework, it is no surprise that these views are similar, and that one can find a common denominator behind them all (albeit a quite general one). As has been argued above, and as James himself maintained, that common denominator is precisely the pragmatist attitude that characterizes Vahinger's, Mach's, and Poincaré's ways of thinking – as much as Nietzsche's.

## 4.4 Perspectivism as a "program of behaviour"

In the light of what has been shown so far, it is now possible to address the question about the consistency between Nietzsche's perspectivism and classic pragmatism. From a historico-philosophical viewpoint, Danto's idea that Nietzsche defended a pragmatic conception of truth can be contextualized, thus proving to be more articulated than what the simple formula "$p$ is true and $q$ is false if $p$ works and $q$ does not" suggests. Broadly speaking, it can be argued that Nietzsche's perspectival thought is in fact one of the "old ways of thinking" that James collects under the name "pragmatism," but this does not mean that the value and scope of Nietzschean philosophy can be reduced to a mere logical formula for assessing the truth-value of ideas. A two-fold remark is worth to be made. Firstly, it is not my aim to argue that Nietzsche's perspectivism and the philosophical view that follows from it should be interpreted as juxtaposing with Jamesian pragmatism. Nietzsche developed an original and – in my opinion – tremendous philosophy, which is consistent with James's pragmatism on some points, but of course cannot be reduced to it. In other words, I believe we can find a *pragmatist feature* in Nietzsche's perspectivism, this feature being important for the development of that philosophical view. Secondly, it must be said that pragmatism itself is not to be interpreted as a mere epistemological stance, for James is rather concerned with ethics and morality, as recent studies suggested.[43] Therefore, to argue that a pragmatist feature pertains to Nietzschean perspectivism

---

[42] For further information on Poincaré, see e.g. Giedymin 1982; Heinzmann 2009; Ben-Menahem 2006; De Paz/Di Salle 2014.
[43] See e.g. Marchetti 2015; Franzese 2008; and Philström 1998.

does not mean at all to reduce his late philosophy, or even only his epistemological concerns, to the "pragmatic maxim" expressed by Danto. On the contrary, that can shed light on Nietzsche's general attitude toward relativism and nihilism, and show how intertwined his theoretical, moral and anthropological reflections in fact are.[44]

The idea that perspectivism and pragmatism are comparable strategies for dealing with relativism can be defended with the help of John Dewey. In 1908, Dewey published in the *Journal of Philosophy, Psychology, and Scientific Methods* a paper titled *What does Pragmatism mean by Practical?* The paper is a review of the recently published *Pragmatism*: Dewey explores some key points of James's position, to which he himself adhered, and aims to outline an accurate image of that view. Firstly, Dewey stresses that the term "pragmatism" has three main meanings: "According to Mr. James, [it] is a temper of mind, an attitude; it is also a theory of the nature of ideas and truth; and, finally, it is a theory about reality." (Dewey 1908, p. 85) Moreover, Dewey argues that the first meaning is the most important, although the scholarship often gives more credit to one of the other two. Indeed, Dewey observes that

> it is pragmatism as method which is emphasized [...] in the subtitle, "a new name for some old ways of thinking." It is this aspect which I suppose to be uppermost in Mr. James's own mind – one frequently gets the impression that he conceives the discussion of the other two points to be illustrative material, more or less hypothetical, of the method. (Dewey 1908, p. 85)

This method in fact consists in the *attitude* described by James of "looking away from first things, principles, 'categories,' supposed necessities; and of looking towards last things, fruits, consequences, facts." (James 1907, p. 54–5) That is, to leave metaphysical disputes aside, and deal with the effects of ideas and theories on our philosophical practice and world-description. Given this premise, Dewey focuses on some issues which are of some interest for the present research. Firstly, he argues that pragmatism shares some fundamental ideas with utilitarianism, nominalism, and empiricism; most importantly, Dewey stresses the role that experimental science played in the development of James's view. The influence of the scientific method in fact led James to the idea that "conceptions, theories, etc., [may be treated] as working hypotheses, as directors for certain experiments and experimental observations." (Dewey 1908, p. 86)[45]

Although pragmatism is based on modern epistemology, Dewey maintains that the application of the pragmatic method to ideas is not limited to the pure theoretical field, thus stressing the philosophical value of James's view. For Dewey (1908, p. 88), "an idea is a draft drawn upon existing things, an intention to act so as to arrange

---

[44] I defended this view in Gori 2017c. More on this will be said in the final chapter.
[45] In the lecture *Humanism and Truth*, first published in 1904 and later included in *The Meaning of Truth* (1909, p. 51 ff.), James especially deals with the connection between pragmatism and the most recent outcomes of scientific research.

them in a certain way." This can be applied to scientific research and theoretical activity, but also to human agency, morality, or to his practical activity in general. In other words, when James argues that "the pragmatic procedure is to set the idea 'at work within the stream of experience'" (Dewey 1908, p. 88), he means that we should look at its effects on the field which this idea pertains, being it theoretical, ethical, or of some other kind. The usefulness of that idea is not to be evaluated on the practical plane as it is ordinarily (mis)conceived. That does not mean that one must look at the concrete consequences of an idea in terms of her *actual* effects on reality. James's argument is more general and, especially, more philosophically relevant. He aims first to *avoid* a kind of evaluation of ideas (being it of their truth-value or more generally of their meaning) which refers to the dimension of metaphysical absolute Truths and Values, that cannot be assessed at all. As James points out in a passage quoted by Dewey, the pragmatic method

> appears less as a solution than as a program for more work, and particularly as an indication of the ways in which existing realities may be changed. Theories [and ideas in general], thus, become instruments. [...] We don't lie back on them, we move forward, and, on occasion, make nature over again by their aid. (James 1907, p. 53)

Dewey especially focuses on this. For him, James is primarily concerned with the consequences of our belief in a definite world-conception, which we assume as given, regardless of it being "true" or not (i.e. an adequate description of reality). What matters is indeed the *value* of that world-conception for our subsequent action, for the consequences it entails on the practical plane. As James remarks in an important passage of his 1907 book (p. 50), a passage that of course Dewey quotes (1908, p. 80), "the whole function of philosophy ought to be to find out what definite difference it will make to you and me, at definite instants of our life, if this world formula or that world formula be true." In commenting this excerpt, Dewey remarks that, if one conceives of ideas as working hypotheses,

> the chief function of philosophy is not to find out what difference ready-made formulae make, *if true*, but to arrive at and to clarify their *meaning as programs of behavior for modifying the existent world*. From this standpoint, the meaning of a world formula is practical and moral, not merely in the consequences which flow from accepting a certain conceptual content as true, but as to that content itself. (Dewey 1908, p. 90)

I find this remark, and especially the idea that our world-descriptions (or "world formulas," as Dewey calls them) can be seen as "programs of behaviour for modifying the existent world," quite helpful in order to interpret Nietzsche's perspectivism as a form of pragmatism. Indeed, I believe that this idea can be applied also to Nietzsche's strategy for dealing with the problem of the value of truth which he tackles especially in the late years. Moreover, Dewey allow us to better compare Nietzsche's view with James's, for it can be argued that perspectivism is consistent at least with the first two meanings of the term "pragmatism" we find in the 1908 paper. According to Dewey, in fact, the pragmatic method is grounded on a definite conception of truth ("a theory of the nature of ideas and truth") and a general "temper of mind" or "attitude," which can also be encountered in Nietzsche.

Let us consider what Nietzsche means by "perspectivism," firstly. As shown in the previous chapters, Nietzsche provides a proper definition of this term only in GS 354, and he makes this precisely by referring to "a theory of the nature of ideas and truth." For Nietzsche, "true perspectivism" consists in the fact that

> due to the nature of *animal consciousness*, the world of which we can become conscious is merely a surface- and sign-world, a world turned into generalities and thereby debased of its lowest common denominator, [...] that all becoming conscious involves a vast and thorough corruption, falsification, superficialization, and generalization.

Consequently, "we simply have no organ for *knowing*, for 'truth'," (GS 354) and, as Nietzsche argues in BGE 34, KSA 5, p. 53–4, we can only refer to "levels of appearance and, as it were, lighter and darker shades and tones of appearance." According to what has been argued above, it is possible to say that Nietzsche's view is consistent with that outlined by Dewey. Nietzsche's perspectivism is in fact a philosophical position grounded on a post-positivist, phenomenalist epistemology (see NL 1886–87, KSA 12, 7[60]; GS 354 and especially chapter 2.5 of this volume). That epistemology arose from a (neo-)Kantian framework and was strongly influenced by the evolutionary viewpoint that during the late nineteenth century became a referential stance (on this, see chapters 1 and 2). Therefore, Nietzsche's view incorporated the outcomes of a debate occurring in his time and that finally put up to question the traditional conception of truth as correspondence to reality (chapter 1.4). Thus, perspectivism seems to be first and foremost a theory about the nature of truth, but its actual meaning may not be reduced to it. That view in fact encloses the moral plane and determines a critique of the value of truth which involves the "eternal idols" one find at the basis of Western culture and civilization. Nietzsche did not only put up to question the theoretical truths, but rather the whole set of values and "moral truths" that man has always believed in, that he uncritically presupposed, as if they were the expression of an order transcending the purely human dimension.[46]

This leads us to the second point to be considered, which concerns the "temper of mind" or "attitude" which, in both James and Nietzsche, follows from their relativism about truth. Nietzsche's perspectivism deals with an epistemological (but also someway ontological) void lying at the basis of the human theoretical and existential

---

[46] The link to the moral level is especially clear from what Nietzsche argues in GS 354, for in that aphorism he ascribes the falsifying character of consciousness to the "herd instinct" (see above, chapter 3). But it also can be inferred from Nietzsche's dealing with the value of truth at the end of the third essay of *On the Genealogy of Morality* (and therefore at the end of the whole *Genealogy*), where he claims that critique to be crucial for the further development of European civilization (see GM III 27; KSA 5, and Gori 2015c).

dimension. During his late period, Nietzsche tackles that void positively, "cheerfully," and deals with it in a creative and fruitful way, developing the multifaceted philosophical position that I call "perspectival thought."[47] That thought fits Dewey's definition of a "program for behaviour," for it draws the practical and existential consequences of the crisis of the value of truth, and show how the human being should be educated (or "bred," in Nietzschean terms), in order to grow stronger and contrast the degenerative anthropology that characterized Europe since the age of Plato and Christianity. As Nietzsche argues especially in *Twilight of the Idols*, our *faith* in absolute value judgements and eternal idols (i.e., the old "truths") produced a weak and mediocre type of man (*Typus Mensch*): the *decadent*. But, if the cause of this degeneration of the human animal is due to the worldview he absorbed, it is possible that a completely different ideal, an opposite view, would produce a healthier and, therefore, "higher" human type.[48] Given that Western metaphysics was grounded on an "unconditional will to truth," on a "faith in a *metaphysical value, a value as such of truth*" (GM III 24; KSA 5, p. 400), Nietzsche apparently argues that the opposite ideal is in fact a pure relativism about that same truth – that is to say, a perspectival conception of knowledge. For Nietzsche, the world-conception that follows from a perspectival epistemology has thus an important influence on human practice, and it can be seen as an actual "program of behaviour." According to Dewey's model, it is possible to say that Nietzsche believes that this view, once accepted, would be capable to "modify the existent world" – namely, the human type – and therefore of making a "practical difference" on both the existential and the anthropological plane.[49]

Nietzsche's view seems to be consistent with James's – as Dewey describes it – in several respects, and it is possible to conclude that it is indeed a form of pragmatism, as the historico-philosophical investigation developed in the previous sections suggested. Both the awareness of the epistemological and ontological void lying at the basis of Western thought, and the attitude aimed at tackling this void through a method admitting that from the positive practical implications of certain ideas, the value of these ideas may be determined, are the characteristic features of a proper "pragmatic" conception. These are in fact the principles that Nietzsche's late philosophy shares with phenomenalism, fictionalism, and conventionalism, as well as

---

[47] Simon (1989) explored the path that, starting from the second *Untimely Meditation*, led Nietzsche to reject the metaphysical value of truth and to outline this perspective-oriented view.
[48] On this, see Schacht 2006; Gori/Piazzesi 2012; Gori 2017c and 2015a.
[49] In a famous passage of *Pragmatism*, James describes the pragmatic method for assessing ideas or notions as the answer to these questions: "What difference would it practically make to any one if this notion rather than that notion *were true*? If no practical difference whatever can be traced, then the alternatives mean practically the same thing, and all dispute is idle." (James 1907, p. 45) As has been argued in the past decades, this should be interpreted primarily in existential terms (see e.g. Pihlström 1998 and Gori 2017c). On the transformative power that knowledge exerts on the type of man, in Nietzsche, see below, chapter 5.3.

with Jamesian pragmatism. Like all these views, Nietzsche's perspectival thought is a strategy for dealing with the problem of the value of truth that follows from modern epistemology.

As a conclusive remark, it can be said that the comparison presented throughout this chapter has not a merely historical significance, but rather sheds light on Nietzsche's late philosophy, thus contributing to its interpretation. Given the aim and scope of pragmatism, Nietzschean perspectival thought can be seen as a positively-oriented, non-nihilistic and non-sceptical relativism.[50] In Nietzsche, as much as in any other historically realized form of pragmatism, the reference points of our world-orientation (being them theoretical or practical) are not abandoned, but rather *re-defined* within a view that leaves no space for absolute and fixed principles.[51] As mentioned above, this is crucial for Nietzsche's late thought, and also fundamental in order to understand properly his editorial and philosophical project of a *Revaluation of all values*, that he outlined as main outcome of his diagnosis of European nihilism (see GM III 24; KSA 5 and TI Preface; KSA 6).

---

**50** Julião (2013) sees perspectivism as a "pragmatic relativism." On whether Nietzsche's perspectivism is a "strong relativism" or not, see Gori/Stellino 2018.
**51** Nietzsche's attempt to a re-valuation of truth on practical basis can be evaluated properly by comparing his conception of truth with James's. I will deal with that in the following chapter.

# 5 A Pragmatist Conception of Truth

## 5.1 Utilitarianism about truth

We finally have reached the problem of truth – or, better, the problem of the *value of truth* – which in the previous chapters has been evoked many times. This problem plays a pivotal role in Nietzsche's late thought. As we read for example in GM III 24 and GM III 27, to provide a critique of truth and tentatively *call into question* "the value of truth" is the "task" that Nietzsche aims to achieve. That issue is in fact crucial for a philosophy whose main purpose is to re-valuate the old cultural system and get rid of Christian morality – which Nietzsche defines as "the danger of dangers," to be blamed if the human type [*Typus Mensch*] "never reached his *highest potential power and splendour*" (GM Preface 6; KSA 5, p. 253) – for the will to truth, the "faith in a metaphysical value, a *value as such of truth*" is the kernel of that morality itself (GM III 24; KSA 5, p. 400).[1] As Nietzsche argues,

> after Christian truthfulness has drawn one conclusion after another, it will finally draw the strongest conclusion, that against itself; this will, however, happen when it asks itself, *"What does all will to truth mean?"* [...] Without a doubt, from now on, morality will be destroyed by the will to truth's becoming-conscious-of-itself. (GM III 27; KSA 5, p. 410)

Nietzsche's dealing with truth has a long story, throughout his writings. The late observations on that topic are focused on the moral and anthropological plane, but they are grounded on some epistemological observations that Nietzsche developed during his whole activity as a philosopher, and which are extremely coherent. In fact, it is possible to argue that Nietzsche's view of truth only slightly changed from the early writing *On Truth and Lie in an Extra-Moral Sense*, through *Human, All Too Human* and *The Gay Science*, to *Twilight of the Idols*. In these writings we find a well-defined conception of knowledge which, influenced by both Schopenhauerian and post- or neo-Kantian epistemology (the role played by Friedrich Lange is of course fundamental), outlines a notion of truth to be re-defined in relative terms. What is worth to be stressed preliminarily is that the concept of "truth" does not play a mere epistemological role, in Nietzsche. Although his early reflections pertain to human (and animal) knowledge, the very meaning of the notion of truth soon involves a wider range. "Truth" is in fact related with "good" and "full of value" (NL 1888, KSA 13, 14[103]); thus, it deals with the general problem of lack of orientation that Nietzsche's madman announces in GS 125, and is not restricted to the problem of knowledge exclusively.[2]

---

1 On this, see e.g. Stegmaier 1985; Schacht 2006; and Gori 2015c.
2 On the problem of human orientation in Nietzsche, see Stegmaier 2008 and 2016.

In the last decades, several scholars dealt with Nietzsche's conception of truth.[3] It is not my intention to re-open that debate, which I believe to be mostly unsolvable. In this chapter, I will try to shed new light on the concept at issue, thus showing its relevance for the history of Western philosophy and for the development of contemporary thought especially. My point is in fact that Nietzsche's view of truth is consistent with late nineteenth-century positions which determined the further development of philosophical investigations. Deeply influenced by post-Kantianism, Nietzsche developed a conception of knowledge, truth, and in general of our valuational activity, which can not only be compared with the most important outcomes of post-empiricist thinkers such as L. Wittgenstein or W.O. Quine,[4] but also provide an original contribution to still heated topics such as realism and naturalism.[5] Moreover, that contribution is pragmatically-oriented – in a sense far from the merely theoretical interpretation of pragmatism provided by analytic thinkers, as much as from the ethical-political conception that imbues neo-pragmatist thinkers. As will be argued, Nietzsche's pragmatism is a strategy for dealing positively with the lack of content of human knowledge that modern epistemology revealed. That strategy consists in particular in claiming that a positive value can be assessed also for concepts or theories with no truth-value – that is, to which we cannot apply the *traditional* categories of "truth" or "false." Nietzsche tackles the epistemological and axiological disorientation which characterizes the European culture of his time, and aims to avoid any kind of sterile relativism, scepticism or nihilism. Nietzsche's late thought is in fact determined to provide *new basis* for us human beings, to help us to *create new values* that would let us find our way out in the world (see e.g. GS 343). The problem is how it can be done. Which should be the fundamental feature of these new values? In order to answer that question, one must first consider how *old* values were claimed to be, and which is the actual character of truth, that philosophers traditionally misconceived.

Nietzsche famously argued that truth has a merely relative value. That idea follows from his view of human knowledge as interpretation, which can especially be related with the *poetic* character of Reason stressed by Friedrich Lange. On this, scholars devoted several studies, also because the topic has important consequences on the philosophical plane.[6] There is no "knowledge in itself" – argues Nietzsche in GM III 24;[7] moreover, the very idea that we can know "things in themselves" is a *con-*

---

[3] Among the most interesting and discussed studies, see Grimm 1977; Clark 1990; and Gemes 1992. Arthur Danto's investigation on that topic is also important for the present research, for he deals with Nietzsche's "perspectivism" claiming that he adopted a "pragmatic criterion of truth." (Danto 1965, p. 54. Danto's view is discussed in the fourth chapter of this volume.)
[4] On twentieth-century post-empiricism, see Hesse 1972.
[5] On Nietzsche's naturalism and its relationship with modern science, see Emden 2014.
[6] See e.g. Abel 1998, chapter VI, and Figl 1982.
[7] See also NL 1881, KSA 9, 15[9]: "Our knowledge is not knowledge in itself, moreover it is not even knowledge, but rather a chain of deductions and spider's webs: it is the result of thousands years of

*tradictio in adjecto*, for we can know only what is "conditioned" (*bedingt*), that is, mediated by our sensorial and/or cognitive apparatus (NL 1885, KSA 12, 2[154]. See also above in this volume, chapter 2.2 and 2.4). Once the term "interpretation" is considered in a wider sense – so to say, with both a physiological and a hermeneutical meaning – it is easy to see that this involves Nietzsche's whole theory of knowledge. His first remarks on the metaphorical value of language (TL; KSA 1, pp. 879-881); the early observations on the physiological 'falsification'[8] of reality; his later perspectivism[9] – all these topics can be related to the idea that to know is to interpret, that the knowing subject plays an active role in its relationship with the external world, thus 'creating' something, instead of merely reproducing a given state of affairs.[10] These principles lead to the view that the ordinary value of truth must be reconceived, if not completely rejected, for it is not possible to defend the idea that truth is an adequate, fixed and undisputable description of reality. On the contrary, according to Nietzsche there is no 'Truth,' but only a huge ("infinite") amount of world-interpretations, of world-descriptions, of viewpoints that cannot be *a priori* labelled as 'absolutely false' (see e.g. GS 374).[11] Most importantly, anything one can say about reality falls within these interpretations. Thus, "the 'apparent' world is the only world," while the "true world" is inconsistent, hollow, a merely logical creation with no ontological value (TI, "Reason" in Philosophy 2; KSA 6, p. 75). According to this view, if we want to keep on describing the world in terms of 'truthfulness' and 'falsehood' (a quite fruitful attitude, indeed, for reasons that will be shown below), that must be done within the human – phenomenal – realm of 'appearances.' Nietzsche stresses this view in BGE 34, and argues that

---

necessary optical errors – necessary, since we basically want to live –, errors, since any perspectival law is basically an error."

**8** Nietzsche's *falsificationism* is maybe one of the most discussed issues explored in M. Clark's seminal work (Clark 1990). On this, see also Hussain 2004a; Clark/Dudrick 2004; and Riccardi 2011.
**9** In chapters 2 and 3 I tried to argue that, although Nietzsche's perspectivism is strictly related with his theory of knowledge and especially with the 'falsification thesis', his meaning is not merely epistemological. The notion of interpretation also reveals this kind of multifaceted meaning: we are interpreting the world when we "falsify" it, by modifying its "true," "absolute" nature through our senses and intellect; but we are also interpreting the world when we judge it from an ethical or moral standpoint. This is well expressed in the definition of "perspectivism" that Nietzsche provides us in *Gay Science* 354. In that aphorism, Nietzsche describes the physiological activity of human (animal) consciousness, which simplifies, falsifies the external data according to the viewpoint of the human *herd*. On this, see above, chapter 3.
**10** In 1885 Nietzsche defined the human being as "a shapes and rhythms moulding creature." (NL 1885, KSA 11, 38[10])
**11** As has been shown in chapter 3.1, although – as Volker Gerhard argues (1989, p. 279) – Nietzsche focuses primarily on the human being, it is not clear who the subject of his perspectivism actually is. In his writings, Nietzsche speaks of the species, the human being, society and cultural communities, but also of the "centres of force," each of which "has a perspective towards the entire external world, i.e., its own valuation, mode of action and resistance." (NL 1888, KSA 13, 14[184]; my translation)

> if, with the virtuous enthusiasm and inanity of many philosophers, someone wanted to completely abolish the 'world of appearances', – well, assuming *you* could do that, – at least there would not be any of your 'truth' left either! Actually, why do we even assume that 'true' and 'false' are intrinsically opposed? Isn't it enough to assume that there are levels of appearance and, as it were, lighter and darker shades and tones of appearance? (BGE 34; KSA 5, p. 53–4)

The conclusion of this aphorism is particularly important, for it helps to understand Nietzsche's attitude towards epistemological as much as axiological nihilism. Once the "true world" is obliterated, its place remains empty. But, given that any traditional principle of human knowledge and agency is rejected as "unattainable," "unprovable," and "superfluous" (TI, How the "True World" Finally Became a Fable; KSA 6, p. 80), it is not easy to fill that gap. Nietzsche's attempt to overcome the old dichotomy between truth and appearance by referring to the phenomenal world only is problematic, for it leads to the well-known paradox of relativism, according to which who claims that no absolute principles can be assessed must admit that also its own principle is disputable. Indeed, if the world is painted with human colours (HH I 16), is it still possible to find reference points for a theoretical and practical orientation? What would be the basic feature of these new principles? Apparently, Nietzsche is aware of that danger. He in fact aims to help the human being to tackle the disorientation that follows from the "death of God" and find a way out of the maze of nihilism. In Nietzsche's late writings, in particular, that "greatest recent event" that casts "its shadows over Europe" (GS 343; KSA 3, p. 573) is interpreted as the starting point of a second sailing that will determine a positive attitude towards life. The future philosophers that would embrace the view according to which "true" and "false" are not to be discarded, but only reassessed, will thus get rid of the chains of nihilism constraining their spirit. That would determine the "cheerfulness" (*Heiterkeit*) Nietzsche speaks of both in GS 343 and in the *Preface* to TI, which is the peculiar feeling he attributes to anyone who proves to be strong enough to bear that weight. Thus, Nietzsche's relativism is not nihilistic at all. He never claims that the rejection of traditional truth-values will leave us with *no* reference points. He never completely accepts that "if nothing is true, everything is permitted."[12] On the contrary, once the value of the "true" world is proved to be illusory, a distinction between "true" and "false" can still be made, but on new basis and within new boundaries. It is only the absolute and fixed Truth that Nietzsche rejects as inconsistent, claiming it to be an "eternal idol" of common-sense and ordinary philosophy.[13] But he does not deny the actual value of the reference points that help us to orient ourselves in the world, whose importance is so great for us that we are allowed to call them "truths." (NL 1888, KSA 13, 14[153]) What is needed is

---

**12** On this, see especially Stellino 2015a.
**13** See EH, Twilight of the Idols 1; KSA 6, p. 354: "What the word 'idols' in the title page means is quite simply what had been called truth so far. *Twilight of the Idols* – in plain language: the end of the old truth…"

a new method to evaluate these reference points and "truths," new principles – that must be as different as possible from the old ones.

Apparently, this is a mostly neglected issue, despite its importance. It is quite common to encounter scholars whose interest in Nietzsche's critique of Western metaphysics is limited to the way he rejects the old conception of knowledge through the falsification thesis. These scholars seem not to admit the possibility (which I am inclined to see as a fact) that Nietzsche uses the term "truth" with two different meanings, and that there is no contradiction between his criticism of Truth as correspondence and his use of "truth" as operational fruitful notion.[14] BGE 34, in particular, allows us to argue that Nietzsche's rejection of the view of truth as adequate reproduction of reality does not entail that no referring points can be encountered. On the contrary, Nietzsche suggests that the relationship between "true" and "false" must be re-defined, that these terms must be re-valuated, in a way that overcomes the traditional contraposition. Moreover, if we hold that knowledge is basically interpretation, and that we only know an illusory, "erroneous" representation of reality,[15]

---

**14** R. Lanier Anderson (2005, p. 193) for example agrees with Schacht 1983 that "the paradoxes generated by Nietzsche's denial of the possibility of truth are to be resolved by distinguishing different senses of 'true' and 'false'." (I owe this quotation to Remhof 2016, p. 242.) According to Maudemarie Clark (1990, p. 33), both Wolfgang Müller-Lauter and Ruediger Grimm "think that Nietzsche discards our ordinary concept of truth and replaces it with a new use of 'true' and 'false'." Clark, on the contrary, focuses on Nietzsche's falsification thesis, and criticizes as contradictory the fact he keeps on talking of truth in his late period, when his rejection of the thing in itself should have been completed. As will be shown shortly below, that involves a discussion of the so-called "correspondence theory" of truth, which has been considered by Nietzsche-scholars such as Danto (1965, p. 54 ff.), Grimm (1977), Stack (1981a), Wilcox (1986), and Cox (1999, p. 28 ff.). Moreover, that issue is the starting point of James's pragmatism. On this, see chapter 1.2 of this volume and below in this section, § 5.3. Remhof 2015 explores a third viable option, in addition to the pragmatist and the correspondence conception of truth, namely the "coherence theory of truth," according to which "the truth of a proposition consists in its coherence with some specified set of propositions." (Remhof 2015, p. 232) That option would solve much trouble, since it holds that "the truth conditions of propositions consist in other propositions rather than mind-independent objects." Consequently, "a true proposition consists in its coherence with a system of beliefs," rather than "in its relation to objects that exist independently of our representations of them." (Remhof 2015, p. 232–3)

**15** This "erroneousness" must be understood in the light of the old notion of truth, i.e. of truth as correspondence to or *adequatio* with reality. The idea that Nietzsche inherits by modern physiologists and cognitive scientists such as Gustav Fechner, Johannes Müller, Hermann von Helmholtz, and Friedrich Lange is that the world we know is but a *product*, in a non-idealist and non-solipsist sense even a *creation* of our perceptual organs. Our senses first, and therefore our intellect, modify the reality they deal with, and leave us with a simplified world that we can manage. (Just think at how our eyes work, allowing us to see light only in a particular range. This is a kind of *falsification* that no one of us would deny: *we only see a portion of reality. Therefore, our image of reality is a false one, when compared with the actual flux of information our senses receive originally.* The fact that we cannot actually perceive that additional information does not contradict our claim, since the selective activity of our sense organs has been demonstrated experimentally.) From these observations, widely debated by Nietzsche's contemporaries, Nietzsche infers that we have no access to the inner reality of things, to their features *in themselves*, *unbedingt*. Moreover, he feels allowed to argue that the world

then our only option is to admit that, within these errors, it is possible to choose the relatively more fruitful one, and take it as (temporary) principle of a world-description, ethical behaviour, or practical activity. If we do not accept that, the only option

---

we know, common sense reality as much as the one described by natural science, is illusory at her core. That is why Nietzsche calls "errors" any outcome of our intellectual activity (e.g. HH I 16 and GS 110), and during his whole philosophical activity he coherently talks of "simplification," "falsification," "schematization," etc. The discussion that especially Maudemarie Clark contributed to develop concerns precisely Nietzsche's apparent confidence that our intellect and sense organs *falsify* reality. How can he be so sure of that, if we have no access to reality *in itself*? How can Nietzsche defend the idea that our concepts are *false* or *erroneous*, if there is no way to compare them with the original datum? Apparently, for Clark the physiological explication according to which the kind of realism we can defend is at most a *hypothetical realism* (see above, chapter 1) is not enough, and the discussion must be developed on the purely logical and philosophical plane. Clark particularly focuses on the fact that Nietzsche keeps on talking of "erroneousness" and "falsification" in his late writings, after having rejected the very idea of a "thing in itself" as a *contradictio in adjecto*. If that is so, if Nietzsche really thinks that the "true world" completely disappeared, then the notion of "error" would be nonsensical. I think that the problem here is that Clark combines the epistemological and the ontological plane. In fact, it seems that she claims that Nietzsche rejected the *existence* of a thing in itself, conceived as the external world in general. But that would be really problematic, for Nietzsche, in particular if his theory of knowledge is grounded on Lange's neo-Kantian physiological observations, which are based on the relationship between a sensorial and intellectual apparatus and an *external datum*. In fact, Nietzsche talks of an *Außenwelt* acting on our sense organs (NL 1886–87, KSA 12, 7[54]), and criticizes the notion of thing in itself on the mere logical plane. The problem he deals with is that of mistaking a pure intellectual creation with the actual features of the world; that is, to claim that we have in the substance-concepts the highest knowledge of reality (see e.g. HH I 11. On this, see above, chapter 2.2 and 2.4). The "thing in itself" is thus a contradiction in terms, for Nietzsche: we cannot even talk of it, for once we do it we transform it in something slightly different, something "for us," moulded by our language and its conceptual schemes. Nietzsche is extremely radical on this, but that does not make neither an idealist nor a solipsist out of him. What he tries to do is to re-define the boundaries of our knowledge. But in order to do that, he needs either to create a new language, or to change the meaning of the terms we already use. Apparently, Nietzsche chose the second way. When he talks of truth, lie, false, error, good, bad, evil, etc., he focuses on the *value* we attribute to these concepts, and aims to re-conceive them, more precisely to *re-valuate* them, without abandoning the ordinary language. As for the notion of truth, I think that his reasoning can be summed up in this way: there is no Truth i.e. adequate knowledge of things; anything we know, any concept we use, is an erroneous representation of reality (*in the light of the traditional notion of truth*); if we want to keep on talking of truth, we must re-valuate that concept, i.e. no more Truth vs. error, but truth *as* error, as relatively more fruitful product of a sensorial and intellectual activity on the external world. I see no contradiction in this view, but only the attempt to develop an argument within the conceptual frame that, as a final result, will be re-valuated. As Nietzsche famously observed, "to err is the condition of living. So strongly err, in fact. To know the error does not delete it! That is nothing bitter! We must love and improve our errors, since they are the basis of our knowledge." (NL 1881, KSA 9, 11[162]) In the light of what has been argued in the previous chapter, it is also worth noting that, as Kaufmann 1974, p. 88 points out, Hans Vaihinger (1925, pp. 84 and 108) conceived truth as "the most expedient error."

we have is to completely give up knowledge and morality, thus supporting a sterile epistemological and axiological nihilism.[16]

The new principles of human orientation may be found precisely embracing that relativism. As shown, it can be argued that, since we cannot refer to a "true world" anymore, our evaluations rest within the boundaries of our actual knowledge only. But since or knowledge is a fundamental means to manage the world, as Nietzsche repeatedly affirms, we are allowed to judge the "levels of appearance" – i.e. to define what is "true" and what "false" for us – on the basis of their operational efficacy, that is, of their *practical usefulness*. Nietzsche reflects on this in an 1888 posthumous note. The passage deals with the origin of human faith in the power knowledge and the role she played in the evolution of humankind. As shown in chapter 1, this biological conception of knowledge determines a relativization of the value of ideas and concepts which leads Nietzsche to a strong anti-realistic view. In fact, Nietzsche argues that

> the aberration of philosophy is that, instead of seeing in logic and the categories of reason means toward the adjustment of the world for utilitarian ends (basically, toward an expedient falsification), one believed one possessed in them the criterion of truth and *reality*. The 'criterion of truth' was in fact merely the *biological utility of such a system of systematic falsification*; and since a species of animal knows of nothing more important than its own preservation, one might indeed be permitted to speak here of 'truth'. The *naiveté* was to take an anthropocentric idiosyncrasy as the *measure of things*, as the rule for determining 'real' and 'unreal': in short, to make absolute something conditioned (NL 1888, KSA 13, 14[153]; my translation).

This is only the final stage of a reflection that started in the 1870s and that Nietzsche developed coherently until his mental collapse. The main thesis, which we find expressed in particular in GS 110, is that human knowledge played a fundamental role in the preservation of the species. According to Nietzsche, the way our intellect modifies the external world, the way it schematizes and simplifies the chaotic flux of data, is an important tool for humankind. Without it, our species would have not preserved. From the first stages of humanity, the usefulness of the categories of reason has been misinterpreted as a sign of their truthfulness, that is, of the fact that these categories *adequately* reproduce reality. Nietzsche seems to agree on the high evaluation of the categories of reason, but there is a limit we must not trespass: these categories are intellectual products, and nothing more; they are no "criterion of reality." As Nietzsche argues, "we cannot cut off [our] head." (HH I 9; KSA 2, p. 29) Therefore, it is not possible to compare the image we have of the world with its inner features. On the contrary, we witness a "system of systematic falsification," that is, we constantly cope with a world which is in fact a sensorial and intellectual creation, grounded on basis which we cannot have access to. As suggested in BGE 34,

---

**16** Richard Bernstein (2012, chapter 1) calls this kind of relativism a "bad" relativism, precisely for it leads nowhere. According to him, the pragmatist attitude is an attempt to avoid this option and look at the problem of objectivity positively, providing us with new principles of orientation.

"true" and "false" can only be assessed within the boundaries of that phenomenal image, within the boundaries of the "apparent" world, and that is it. "Truth" is not "real"; "truth" is only "biologically useful." Or, as Nietzsche stated some years earlier:

> Truth does not signify the antithesis of error but the status of certain errors vis-à-vis others, such as being older, more deeply assimilated, our not knowing how to live without them, and so on. [...] The valuations must stand in some kind of relation to the conditions of existence, but by no means that of being *true*, or *exact*. The essential thing is precisely their inexactitude, indeterminacy, which gives rise to a kind of *simplification of the external world* – and precisely this sort of intelligence favours survival. (NL 1885, KSA 11, 34[247])[17]

This is a biologically grounded utilitarian view of truth, which reveals a broader idea. Nietzsche deals with human knowledge for he is primarily interested in the origin of the metaphysical realm. The fruitfulness of language for the development of humankind can in fact explain why man "conceived that with words he was expressing supreme knowledge of things." (HH I 11; KSA 2, p. 31) According to Nietzsche, our world-picture has been elaborated during the development of our species (HH I 16), and what we now believe to be a truthful i.e. adequate reproduction of reality is in fact only a very useful, indeed fundamental, elaboration of the external datum. This utilitarian view is not to be applied to natural events such as the development of human brain solely; rather, it works also for world-descriptions and world-interpretations of other kinds, being them either theoretical or ethical. The biological criterion in fact can be assumed as principle of evaluation for truths as much as for values in general, thus making sense of the proposed naturalization of morality that has been recently debated. "True," or "valuable," is thus what is relatively more useful i.e. fruitful and operational efficient. It is what "pays," whose effects are "better" – depending on what one needs. Given the importance of human life, Nietzsche mostly focuses on that (see e.g. NL 1881, KSA 9, 6[421]). But the utilitarian principle can be applied at different levels: for example, it is possible to argue that "truth" in science is the most economic idea or theory, the idea which explains the larger number of phenomena with the smaller number of principles; or that "good" is the value that better helps to develop a social community to grow. In both these cases, we deal with values that are not absolute, but merely relative – but which nonetheless are there, as principles of orientation.

This outcome of Nietzsche's conception of knowledge – the idea that the truth-value on any idea or concept is merely relative, and that it results, in fact, from a utilitarian evaluation – persuaded some scholars to compare Nietzsche's view with William James's pragmatism.[18] As I will try to show, a strong consistency between

---

[17] Nietzsche also states the biological value of truth in NL 1880, KSA 9, 6[421]; NL 1884, KSA 11, 25[372]; and NL 1888, KSA 13, 14[105].
[18] See e.g. Marcuse 1950 and 1959; Hingst 1998 and 2000; Fabbrichesi 2009; and Karakaş 2013.

Nietzsche's and James's views of truth can be found, and the nineteenth-century debate on epistemology casts light on that correspondence. The influence of that debate on Nietzsche's thought has already been mentioned in the previous chapters.[19] For what concerns his view of knowledge and truth, post-Kantian epistemology especially focused that "truth" is something to be determined from a theoretical viewpoint, and not a property of things, to be discovered. The development of modern science is in fact grounded on that observation. During the second half of the nineteenth century, in particular, scientists dealt with the explicatory power of their own disciplines, stimulated by the new discoveries developed within the natural sciences, mathematics and theoretical physics. In general, science tried to get rid of the metaphysical remnant that was still involved in the mechanical world-conception. Newtonian physics proved not to be the better explanation of how our world works. More importantly, it proved not to be the *only fruitful one*. In fact, the development of non-Euclidean mathematical models proved that Newtonian physics and its Euclidean ground did not *discover* anything of the real world. They were only very good models to manage the data of our experience, and let us orient in the world. But they were "true" as much as Riemannian or Hyperbolic geometry: each one of these three models is better – that is, operationally more efficient or useful – than the other two *depending on what one aims to explain*. Therefore, their value cannot be assessed independently of the research that we are developing and of the results these models allow us to achieve. On the purely theoretical level, each one of them is a humanly created attempt to describe reality.

Of course, these new discoveries deeply impacted modern science and culture. At the beginning of the twentieth century, science had to face a potentially nihilistic relativism about its principles. If one wanted not to abandon the ship, a re-conception of those very principles was needed – and that is precisely the starting point of James's reflection on pragmatism and truth (see e.g. James 1909, p. 57 f.). Among the scientists and thinkers who dealt with this problem, Ernst Mach is an interesting figure, for several reasons. He directly influenced James on the value of truth;[20] he determined the further development of the philosophy of science (in particular, of the movement for *scientific philosophy* and of the early *Vienna Circle*);[21] he was also known by Nietzsche, as I already mentioned in the previous chapters.[22] My aim in

---

**19** The seminal studies on the scientific sources of Nietzsche's thought are Mittasch 1950 and 1952. More recently, important papers on that topic have been published in Brobjer/Moore 2004; Heit/Abel/Brusotti 2012; and Heit/Heller 2014.
**20** On this, see e.g. Holton 1992 and 1993; and Banks 2003, p. 143 ff.
**21** See e.g. Frank 1949; Blackmore 1972; Stadler 1982 and 1993.
**22** As for the comparison between Nietzsche and Mach, it has been recently shown that it is not possible to consider Mach as a direct source of Nietzsche's thought. In fact, Nietzsche bought Mach's *Beiträge zur Analyse der Empfindungen* in 1886, but as early as 1878 (e.g. in HH I 13) he already expressed some ideas that we also find in that book (on this, see Gori 2009b, 111 ff.). The consistency between Nietzsche and Mach can be explained by referring to the common ground of their views. In fact, both of them have been influenced by post- and neo-Kantian thinkers such as F. Lange, G. Lichtenberg, G.

this chapter is to explore the principles of Mach's epistemology and compare them with Nietzsche's view on knowledge and truth. Then, I will deal with James's pragmatism and show that it is consistent with both Mach's and Nietzsche's view, under several respects. Finally, I will say something about Nietzsche's pragmatism, with special attention to the role that this feature or attitude played in his late thought.

## 5.2 Anti-metaphysical principles

The guiding lines of Ernst Mach's epistemology are well expressed in the 1871 lecture held at the Royal Bohemian Society of Sciences: *History and Root of the Principle of Conservation of Work* (or *energy*, as one reads in some translations).[23] In that text we find the fundamental ideas of Mach's anti-metaphysical view of science, namely the idea that physical concepts, laws and theories have a merely relative and historical value. This of course contrasts the traditional conception of science, and in fact Mach aims to stress the fundamental error of his colleagues, who attribute to the scientific enterprise a value which she does not have. Science does not provide us with a "true" description of the world, but only with a set of tools, of instruments that allow science "to provide the fully developed human individual with as perfect means of orientating himself as possible." (Mach 1914 [1886], p. 37) Moreover, scientific concepts are the product of a biological and cultural development, therefore they change constantly, according to the development of the environment they are part of. According to that view, "metaphysical" are for Mach those notions that we isolate from their developing framework, the concepts that we assume from the tradition as if they were always been there. More precisely, Mach argues that "we are accustomed to call concepts metaphysical, if we have forgotten how we reached them." (Mach 1911 [1872], p. 17) In doing so, Mach does not aim to reject the value of those concepts from a practical/utilitarian point of view; he only stresses the fact that they are the product of a historical development, and warns his colleagues

---

Fechner etc. (for more on this, see Hussain 2004b and Gori 2009a). The similarity between Nietzsche's and Mach's conceptions of knowledge has also been explored by Hans Kleinpeter, at the beginning of the twentieth century (I dealt with this in chapter 4.1). Kleinpeter especially argues that both Mach and Nietzsche share the principles of Jamesian pragmatism, and that the epistemological views of the three of them represent an important development of Kantianism by means of a biological (evolutionary) conception of truth (Kleinpeter 1913 and 1912b, p. 100). The relationship between Mach, Nietzsche and pragmatism is also mentioned in a letter that Kleinpeter sent to Mach on 22.12.1911 (available in the archive of the *Deutsches Museum*, Munich, and published in Gori 2011c).

**23** Mach published that lecture the following year (1872), but he also included a revised version of it in his *Popular Scientific Lectures* (1895). In a 1882 note which is not included within the posthumous fragments, but that can be found in the critical apparatus of Nietzsche's complete works (KGW VIII/4/2, p. 67), one encounters the title of Mach's 1872 essay, within a list of books that Nietzsche read earlier (cf. Mittasch 1950, p. 186).

not to mistake the pure logical function of the notions they use with their ontological content.[24] Consequently, Mach thinks that an inquiry on the genesis of scientific concepts (in particular on the concepts used in physics and psychology), would help us to get rid of any dogmatic heritage, for it sheds light on their essence.[25]

Mach first expressed his view of the importance of a genealogical investigation in the early paper *Über die Definition der Masse* (1868). In that text, we find the fundamental ideas later developed in the *Conservation of Energy* essay, namely that "one can never lose one's footing, or come into collision with facts, if one always keeps in view the path by which one has come." (Mach 1911 [1872], p. 17) These anti-metaphysical principles are the seeds of Mach's famous works such as *The Science of Mechanics* (1919 [1883]) and the *Analysis of Sensations* (1886 as *Beiträge zur Analyse der Empfindungen*). The 1883 book is maybe the most representative, since it aims to provide "a critical and historical account of [the] development" of Mechanics (as the whole title says). It is worth exploring what Mach means with "critical" here. This term in fact recalls the Kantian enterprise, which Mach has most likely in mind, although his aim is not the same as Kant's. In the *Preface to the first edition* of his *Mechanics*, Mach writes that "the present volume is not a treatise upon the application of the principles of mechanics. Its aim is to clear up ideas, expose the real significance of the matter, and get rid of metaphysical obscurities." (Mach 1919 [1883], p. ix) If we look at the original German text, we see that Mach talks of a "*aufklärende oder antimetaphysische Tendenz*"; the critique he aims to develop is therefore an attempt to cast light on the principles of mechanics, in order to get rid of the shadows of the old metaphysics.[26] Furthermore, Mach observes that

> the gist and kernel of mechanical ideas has in almost every case grown up in the investigation of very simple and special cases of mechanical processes; and the analysis of the history of the discussions concerning these cases must ever remain the method at once the most effective and the most natural for laying this gist and kernel's bare. Indeed, it is not too much to say that it is the only way in which a real comprehension of the general upshot of mechanics is to be attained. (Mach 1919 [1883], p. ix-x)

According to Mach, a historical inquiry allows us to get "the positive and physical essence of mechanics" rid of the "mass of technical considerations" beneath which it is buried, and which casts light on how the principles of mechanics

---

[24] Mach's argument is strikingly similar to Nietzsche's critique to the philosophers of his time, who "dehistoricize" the products of reason and "turn them into a mummy." (TI, "Reason" in Philosophy 1; KSA 6, p. 74) I will deal with the compliance of these approaches shortly below.

[25] Mach also remarks: "Quite analogous difficulties lie in wait for us when we go to school and take up more advanced studies, when propositions which have often cost several thousand years' labour of thought are represented to us as self-evident. Here too there is only one way to enlightenment: historical studies." (Mach 1911 [1872], p. 16)

[26] Accordingly, the opening section of the first chapter of *The Analysis of Sensations* is also titled "first anti-metaphysical principles."

"have been ascertained, from what sources they take their origin, and how far they can be regarded as permanent acquisitions." (Mach 1919 [1883], p. ix) Moreover, that inquiry reveals the essence of scientific notions, namely it shows that they are mere intellectual products and thought-symbols (*Gedankensymbol*)[27] mankind elaborated throughout its biological and cultural development. In the lecture on the *Conservation of Energy*, the importance of history is especially stressed, insofar as Mach argues that only an historical investigation can allow us to see that views, concepts, theories etc. constantly change, thus letting us "get used to the fact that science is unfinished and variable." (Mach 1911 [1872], 17)

The outcome of Mach's early epistemological reflections already reveals his instrumentalism vs. realism about scientific concepts.[28] This is a fundamental feature of his approach to that issue, and in his further writings he maintains that concepts and ideas are only resting points of our mind, symbols that the scientists elaborate for economical and practical purposes. They are no end of the research, but rather only momentary steps of an unceasing process of "adaptation of thoughts to facts and to each other." (Mach 1910 and 1976 [1905], p. 120) These "labels" in fact allow the scientists to save experience and to better communicate the outcomes of their inquiries to other scientists who will further develop their work. As Mach claims in *The Science of Mechanics*, "science is communicated by instruction, in order that one man may profit by the experience of another and be spared the trouble of accumulating it from himself." (Mach 1919 [1883], p. 481) But he expressed this idea already in 1872, when he observed that a scientific law has "no more real value than the aggregate of the individual facts" it aims to explain (Mach 1911 [1872], p. 55), and argued that "in science we are chiefly concerned with the convenience and saving of thought" and that "the moment of inertia, the central ellipsoid, and so on, are simply examples of substitutes by means of which we conveniently save ourselves the consideration of the single mass-points." (Mach 1911 [1872], p. 88)

This instrumental and conventional conception is rooted in Mach's view of science as a cultural product. For him, concepts are not the result of an actual discovery, but rather the product of an attempt to outline a world-description that could "explain" the events we observe as fruitfully and economically as possible. Consequently, the value of these concepts must be re-assessed: their usefulness remains untouched, but their "truthfulness" is to be put up to question. For Mach, it is not even possible to conceive the idea of a correspondence theory of truth. As a phenomenalist, he particularly insists on the fact that we are not allowed to trespass the limits of the "apparent" world – of our actual knowledge – and any attempt to describe

---

[27] Mach talks of *Gedankensymbol* for example in *The Analysis of Sensations* (Mach 1914 [1886], p. 254 and 296). This notion plays an important role in James, as will be shown in the following section.
[28] The discussion whether Mach was an instrumentalist (or pragmatist) or a direct realist about scientific concepts and theories is still open. On this, see e.g. Banks 2004 and Gori 2018a.

the inner feature of things is destined to lead us far from proper science.[29] All that we can do is find new principles within the realm of the appearances, of the intellectual products, whose value will be judged from their positive practical outcomes.

On this, Mach's view seems to be consistent with Nietzsche's. The very definition of "metaphysical concepts" that we find in the *Conservation of Energy* essay can be compared with Nietzsche's early observations on truth. The idea that we "call concepts metaphysical, if we have forgotten how we reached them" in fact reminds the famous statement of *On Truth and Lie in an Extra-Moral Sense*, according to which "truths are illusions of which one has forgotten that they are illusions." (TL; KSA 1, p. 881) In that unpublished writing, Nietzsche argues that "truths" are mere schematizations of the external data that proved to be extremely helpful for the preservation of the species. That is why we attributed a great value to them and we finally mistake their practical efficacy with their explicatory power. Because of its fruitfulness, we never put up to question these concepts and, after long time, we now take them as granted – as "truths" – completely neglecting their origin. Nietzsche especially talks of "metaphors that have become worn-out and deprived of their sensuous force, coins that have lost their imprint and are now no longer seen as coins but as metal" (TL; KSA 1, p. 881), but the sense of his observations is the same as Mach's. They both stress that we daily work with mental products that are interpreted *as* adequate reproduction of reality. On the contrary, the world we know is a manmade creation whose value rests only on the usefulness of these thought-symbols for the sake of orientation.

Furthermore, Nietzsche focuses on the genealogical reconstruction as critical tool, too. In the first part of *Human, All Too Human*, he develops some ideas from *On Truth and Lie* and contrasts "metaphysical philosophy" with "historical philosophy." (HH I 1; KSA 2, p. 23) "There are *no eternal facts*, just as there are no absolute truths. – argues Nietzsche – Consequently what is needed from now on is *historical philosophizing*, and with it the virtue of modesty." (HH I 2; KSA 2, p. 25) Thus, the "historical sense" is the means to shed light on the illusory "mobile army of metaphors, metonyms, and anthropomorphisms" (TL; KSA 1, p. 881) that we mistake as a truthful world-description. More on this can be found in the important aphorism 16 of *Human, All Too Human*, where Nietzsche focuses on the origin of the realm of appearances and stresses that ordinary concepts are gradually evolved and still evolving intellectual products. For Nietzsche,

> it is the human intellect that has made appearance appear and transported its erroneous basic conceptions into things. Late, very late – it has reflected on all this: and now the world of experience and the thing in itself seem to it so extraordinarily different from one another and divided apart that it rejects the idea that the nature of one can be inferred from the nature of the other. (HH I 16; KSA 2, p. 37)

---

**29** On this, see e.g. Mach 1914 [1886], chapter 1, § 13; Mach 1976 [1905], chapter 1; and above in this volume, chapter 2.5.

Moreover, the world of phenomena is an "inherited idea, spun out of intellectual errors." (HH I 16; KSA 2, p. 37) Once we realize that, we are just one step to the goal: if one admits that the world we know is a man-made product, the result of the biological and cultural history of mankind, then its ontological lack of content, its merely logical value can be revealed through a genealogical inquiry. Nietzsche in fact continues this way:

> With all these conceptions the steady and laborious process of science, which will one day celebrate its greatest triumph in a *history of the genesis of thought*, will in the end decisively have done; for the outcome of this history may well be the conclusion: that which we now call the world is the outcome of a host of errors and fantasies which have gradually arisen and grown entwined with one another in the course of the overall evolution of the organic being, and are now inherited by us as the accumulated treasure of the entire past – as a treasure: for the value of our humanity depends upon it. (HH I 16; KSA 2, p. 37)

Nietzsche never rejected the conception of knowledge that in *Human, All Too Human* is expressed with great clarity. His view changed a little bit throughout the years, but its principles remained the same. Most importantly, Nietzsche buildt an original antimetaphysical philosophy on that conception, a "counter-movement" against European nihilism. In his late years he in fact focuses on the "metaphysical value, a value as such of truth" as the kernel of the ascetic ideal, which is the expression of Western metaphysics. This can be traced back to his reflections on the origin of the realm of absolute and fixed concepts, the realm that Nietzsche finally called the "true world" and which is in fact the dimension of the "eternal idols" he aims to sound out, in order to show how empty they are. These idols are the "means toward the adjustment of the world for utilitarian ends" which are mistakenly seen as the "criterion of truth and reality" (NL 1888, KSA 13, 14[153]), and their origin rests in our language, as Nietzsche argued in *Human, All Too Human*. For Nietzsche, language plays an important role "for the evolution of culture," precisely for "mankind set up in language a separate world beside the other world, a place it took to be so firmly set that, standing upon it, it could lift the rest of the world off its hinges and make itself master of it." (HH I 11; KSA 2, p. 30) The operational efficiency of language determined that mankind trusted it uncritically, and finally forgot the origin of the intellectual world, which is valued as the *real* world. Defending a sort of nominalism and antirealism, Nietzsche argues that "the shaper of language was not so modest as to think that he was only giving things labels; rather, he imagined that he was expressing the highest knowledge of things with words; and in fact, language is the first stage of scientific effort." (HH I 11; KSA 2, p. 30–1)

From these observations it can be argued that, for Nietzsche, metaphysics is a matter of faith in the value of our knowledge, and we can get rid of it just becoming aware of this. All we have to do is thus to re-valuate our world-image and stress the practical usefulness of our concepts – which is something that Nietzsche never rejects. As above stated, Nietzsche's critique of truth does not lead to an epistemological nihilism; in fact, he is well aware that our intellect is physiologically structured to produce "errors" and "illusions" (see e. g. HH I 9), and we should just accept it and use these products insofar as they are fruitful for us. What is important is not to forget that they are only useful fictions, whose value is relative and dependent on the environment from which they arose. That would be possible if we merge philosophy with history and never leave the path of the genealogical inquiry. As Nietzsche argues in an 1885 note, "what distinguishes us in the deepest way from all the Platonic and Leibnitzean way of thinking, is this: we do not believe in eternal concepts, eternal values, eternal shapes, eternal souls; and philosophy, as far as it is science and not legislation, is for us just the broadest extension of the concept of 'history'." (NL 1885, KSA 11, 38[14])[30]

Apparently, the way Nietzsche reflects on the value of the categories of reason is consistent with Mach's observation on scientific concepts. As much as any other human "truth," these concepts have a merely relative and historical value. But they are so fruitful, they help us to manage the world so well, that it is not possible for us to live and work without them. It is precisely this practical usefulness that allows us not to remain stuck in a nihilistic relativism. Our concepts, ideas, scientific theories etc. actually provide us with reference points for finding our way in the world. Their value being relative does not change this, and our need of finding principles of orientation is still satisfied. In other words, once we put up to question the value of ordinary truth, we do not necessary eliminate any possibility of assessing truth. The result of our critique is only that the "metaphysical value" of truth is rejected, and *not* that *there is no truth*. But we still need a criterion for assessing truth; otherwise, we would be unable to manage the world as we did in past-time. If we consider natural sciences, we can easily understand how important this is. The researcher *needs* principles and theories in order to develop a world-description. If a theory is proved to be false, if someone demonstrates that a concept is erroneous (just think at the notion of *aether*, which for decades worked so well!), *new theories and concepts are needed*. The scientific enterprise does not stop at that point; rather, she works out other principles and determines a new "paradigm" (to use the famous Kuhnian concept). But this can be applied also to the moral and ethical plane. The human being *needs* principles of practical orientation, in order to be part of a social community. Once we put up to question the value of ordinary principles, we cannot stop and say: "there is no truth, then everything is permitted!" Nihilism is not an option, if we aim to keep on living in a human community. On the contrary, we have to find new principles, and firstly we need a method to determine them in a way that must be different from the old one. If, as has been argued above, the phenomenal plane is the only one we live in, if our world is only a humanly-categorized world (if, in other words, we completely get rid of the dualism between "true" and "appa-

---

[30] This is consistent with the observation on "historical philosophy" expressed in HH I 1 and HH I 2. In TI, "Reason" in Philosophy 1, Nietzsche deplores the philosopher's "lack of historical sense," too, thus proving that his late remarks on the eternal idols are related with the early observations on knowledge and truth. On this, see also Gori 2009c.

rent" world), then the criterion for assessing new "truths" must be a phenomenal and human one, too. Non-metaphysical truths will therefore be determined by making reference to their fruitfulness and operational efficiency, that is, to their practical usefulness. This is what we find in Mach and, apparently, also in Nietzsche. But this is precisely what William James thinks about truth, as will be shown in the following section.

## 5.3 William James on truth

William James's pragmatism is deeply influenced by Ernst Mach's empiricism, his neutral monism and, more generally, his epistemology. Moreover, Jamesian conception of truth is grounded on the outcomes of nineteenth-century science and can be interpreted as a strategy for dealing with the relativism implied in these outcomes.[31] In this section, I will outline some similarities between James's and Nietzsche's views

---

[31] Gerald Holton (1992, p. 36) stressed the "state of elective – but also selective – affinity" that characterized the relationship between Mach and James. He observes that "James's copies of Mach's book graphically demonstrate the intense impression they made on him during the period in which he was engaged in writing his own major works." That impression is particularly evident in James's *Pragmatism*, where the debt to Mach is explicitly mentioned (see e.g. James 1907, p. 57 and 190). Mach himself, in a famous letter written to James on 28 June 1907, once admitted: "Although I am by my entire training a scientist and not at all a philosopher, nevertheless I stand very close to pragmatism in my ways of thinking, without ever having used that name." (Thiele 1978, p. 175) On Mach's influence on James, see also Banks 2003. For what concerns the origins and actual meaning of pragmatism, two excerpts from James's wrings are worth to be considered. The first one is published in *The Meaning of Truth*. In this 1909 book, James argues that "the pragmatist way of seeing things owes its being to the break-down which the last fifty years have brought about in the older notion of scientific truth. 'God geometrizes,' it used to be said; and it was believed that Euclid's elements literally reproduced his geometrizing. [...] So also for the 'laws of nature,' physical and chemical, so of natural history classifications – all were supposed to be exclusive duplicates of pre-human archetypes buried in the structure of things, to which the spark of divinity hidden in our intellect enables us to penetrate. [...] Up to about 1850 almost every one believed that sciences expressed truth that were exact copies of a definite code of non-human realities. But the enormously rapid multiplication of theories in these latter days has well-night upset the notion of any one of them being a more literally objective kind of thing than another. There are so many geometries, so many logics, so many physical and chemical hypotheses, so many classifications, each one of them good for so much and yet not good for everything, that the notion that even the truest formula may be a human device and not a literal transcript has dawn upon us. We hear scientific laws now treated as so much 'conceptual shorthand,' true so far as they are useful but no farther." (James 1909, p. 57–8. On this, see also Ferrari 2015, p. 256 f.) The second excerpt is from a review of Ferdinand Schiller's *Humanism* written by James. Here, we read that "the enormous growth of the sciences in the past fifty years has reconciled us to the idea that 'not quite true' is as near as we can ever get." For James, Schiller's conception of the relative character of theories and laws of nature is the framework out of which "has arisen the pragmatism of Pearson in England, of Mach in Austria, and of the somewhat reluctant Poincaré in France, all of whom say that our sciences are but *Denkmittel* – 'true' in no other sense than that of yelding a conceptual short-hand, economical for our description." (James 1920, p. 449)

of truth and knowledge. My point is that we can make sense of this compliance by referring to the broad context of their reflections. James and Nietzsche in fact shared a post- and neo-Kantian framework, whose main outcome was precisely to put up to question the ordinary value of both human and scientific knowledge. Therefore, they dealt with the same problem – that of the *value of truth*. As will be argued, the strategies they developed are also comparable, for they both aimed to avoid metaphysic and nihilism, and tried to provide us with new principles of knowledge and action.

The starting point of Jamesian pragmatism is the rejection of the correspondence theory of truth, namely the idea that truth expresses what reality is in itself.[32] At the beginning of the lecture *Pragmatism's Conception of Truth*, James argues that "the popular notion that a true idea must copy its reality" must be discarded insofar as it is a bad interpretation of the conception of truth as "agreement" with "reality" defended by the intellectualists (James 1907, p. 198–9). On the contrary, James holds that truth is not a "static" predicate of things, but rather a dynamic, developing property of them. In fact, he argues that "the truth of an idea is not a stagnant property inherent in it. Truth *happens* to an idea. It *becomes* true, is *made* true by events. Its verity is in fact an event, a process: the process namely of its verifying itself, its veri-fication." (James 1907, p. 201)[33] The idea that "truth is simply a collective name for verification-processes" (James 1907, p. 218) can already be compared with Nietzsche's conception of truth, and especially with his view of the truth-value of "facts." In an 1887 notebook, for example, Nietzsche argues that

> truth is not something that's there and must be found out, discovered, but something *that must be made* and that provides the name for a *process* – or rather for a will to overcome, a will that left to itself has no end: inserting truth as a *processus in infinitum*, an *active determining*, not a becoming conscious of something that is 'in itself' fixed and determinate. (NL 1887, KSA 12, 9[91])

At the basis of this reflection one finds the critique to the notion of thing in itself as principle of our world-description, that Nietzsche and James share. If a thing in itself exists (both Nietzsche and James deal with it on the purely theoretical plane only), it would be neither "true" nor "false." Reality has no truth-value in itself; it is only *us* that give meaning to the world. In a way that strongly resembles Nietzsche's dichotomy between facts and interpretations, James argues that "the 'facts' themselves are

---

[32] On this, see Hingst 2000, p. 293f.
[33] In the light of what has been shown about evolutionary epistemology in the first chapter of this volume, and since James can be considered as a forerunner of that research program, it is worth mentioning Sergio Franzese's observation that "the pragmatist conception of truth is a process for selecting hypotheses that constantly needs to be confirmed; that is, the coincidence between the truthfulness of an idea and the process of its verification" corresponds to and follows from "Darwinian natural selection," according to which "any mutation is [a sort of 'hypotheses' to be accepted or rejected by] the environment." (Franzese 2009, p. 23)

not *true*. They simply *are*," and "truth is the function of the beliefs that start and terminate among them." (James 1907, p. 225)³⁴

This view is grounded on a Machian basis, a sort of sensualism that Nietzsche apparently shares, too. In fact, James (1907, p. 244) argues that

> the *first* part of reality [...] is the flux of our sensations. Sensations are forced upon us, coming we know not whence. Over their nature, order, and quantity we have as good as no control. *They* are neither true nor false; they simply *are*. It is only what we say about them, only the names we give them, our theories of their source and nature and remote relations, that may be true or not.

This is one of the fundamental assumptions of Mach's *Analysis of Sensations* and his so-called "neutral monism." According to Mach, (our) reality is made out of *elements* or *sensations*, which have no qualities in themselves; they are neither physical nor psychical entities, but are rather "neutral." The elements rest at the origin of our world-description, and it is *us* who call them physical or psychical, depending on the particular perspective from which we look at them.³⁵ But this interest in our senses can be also found in the late Nietzsche.³⁶ In *Twilight of the Idols*, Nietzsche argues that senses "do not lie at all," and it is "what we *do* with the testimony of the senses, where the lies begin. [...] 'Reason' makes us falsify the testimony of the senses." (TI, "Reason" in Philosophy 2; KSA 6, p. 75)³⁷ The meaning of this observation is still disputed. In my view, given the general topic of the third chapter of TI, it can be argued that Nietzsche aims to stress the interpretive character of our knowledge, that is, the fact that "Reason" modifies something which is essentially "neutral." We find this view also in James, for example when he quotes Ferdinand Schiller's idea that "our truths are a man-made product" (James 1907, p. 242),³⁸ or when he

---

**34** Accordingly, in *The Meaning of Truth* James observes that "realities are not *true*, they *are*; and beliefs are true *of* them." (James 1909, p. 196) On the similarity between James's theory of truth and Nietzsche's perspectivism see Fabbrichesi 2009, p. 26 ff.
**35** On neutral monism in Mach and James, and also on Mach's elements/sensations, see Banks 2003 and 2014.
**36** On Nietzsche's "sensualism" see Riccardi 2013 and Small 2001. This issue, with regard to Mach's view, is also explored in Hussain 2004a and 2004b; and Gori 2009b.
**37** Nietzsche's positive attitude towards sensualism is also expressed in BGE 15 and GS 272.
**38** The name of Ferdinand Schiller deserves a short digression. Schiller developed his humanistic view when James was working on his pragmatism. The similarities between their conceptions become immediately clear to both of them, and James in fact talks about humanism as a pragmatist view and vice versa (in other words, humanism is another of the "old ways of thinking" James thinks of in the title of his book). In 1982, George Stack published a paper on *Nietzsche's Influence on Pragmatic Humanism*, arguing that Schiller's view may not have been so original. In fact, Stack noticed that Schiller admired Nietzsche, and it is possible that the latter influenced him, although Schiller never mentions Nietzsche in his works. Stack's conclusion is that Nietzsche may be a direct (but hidden) source of Schiller. But if this is so, Schiller's *Humanism* would have arisen from purely Nietzschean basis – a thesis which casts new light on the present research. Given the relationship between Schiller and James, we should not merely compare Nietzsche's view of truth with James's, but it could be argued

argues that "in our cognitive as well as in our active life we are creative. We *add*, both to the subject and to the predicate part of reality." (James 1907, p. 256–7) In claiming this, James invites us to restrict the range of out epistemological observations to the human plane only, to that same "apparent world" world Nietzsche talks of in *Twilight of the Idols*.[39]

Speaking of Nietzsche's 1888 book, in the lecture on *Pragmatism and Humanism* (James 1907, chapter 7) we find some interesting remarks on the rationalistic view of truth that can be compared with Nietzsche's late critique to the "prejudices of reason." For example, James argues that "the notion of *the* Truth, conceived as the one answer, determinate and complete, to the one fixed enigma which the world is believed to propound," is a "*typical idol of the tribe*." (James 1907, p. 242, my emphasis) Moreover, he observes that "by amateurs in philosophy and professional alike, the universe is represented as a queer sort of petrified sphinx whose appeal to man consists in a monotonous challenge to his divining powers. *The* Truth: what a perfect idol of the rationalistic mind!" (James 1907, p. 242–3) With all likelihood, James's reference in speaking of an "idol of the tribe" is just Francis Bacon's *idola tribus*, but his view is nevertheless consistent with Nietzsche's. The "eternal idols" Nietzsche deals with in TI are in fact the old truths which we ordinarily attributed a metaphysical value to; Nietzsche's idols are a product of the "philosophers's idiosyncrasy" and their faith in the "prejudices of reason" (e. g. TI, "Reason" in Philosophy 1 and 5; KSA 6, p. 74 f.); finally, as has been argued above, Nietzsche's idols are intellectual creations of which we forgot their historical character, concepts developed during the biological and cultural history of humankind, and that are now misinterpreted as fixed, non-becoming, adequate descriptions of reality.

As argued above, James is concerned with the disorientation following from the outcomes of nineteenth-century epistemology. In fact, his view of truth is grounded on that epistemology, as the above quoted passages show. James holds that truth is not a property of things, but rather something that we add to them. Thus, for him there is nothing to discover, and we can call "true" or "false" only elements of a man-made image of reality, a human interpretation of it.[40] Within this picture, concepts are defined according to the epistemological conception provided by Mach and

---

that James's conception of truth is – partially as much as indirectly – influenced by Nietzsche! Furthermore, if Stack is right, it is also arguable that Schiller has been the one who sparked Hans Kleinpeter's interest in Nietzsche. As shown in chapter 4.1, Kleinpeter published some papers on Nietzsche's conception of knowledge, and compared it with the principles of Mach's epistemology. Moreover, Kleinpeter (1912c) argued that "Nietzsche's view of truth is consistent with both James's and Schiller's pragmatism." Now, Kleinpeter started dealing with Nietzsche in 1911, after having participated to the International Congress of Philosophy held in Bologna – when he first met Schiller (see Gori 2011). Unfortunately, there is no evidence to confirm this. But all these coincidences put together lead us to that conclusion.

**39** On our role of world- and truth-makers, according to Jamesian pragmatism, see Philström 2009. On Nietzsche's perspectivism and pragmatic humanism, see Gori 2017c.

**40** On this, see Franzese 2009, p. 34.

his school (Duhem, Ostwald, etc.): "All our conceptions are what the Germans call *Denkmittel*, means by which we handle facts by thinking them. Experience as such doesn't come ticketed and labelled, we have first to discover what it is." (James 1907, p. 171–2) These *Denkmittel* are precisely the *Gedankensymbol* Mach speaks of. But they are also similar to Nietzsche's "fictions" that make the world manageable for us, thus proving their practical usefulness. For James, concepts are in fact "artificial short-cuts for tacking us from one part to another of experience's flux" and "sovereign triumph of economy in thought." (James 1907, p. 191. The reference to Mach in the last excerpt is particularly clear.)

The similarity between James's and Nietzsche's views can be further stressed, by looking at their attitude towards the ordinary world-description (that of common-sense). For James, the *Denkmittel* become the principles of our worldview because of their fruitfulness, for they played an important role in the development of mankind. Furthermore, James (1907, p. 181) calls "common sense [...] a perfectly definite stage in our understanding of things, a stage that satisfies in an extraordinarily successful way the purposes for which we think." This "great stage of equilibrium in the human mind's development" arose from "*our fundamental ways of thinking about things,*" that James claims to be "*discoveries of exceedingly remote ancestors, which have been able to preserve themselves through the experience of all subsequent time.*" (James 1907, p. 170) James's conclusion is that "We are now so familiar with the order that these notions have woven for us out of the everlasting weather of our perceptions that we find it hard to realize how little of a fixed routine the perceptions follow when taken by themselves." (James 1907, p. 173)[41] Once more, James's view seems to be consistent with Nietzsche's. In GS 110, Nietzsche in fact speaks of the role played by human knowledge for the preservation of our species and argues especially that

> through immense periods of time, the intellect produced nothing but errors; some of them turned out to be useful and species-preserving [...]. Such erroneous articles of faith, which were passed on by in inheritance further and further, and finally almost became part of the basic endowment of the species, are for example: that there are enduring things; that there are identical things; that there are things, kinds of material, bodies; that a thing is what it ap-

---

**41** See also James 1909, p. 61–2: "Experience is a process that continually gives us new material to digest. We handle this intellectually by the mass of beliefs of which we find ourselves already possessed, assimilating, rejecting, or rearranging in different degrees. Some of the apperceiving ideas are recent acquisitions of our own, but most of them are common-sense traditions of the race. [...] All these were once definite conquests made at historic dates by our ancestors in their attempt to get the chaos of their crude individual experiences into a more shareable and manageable shape. They proved of such sovereign use as *Denkmittel* that they are now a part of the very structure of our mind."

pears to be; that our will is free; that what is good for me is good in and for itself. (GS 110; KSA 3, p. 469)⁴²

In the light of what has been argued so far, I believe that the compliance between Nietzsche's conception and that of James on this point does not need to be argued any further.

In the lecture on *Pragmatism and Common Sense*, James reveals the ideas that inspired his conception of truth. Moreover, he argues that twentieth-century science finally stressed the merely practical value of ordinary concepts. Firstly, James deals with the "*naif* conception of things" which, for him, "get superseded, and a thing's name is interpreted as denoting only the law or *Regel der Verbindung* by which certain of our sensations habitually succeed or coexist." (James 1907, p. 185–6) But

> science and critical philosophy burst the boundaries of common sense. With science *naif* realism ceases: "secondary" qualities become unreal; primary ones alone remain. With critical philosophy, havoc is made of everything. The common-sense categories one and all cease to represent anything in the way of *being*; they are but sublime tricks of human thought, our ways of escaping bewilderment in the midst of sensation's irremediable flow.⁴³

A few pages below, in a purely Nietzschean style, James also argues:

> Scientific logicians are saying on every hand that these entities and their determinations, however definitely conceived, should not be held for literally real. It is *as if* they existed; but in reality they are like co-ordinates or logarithms, only artificial short-cuts for taking us from one part to another of experience's flux. [...] Just now, if I understand the matter rightly, we are witnessing a curious reversion of the common-sense way of looking at physical nature, in the philosophy of science favoured by such men as Mach, Ostwald and Duhem. According to these teachers no hypothesis is truer than any other in the sense of being a more literary copy of reality. They are all but ways of talking on our part, to be compared solely from the point of view of their use. (James 1907, p. 189–90)

For James, nineteenth-century epistemologists contributed to radically re-conceive the principles of our world-description. In fact, they undermined the value of that description itself. Mach, Ostwald, Duhem, etc. invited us to go searching (or to develop) new, anti-metaphysical, principles, that could make sense of our fundamental need to "find our way in the bewildering tangle of fact." (Mach 1976 [1905], p. 98)

---

**42** According to James (1907, p. 173), the most important concepts we inherited, the concepts that constitute the common-sense world-conception, are: "thing; the same or different; kinds; minds; bodies; one time; one space; subjects and attributes; causal influence; the fancied; the real."
**43** This is another hidden reference to Mach, which most likely James believed his readers would have easily recognized, given the impact of Mach's ideas in the contemporary debate. Mach, for example, talks of the ordinary view as a "naïve realism" in the *Analysis of Sensations* (Mach 1914 [1886], p. 37). For more on this, see Holton 1992 and Ferrari 2010. On the philosophical-critical approach to the metaphysical (realist) commitment of common-sense in James, Mach, Vaihinger, and Nietzsche, see Gori 2017b.

On both the theoretical and the ethical/moral plane, this need is referential. Therefore, truth should not be assessed as a more or less adequate representation of reality, but rather as a more or less fruitful means for our orientation.

Before turning to the consequences of this view, let me briefly explain why I believe that the above quoted passage from James's *Pragmatism* is written in a Nietzschean style. In his writings, sometimes Nietzsche argues that the development of logic and physics would lead us to a new evaluation of the explanatory power of science. In the first section of *Beyond Good and Evil*, for example, Nietzsche copes with the "prejudices of philosophers," and focuses on the outcomes of modern science. His criticism especially deals with the mechanistic world-conception and its metaphysical commitment (the faith in material elements such as matter, atom, and soul. See e.g. BGE 12 and BGE 17), but Nietzsche also observes that "now it is beginning to dawn on maybe five or six brains that physics too is only an interpretation and arrangement of the world […] and *not* an explanation of the world." (BGE 14; KSA 5, p. 28) This passage recalls an early statement published in *Human, All Too Human I*, where Nietzsche declares that "only now it dawns on men that in their belief in language they have propagated a tremendous error." (HH I 11; KSA 2, p. 31) Thus, Nietzsche seems to think that the common-sense metaphysical world-conception, the ordinary view that one finds also expressed by scientific ideas and theories, is nowadays discredited, thanks to modern logicians and epistemologists. Nietzsche therefore witnesses the same change James describes in *Pragmatism*. Both of them reflect on the impact of critical thinking on the ordinary conception of knowledge and truth, and, as will be argued shortly below, both of them stress the importance of this impact for the ethical and anthropological development of the human being.

The view of ordinary concepts as *Denkmittel* and the rejection of the correspondence theory of truth are the principles of James's "pragmatic method." Given that we have no access to any metaphysical Truth, that everything we know is a man-made world of intellectual symbols, James invites us to look at the practical plane and, more precisely, at the consequences of *our believing something to be true*, in order to grant value to logically irrelevant views.

> Pragmatism asks its usual question. "Grant an idea or belief to be true", it says, "what concrete difference will its being true make in anyone's actual life? How will the truth be realized? What experiences will be different from those which would obtain if the belief were false? What, in short, is the truth's cash-value in experiential terms?" (James 1907, p. 200)

As Rossella Fabbrichesi observes (2009, p. 31), James's fundamental idea is that "a belief *counts* as true when it *satisfies* us, it *pays*, also, in the cash-value of the word, it *gratifies* us, is *held as* true, proves itself *useful* if considered true, *functions* in orienting us along the road of research, that is, is *advantageous* as related to our vital power." What is worth noting is that, in providing us a definition of the pragmatic method, James is particularly interested in the ethical dimension. In fact, he focuses on how an idea affects *our life*, our existence, thus proving that pragmatism should not be interpreted from an analytical point of view solely.[44] Moreover, this is something that can be compared with Nietzsche's approach to the problem of the value of truth and especially with the aims of his late philosophy. As argued above, in his late period Nietzsche criticizes the faith in the metaphysical value of truth as kernel of the ascetic ideal, that is of Christian morality, which he blames if the human type (*der Typus Mensch*) "never reached his *highest potential power and splendour.*" (GM Preface 6; KSA 5, p. 253) The idea that "true" and "false" – as much as "good" and "bad" – are only "levels of appearance and, as it were, lighter and darker shades and tones of appearance" (BGE 34; KSA 5, p. 33–4) is intended to have an impact on the anthropological plane, to actually *modify* the human being. At the basis of this idea, we find the same epistemological principles as James's, as much as the same attitude towards the relativism implied in modern science. Both Nietzsche and James aim not to leave us without reference points for an either theoretical or practical orientation. Given that no absolute principles can be found, both of them look at the practical plane in order to develop a re-valuation of the old "truths," this re-valuation depending on the ethical and anthropological effects of the ideas we believe in. Nietzsche's pragmatism can be in fact defined by stressing this last point and by focusing on Nietzsche's attempt to develop an experimental philosophy which aims to contrast the anthropological degeneration determined by European nihilism.[45]

## 5.4 Nietzsche's pragmatism

In section 5.1 I quoted the posthumous fragment 1888, 14[153], which I find extremely important in order to display Nietzsche's approach to truth. That note in fact shows us that, for Nietzsche, the fundamental problem is the *value* we attribute to that notion, while he is scarcely interested in the proper theoretical issue. That is to say, Nietzsche warns us not to mess the usefulness of the categories of reason with their truthfulness (in the ordinary, correspondentist sense). The categories of reason are only "means toward the adjustment of the world for utilitarian ends (basically, toward an expedient falsification)," and we are wrong in believing that we "possessed in them the criterion of truth and reality. The 'criterion of truth' – continues Nietzsche – was in fact merely the biological utility of such a system of systematic falsification; and since a species of animal knows of nothing more important than

---

[44] On the ethical core of Jamesian pragmatism, see e.g. Franzese 2008 and Philström 2007.
[45] In his seminal book, Walter Kaufmann drew parallels between Nietzsche's experimentalism (i.e. "testing an answer by trying to live according to it") and pragmatism, but he remained sceptic about the actual consistency between these views, mostly for he believes that Nietzsche never developed properly the pragmatists features that can be found in his thought (Kaufmann 1974, e.g. p. 66 and 68; Ratner-Rosenhagen 2012, chapter 5; and Karakaş 2013, p. 87 ff.). On pragmatism, perspectivism and philosophical anthropology, see Gori 2017c.

its own preservation, one might indeed be permitted to speak here of 'truth'." Apparently, Nietzsche does not completely reject the very notion of "truth;" he rather revaluates it according to new principles. More precisely, for him truth is not what corresponds to reality, but rather what helps us to orient ourselves in the world, what is fruitful and operational efficient for us.[46] Thus, Nietzsche adopts a sort of pragmatic method: the truth-value of ideas cannot be assessed theoretically, but I do not give up! Instead of getting rid of these ideas, which would be hard to replace, let's try with different principles of evaluation.[47] In this fragment, Nietzsche focuses on the preservation of the species, and looks at it as the "cash-value" of a truthful idea. But this is not the point. What is worth is the attitude towards truth that one finds stated here, which is non-nihilistic and pragmatic at her very core. Nietzsche in facts argues that *there can be* a truth of some sort, even when the value of truth has been put up to question. This follows also from Nietzsche's observations on perspectivism. The idea that the "true world" is an illusory realm, that our "knowledge" is merely phenomenal and, consequently, that no radical theoretical contraposition between "true" and "false" can be admitted, does not lead to an epistemological nihilism. In BGE 34 Nietzsche in facts asks to himself (and to ourselves) why not to follow the easier way, which is to consider "true" and "false" as "levels of appearance." Therefore, the relativism he defends is not a sterile form of scepticism. Nietzsche does not argue that "if nothing is true, everything is permitted"; he rather affirms: "if nothing is True, *we have to create new truths*." On what basis? Well, that is the question I will try to answer in these final pages.

In my opinion, the key to interpret Nietzsche's pragmatic perspectivism is to look at it in the light of the anthropological problem.[48] As has been stated above,

---

[46] Franzese (2009, p. 47) speaks of "fruitful relationship" between man and world as the principle of the pragmatist assessment of truth. According to him, pragmatists such as James think that "truth" is only "a human truth, that is, a truth which satisfies our human needs." The concept of "fruitful relationship" is interesting as much as viable, for it allows us to conceive different forms of pragmatisms, each one depending on the aims and scopes of the thinker who supports it, but also to stress the complex and transient nature of the pragmatist concept of truth.

[47] This view is well expressed by Christophe Bouriau, which I already mentioned in the previous chapters: pragmatist thinkers are those who think that "a logically irrelevant view [can] assume some practical value insofar as it gives rise to a fruitful process." (Bouriau 2009, p. 227)

[48] Sami Philström (2007, § 66), argues that "for James as much as for Kant, philosophy culminates in the question, 'What is man?' (or more politically correctly, 'What is a human being?'), that is, the key question of philosophical anthropology, which is the starting point for any pragmatically conceivable metaphysical inquiry." In an early essay, Philström observed that "the pragmatist urges to take seriously the role that our purposive, goal-oriented, and value-laden practices play as the background of our ways of dealing with the problems" in many fields in philosophy; therefore, "the question of human nature should be in the focus of all pragmatistic philosophy." (Philström 1998, p. ix) Insofar as "it is humanity with reference to which reality is structured," and "the conceptual schemes and practical viewpoints through which alone things can be meaningfully said to exist (or fail to exist), to be real or unreal, are [...] human-made," Pihlström argues that "the Kantian question 'What is man?' is the core of [...] pragmatism in general." (Philström 1998, p. 132)

## 5.4 Nietzsche's pragmatism

Nietzsche's attempt in the late years is to put up to question the value of truth, for it determined an anthropological degeneration of the human type. Thus, his interest seems not to be merely theoretical; on the contrary, it can be argued that Nietzsche aims to develop a new culture that would allow the human being to grow stronger. This viewpoint is also helpful to tackle the question of the validity of Nietzschean perspectivism that has been posed in past times by Brian Leiter (2000). Leiter argues that it does not seem possible to attribute to Nietzsche's criticism of Christian morality an "epistemic privilege – being veridical, being better justified – over its target." (Leiter 2000, p. 277) I agree with Leiter that the revaluation of values that follows from Nietzsche's perspectivism has no metaphysical privilege, for it cannot be demonstrated that it is more "truthful" or better justified (in absolute terms) than the rejected morality. But this does not mean that no privilege at all can be found. Rather, as said, I believe that Nietzsche's perspectivism can prove its validity on purely pragmatic and anthropological grounds.[49] Consider these remarks that Sami Philström makes on pragmatism:

> Pragmatism is true precisely by its own lights, on its own standards of acceptance, on those very same standards related to the satisfactoriness and moral consequences of a belief by which other beliefs must, according to James, be evaluated. In choosing her or his philosophical orientation (say, pragmatism), an individual makes an existential choice, in which her or his unique existence as the particular individual she or he happens to be is at stake. (Pihlström 1998, p. 125–6)

This observation can be easily applied also to Nietzsche's view, and it can be argued that perspectivism is true "on its own standards of acceptance [...] related to the satisfactoriness and moral consequences of a belief." Moreover, there is hardly no doubt that Nietzsche thought that "in choosing her or his philosophical orientation [...], an individual makes an existential choice, in which her or his unique existence as the particular individual she or he happens to be is at stake." Now, this evaluation of perspectivism in pragmatic terms is two-fold. First, perspectivism itself is perspectival, that is, it is not – and does not pretend to be – metaphysically-valid.[50] The "truth" it set forth is as relative as the one put forward by rival views; therefore, its validity can only be affirmed on the basis of its fruitfulness, of its outcomes. Sec-

---

[49] Volker Gerhard (1989) also argued that the value of Nietzsche's pragmatism should be assessed on the practical plane instead of on the theoretical one. My interpretation follows Gerhard's; I just stress and develop an idea that he expresses at the end of his paper, namely the connection of perspectivism with the anthropological question (in Kantian terms).

[50] It is not necessary to complain that Nietzsche "does consider his own position superior," as Maudemarie Clark did (Clark 1990, p. 140f.). Nietzsche, of course, defended his view – as anyone does with his own ideas. But he never pretended to find absolute principles for that, nor did he claim his position to be universally valid. Nietzsche developed a diagnosis of modern European culture, and he focuses on what should be avoided, in order to allow the proper development of the human being. The evaluation of Nietzsche's view must not neglect that, and one should never forget the contingent and experimental character of his philosophy.

ondly, it can be argued that the "criterion of truth" to be adopted for Nietzschean perspectivism is a sort of "biological utility." That is to say, one must look at the existential and anthropological consequences that believing in that view produces. This can be inferred from Nietzsche's observations, although he never affirmed that one must choose perspectivism for a *positive* outcome. In fact, Nietzsche only suggested that his view is alternative to the view he invites us to avoid. More precisely, perspectivism is for Nietzsche a view antithetical to the one which determined the declined type of man, the herd animal. If one wants to avoid that anthropological degeneration – and there are no absolute reasons for *preferring* it – *one possible way* is to accept the perspectival character of existence, and to call into question the value of truth.[51]

On this point, Nietzsche's view seems to be particularly consistent with James's observations on the anthropological value of the ideas we believe in. In the first lecture of *Pragmatism*, James talks of ideas which are "helpful in life's practical struggles," and then argues: "If there be any life that it is really better we should lead, and if there be any idea which, if believed in, would help us to lead that life, then it would be really better for us to believe in that idea, unless, indeed, belief in it incidentally clashed with other greater vital benefits." (James 1907, p. 76) As James-scholars observed in past times, it can be argued that, for James, the ethical commitment is more important than the metaphysical one. In particular, Pihlström stressed that, in James, the acceptance of a metaphysical stance depends upon the "ethical evaluation" of that position "in terms of [its] potential humanly significant outcome." (Pihlström 2007, § 19)[52] Therefore, since we cannot demonstrate the validity of any idea on purely intellectual grounds, the means to find our way in the world can only be justified by their practical usefulness – in anthropological terms. Nietzsche could be interpreted as supporting that position, too. His rejection of common-sense realism and his affirmation of the purely phenomenal character of human knowledge in fact constitute a metaphysical commitment that Nietzsche cannot demonstrate. But it leads us to a different world-conception and, consequently, to a different practical behaviour (the "cash-value" of Nietzschean perspectivism). That metaphysical commitment can therefore only be justified in terms of its outcomes, depending on the interest of the individual who affirms that particular view. From what has been shown above, it is possible to say that Nietzsche's interest was to criticize the Christian type of man, that he conceived as the product of the faith in "a metaphysical

---

[51] Ken Gemes (1992) also observes that Nietzsche focused on the idea that certain ideas promote life (see e.g. NL 1885, KSA 11, 34[253]). Gemes (1992, p. 57) especially argues that Nietzsche "is involved in promoting a perspective that promotes his ideal kind of life [not-declining] at the price of thereby suppressing other, possibly equally, valid perspectives." On Nietzsche's evaluation of values, see also Richardson 2004, chapter 2.

[52] For Philström (2007, § 19), the "core pragmatic question" is actually: "What will our human life in this human world be like, if we conceptualize our world in terms of a particular metaphysical position?"

value, a value as such of truth." Therefore, Nietzsche evaluated the outcomes of a metaphysical commitment in purely anthropological terms, as James did.

The compliance between Nietzsche's perspectivism and Jamesian pragmatism is therefore multifaceted. They both tackle a fundamental epistemological problem, inspired by the results of modern science and the way she re-defines the very notions of truth and knowledge. But the similarity does not only rest on their premises, on the major question they face. On the contrary, Nietzsche and James shared a well-defined attitude towards the problem of truth, an attitude which is relativistic in a positive, anti-nihilistic sense, and that take cares of man (of *der Typus Mensch*) as "cash-value" of our world-conception. As I tried to show in this volume, perspectivism can conclusively be interpreted as a philosophical position grounded on a post-positivistic phenomenalist conception of knowledge, which can play an important role on the development of the human being. For Nietzsche, to hold the perspectival viewpoint, that is, to accept the merely relative value of truth, will in fact determine the "counter-movement" that he calls *Revaluation of all Values* (NL 1887–88, KSA 12, 11[411]), which in GM III 27 is precisely connected with the attempt at a critique of the value of truth. This is Nietzsche's late task. A task aimed at getting rid of Western metaphysics and finally allow the human being to reach "his *highest potential power and splendour.*"

# References

## Nietzsche's writings

Nietzsche, Friedrich (1967–): *Werke. Kritische Gesamtausgabe*. Eds. Colli, Giorgio/Montinari, Mazzino/Gerhard, Volker/Miller, Norbert/Müller-Lauter, Wolfgang/Pestalozzi, Karl. Berlin, Boston: De Gruyter. (KGW)

Nietzsche, Friedrich (1980): *Sämtliche Werke. Kritische Studienausgabe in 15 Bänden*. Eds. Colli, Giorgio/Montinari, Mazzino. Munich: DTV/De Gruyter. (KSA)

Nietzsche, Friedrich (1975–): *Briefwechsel. Kritische Gesamtausgabe*. Eds. Colli, Giorgio/Montinari, Mazzino/Miller, Norbert/Pieper, Annemarie. Berlin, Boston: De Gruyter. (KGB)

*English translations*

Nietzsche, Friedrich (1999): *The Birth of Tragedy and Other Writings*. Eds. Geuss, Raymond/Speirs, Ronald. Cambridge: Cambridge University Press.

Nietzsche, Friedrich (2001): *The Gay Science*. Ed. Williams, Bernard. Cambridge: Cambridge University Press.

Nietzsche, Friedrich (2002): *Beyond Good and Evil*. Ed. Horstmann, Rolf-Peter. Cambridge: Cambridge University Press.

Nietzsche, Friedrich (2003): *Writings from the Late Notebooks*. Ed. Bittner, Rüdiger. Cambridge: Cambridge University Press.

Nietzsche, Friedrich (2005a): *Human, All Too Human*. Ed. Hollingdale, R.J. Cambridge: Cambridge University Press.

Nietzsche, Friedrich (2005b): *The Anti-Christ, Ecce Homo, Twilight of the Idols, and Other Writings*. Ed. Ridley, Aaron. Cambridge: Cambridge University Press.

Nietzsche, Friedrich (2006): *On the Genealogy of Morality and Other Writings*. Ed. Ansell-Pearson, Keith. Cambridge: Cambridge University Press.

Nietzsche, Friedrich (2009): *Writings from the Early Notebooks*. Eds. Geuss, Raymond/Nehamas, Alexander. Cambridge: Cambridge University Press.

## Secondary literature

Abel, Günter (2010): *Zeichen- und Interpretationsethik*. In: Przylebski, Andrzej (Ed.): *Ethik im Lichte der Hermeneutik*. Würzburg: Königshausen & Neumann, pp. 91–119.

Abel, Günter (1998): *Nietzsche. Die Dynamik der Willen zur Macht und die ewige Wiederkehr*. Berlin, New York: De Gruyter.

Anderson, R. Lanier (2005): "Nietzsche on Truth, Illusion and Redemption". In: *European Journal of Philosophy* 13. No. 2, pp. 185–225.

Anderson, R. Lanier (1998): "Truth and Objectivity in Perspectivism". In: *Synthese* 115. No. 1, pp. 1–32.

Anderson, R. Lanier (1996): "Overcoming Charity: The Case of Clark's *Nietzsche on Truth and Philosophy*". In: *Nietzsche-Studien* 25, pp. 307–341.

Babich, Babette/Cohen, Robert (Eds.) (1999): *Nietzsche and the Sciences* (2 vols.). Dordrecht: Kluwer.

Banks, Erik (2015): *The Realistic Empiricism of Mach, James, and Russell. Neutral Monism Reconceived*. Cambridge: Cambridge University Press.

Banks, Erik (2004): "The Philosophical Roots of Ernst Mach's Economy of Thought". In: *Synthese* 139, pp. 23–53.

Banks, Erik (2003): *Ernst Mach's World Elements. A Study in Natural Philosophy*. Dordrecht: Kluwer.
Bayertz, Kurt/Gerhard, Myriam/Jaeschke, Walter (Eds.) (2007): *Weltanschauung, Philosophie und Naturwissenschaft im 19. Jahrhundert*. Vol. 3: *Der Ignorabimus-streit*. Hamburg: Meiner.
Ben-Menahem, Yemima (2006): *Conventionalism*. Cambridge: Cambridge University Press.
Bernstein, Richard (2010): *The Pragmatic Turn*. Cambridge: Polity.
Blackmore, John (Ed.) (1972): *Ernst Mach. His Work, Life, and Influence*. Berkeley: University of California Press.
Blackmore, John et alia (Eds.) (2001): *Ernst Mach's Vienna 1895–1930. Or Phenomenalism as Philosophy of Science*. Dordrecht, Boston, London: Kluwer.
Bornedal, Peter (2010): *The Surface and the Abyss*. Berlin, Boston: De Gruyter.
Bouriau, Christophe (2009): "Vaihinger and Poincaré: An Original Pragmatism?". In: Heidelberger, Michael/Schiemann, Gregor (Eds.): *The Significance of the Hypothetical in the Natural Sciences*. Berlin, Boston: De Gruyter, pp. 221–250.
Bradie, Michael (2012): "Evolutionary Epistemology". In: *The Stanford Encyclopedia of Philosophy* (Winter 2012 Edition). Ed. Zalta, Edward N. http://plato.stanford.edu/archives/win2012/entries/epistemology-evolutionary/.
Bradie, Michael (1986): "Assessing Evolutionary Epistemology". In: *Biology & Philosophy* 1, pp. 401–459.
Brobjer, Thomas (2008): *Nietzsche's Philosophical Context. An Intellectual Biography*. Urbana: University of Illinois Press.
Buzzoni, Marco (2011): "Verità ed epistemologia evoluzionistica". In: *Philosophical News* 2, pp. 78–83.
Campioni, Giuliano (2009): *Der französische Nietzsche*. Berlin, Boston: De Gruyter.
Campioni, Giuliano et alia (Eds.) (2003): *Nietzsches persönliche Bibliothek*. Berlin, New York: De Gruyter.
Caygill, Howard (2003): "Kant's Apology for Sensibility". In: Jacobs, Brian (Ed.): *Essays on Kant's Anthropology*. Cambridge: Cambridge University Press, pp. 164–193.
Ceynowa, Klaus (1993): *Zwischen Pragmatismus und Fiktionalismus. Hans Vaihingers 'Philosophie des Als Ob'*. Würzburg: Königshausen & Neumann.
Clark, Maudemarie (1990): *Nietzsche on Truth and Philosophy*. Cambridge: Cambridge University Press.
Clark, Maudemarie/Dudrick, David (2004) "Nietzsche's Post-Positivism". In: *European Journal of Philosophy* 12. No. 3, pp. 369–385.
Constâncio, João (2011): "On Consciousness: Nietzsche's Departure from Schopenhauer". In: *Nietzsche-Studien* 40, pp. 1–42.
Cox, Christoph (1999): *Nietzsche. Naturalism and Interpretation*, Berkeley: University of California Press.
Cox, Christoph (1997): "The 'Subject' of Nietzsche's Perspectivism". In: *Journal of the History of Philosophy* 35, pp. 269–291.
Čapek, Milič (1968): "Ernst Mach's Biological Theory of Knowledge". In: *Synthese* 18, pp. 171–191.
Danto, Arthur (1965): *Nietzsche as Philosopher*. New York: Columbia University Press.
Dellinger, Jachob (2012): "Relendo a perspectividade. Algumas notas sobre 'o perspectivismo de Nietzsche'". In: *Cadernos Nietzsche* 31, pp. 127–155.
De Paz, María/DiSalle, Robert (Eds.) (2014): *Poincaré, Philosopher of Science. Problems and Perspectives*. Heidelberg: Springer.
D'Iorio, Paolo (1993): *La superstition des philosophes critiques. Nietzsche et Afrikan Spir*. In: *Nietzsche-Studien* 22, pp. 257–294.
Dickopp, Karl-Heinz (1970): "Zum Wandel von Nietzsches Seinsverständnis – Afrikan Spir und Gustav Teichmüller". In: *Zeitschrift für philosophische Forschung* 24, pp. 50–71.

Emden, Christian J. (2014): *Nietzsche's Naturalism: Philosophy and the Life Sciences in the Nineteenth Century*. Cambridge: Cambridge University Press.

Emden, Christian J. (2005): *Nietzsche on Language, Consciousness, and the Body*. Urbana, Chicago: University of Illinois Press.

Fabbrichesi, Rossella (2015): "Gesture, Act, Consciousness. The Social Interpretation of the Self in George Herbert Mead". In: *Philosophical Readings* 7. No. 2, pp. 98–118.

Fabbrichesi, Rossella (2012): *In comune. Dal corpo proprio al corpo comunitario*. Milan: Mimesis.

Fabbrichesi, Rossella (2009): "Nietzsche and James. A Pragmatist Hermeneutic". In: *European Journal of Pragmatism and American Philosophy* 1, pp. 25–40.

Fazio, Domenico (1991): *Nietzsche e il criticismo*. Urbino: Quattroventi.

Ferrari, Massimo (2017): "William James and the Vienna Circle". In: Pihlström, Sami/Stadler, Friedrich/Weidtmann, Niels (Eds.): *Logical Empiricism and Pragmatism*. Dordrecht: Springer, pp. 15–42.

Ferrari, Massimo (2015): "William James navigava con Otto Neurath?". In: *Rivista di Filosofia* 2/2015, pp. 235–266.

Ferrari, Massimo (2010): "Well, and Pragmatism?". In: Stadler, Friedrich (Ed.): *The Present Situation in the Philosophy of Science*. Heidelberg: Springer, pp. 75–85.

Figl, Johann (1982): *Interpretation als philosophisches Prinzip. F. Nietzsches universale Theorie der Auslegung im späten Nachlaß*. Berlin, New York: De Gruyter.

Fornari, Maria Cristina (2009): *Die Entwicklung der Herdenmoral. Nietzsche liest Spencer und Mill*. Wiesbaden: Harrassowitz.

Franzese, Sergio (2009): *Darwinismo e pragmatismo e altri studi su William James*. Milan: Mimesis.

Franzese, Sergio (2008): *The Ethics of Energy. William James's Moral Philosophy in Focus*. Heusenstamm: Ontos.

Gabriel, Gottfried (2014): "Fiktion und Fiktionalismus. Zur Problemgeschichte des 'Als-Ob'". In Neuber, Matthias (Ed.): *Fiktion und Fiktionalismus: Beiträge zu Hans Vaihingers 'Philosophie des Als Ob'*. Würzburg: Königshausen & Neumann, pp. 65–87.

Gemes, Ken (2013): "Life's Perspectives". In: Gemes, Ken/Richardson, John (Eds.): *The Oxford Handbook of Nietzsche*. Oxford: Oxford University Press, pp. 553–575.

Gemes, Ken (1992): "Nietzsche's Critique of Truth". In: *Philosophy and Phenomenological Research* 52. No. 1, pp. 47–65.

Gentili, Carlo (2015): "'Mein Urtheil ist mein Urtheil'. Le radici kantiane del prospettivismo in Nietzsche". In: Failla, Marianna (Ed.): *Leggere il presente: questioni kantiane*. Rome: Carocci, pp. 153–165.

Gentili, Carlo (2014): "Nietzsche y el Cristianismo". In: Conill Sancho, Jesus/Sánchez Meca, Diego (Eds.): *Guía Comares de Nietzsche*. Granada: Comares, pp. 93–122.

Gentili, Carlo (2013): "Kant, Nietzsche und die 'Philosophie des Als-ob'". In: *Nietzscheforschung* 20, pp. 103–116.

Gerhardt, Volker (1989): "Die Perspektive des Perspektivismus". In: *Nietzsche-Studien* 18, pp. 260–281.

Gerhardt, Volker/Reschke, Renate (Eds.) (2010): *Nietzsche, Darwin und die Kritik der Politischen Theologie* (Nietzscheforschung 17). Berlin: Akademie Verlag.

Giedymin, Jerzy (1982): *Science and Convention: Essays on Henri Poincaré's Philosophy of Science and the Conventionalist Tradition*. Oxford: Pergamon Press.

Gori, Pietro (2018a): "Ernst Mach and Pragmatic Realism". In: *Revista Portuguesa de Filosofia* 74. No. 1, pp. 151–172.

Gori, Pietro (2018b): "What Does It Mean to Orient Oneself in Science? On Ernst Mach's Pragmatic Epistemology". In: Stadler, Friedrich (Ed.): *Ernst Mach – Life, Work, Influence* (Vienna Circle Institute Yearbook). Heidelberg: Springer, p. 299–310.

Gori, Pietro (2017a): "Volontà del nulla e volontà di verità. Una riflessione sul realismo di Nietzsche". In: *Consecutio Rerum* 2, p. 115–126.

Gori, Pietro (2017b): "On Nietzsche's Criticism Towards Common Sense Realism in Human, All Too Human I, 11". In: *Philosophical Readings* 9. No. 2, pp. 207–213.

Gori, Pietro (2017c): "Pragmatism, Perspectivism, Anthropology. A Consistent Triad". In: *Internationales Jahrbuch für Philosophische Anthropologie* 7, p. 81–99.

Gori, Pietro (2015a): "Nietzsche's Late Pragmatic Anthropology". In: *Journal of Philosophical Research* 40, pp. 377–404.

Gori, Pietro (2015b): "Psychology without a Soul, Philosophy without an I. Nietzsche and 19th Century Psychophysics (Fechner, Lange, Mach)". In: Constâncio, João/Mayer Branco, Maria João/Ryan, Bartholomew (Eds.): *Nietzsche and the Problem of Subjectivity*. Berlin, Boston: De Gruyter, pp. 166–195.

Gori, Pietro (2015c): "Porre in questione il valore della verità. Riflessioni sul compito della tarda filosofia di Nietzsche a partire da GM III 24–27". In: Giacomini, Bruna/Gori, Pietro/Grigenti, Fabio (Eds.): *La Genealogia della morale. Letture e interpretazioni*. Pisa: ETS, pp. 269–292.

Gori, Pietro (2015d): "Leaving the Soul Apart. An Introductory Study". In: *Philosophical Readings* 7. No. 2, pp. 3–13.

Gori, Pietro (2014): "Nietzsche and Mechanism. On the Use of History for Science". In: Heit, Helmut/Heller, Lisa (Eds.): *Handbuch Nietzsche und die Wissenschaften*. Berlin, Boston: De Gruyter, pp. 119–137.

Gori, Pietro (2013): "Nietzsche on Truth. A Pragmatic View?". In: *Nietzscheforschung* 20, pp. 71–89.

Gori, Pietro (2012a): "Nietzsche as Phenomenalist?". In Heit, Helmut/Abel, Günter/Brusotti, Marco (Eds.) *Nietzsches Wissenschaftsphilosophie*. Berlin, Boston: De Gruyter, pp. 345–356.

Gori, Pietro (2012b): "Small Moments and Individual Taste". In: Caysa, Volker/Schwarzwald, Konstanze (Eds.): *Nietzsche – Macht – Größe. Nietzsche – Philosoph der Größe der Macht oder der Macht der Größe*. Berlin, Boston: De Gruyter, pp. 155–167.

Gori, Pietro (2011a): "Nietzsche, Mach y la metafísica del yo". In: *Estudios Nietzsche* 11, pp. 99–112.

Gori, Pietro (2011b): "Il 'prospettivismo', epistemologia ed etica". In: Gori, Pietro/Stellino, Paolo (Eds.): *Teorie e pratiche della verità in Nietzsche*. Pisa: ETS, pp. 101–123.

Gori, Pietro (2011c): "Drei Briefe von Hans Kleinpeter an Ernst Mach über Nietzsche". In: *Nietzsche-Studien* 40, pp. 290–298.

Gori, Pietro (2009a): *Il meccanicismo metafisico. Scienza, filosofia e storia in Nietzsche e Mach*. Bologna: Il Mulino.

Gori, Pietro (2009b): "The Usefulness of Substances. Knowledge, Metaphysics and Science in Nietzsche and Mach". In: *Nietzsche-Studien* 38, pp. 111–144.

Gori, Pietro (2009c): "'Sounding out Idols'. Knowledge, History and Metaphysics in *Human, All Too Human* and *Twilight of the Idols*". In: *Nietzscheforschung* 16, pp. 239–247.

Gori, Pietro (2007): *La visione dinamica del mondo. Nietzsche e la filosofia naturale di Boscovich*. Naples: La Città del Sole.

Gori, Pietro/Piazzesi, Chiara (2012): "Commento al *Crepuscolo degli idoli*". In: Nietzsche, Friedrich: *Crepuscolo degli idoli*. Italian trans. ed. by Gori, Pietro and Piazzesi, Chiara. Rome: Carocci, pp. 125–261.

Gori, Pietro/Stellino, Paolo (2018): "Moral Relativism and Perspectival Values." In: Marques, António/Sàágua, João (Eds.): *Essays on Values and Practical Rationality – Ethical and Aesthetical Dimensions*. Berlin: Peter Lang, p. 155–174.

Gould, Stephen J./Vrba, Elisabeth S.: 1982. "Exaptation – A Missing Term in the Science of Form". In: *Paleobiology* 8. No. 1, pp. 4–15.

Green, Michael Steven (2002): *Nietzsche and the Transcendental Tradition*. Champain: University of Illinois Press.
Grimm, Rüdiger Hermann (1977): *Nietzsche's Theory of Knowledge*. Berlin, New York: De Gruyter.
Guzzardi, Luca (2010): *Lo sguardo muto delle cose*. Milan: Raffaello Cortina.
Guzzardi, Luca (2002): "Teorie stravaganti di un redattore invadente. Un positivista italiano nel dibattito scientifico europeo". In: *Intersezioni* 3/2002, pp. 419–422.
Hahlweg, Kai (1986): "Popper versus Lorenz: An Exploration into the Nature of Evolutionary Epistemology". In: *Proceedings of the Biennal Meeting of the Philosophy of Science Association* 1, pp. 172–182.
Halbfass, Wilhelm (1989): "Phänomenalismus". In: *Historisches Wörterbuch der Philosophie*. Vol. 7. Basel: Schwabe, pp. 483–485.
Hatab, Lawrence (1995): *A Nietzschean Defense of Democracy*. Chicago: Open Court.
Heidelberger, Michael (2014): "Hans Vaihinger und Friedrich Albert Lange. Mit einem Ausblick auf Ludwig Wittgenstein". In: Neuber, Matthias (Ed.): *Fiktion und Fiktionalismus: Beiträge zu Hans Vaihingers 'Philosophie des Als Ob'*. Würzburg: Königshausen & Neumann, p. 43–63.
Heinzmann, Gerhard (2009): "Hypotheses and Conventions: On the Philosophical and Scientific Motivations of Poincaré's Pragmatic Occasionalism". In: Heidelberger, Michael/Schiemann, Gregor (Eds.): *The Significance of the Hypothetical in the Natural Sciences*. Berlin, Boston: De Gruyter, pp. 169–192.
Heit, Helmut/Abel Günter/Brusotti, Marco (Eds.) (2012): *Nietzsches Wissenschaftsphilosophie*. Berlin, Boston: De Gruyter.
Heit, Helmut/Heller, Lisa (Eds.) (2014): *Handbuch Nietzsche und die Wissenschaften*. Berlin, Boston: De Gruyter.
Hesse, Mary (1972): "In Defence of Objectivity". In: *Proceedings of the British Academy* 57, pp. 275–292.
Himmelmann, Beatrix (Ed.) (2005): *Kant und Nietzsche im Wiederstreit*. Berlin, New York: De Gruyter.
Hingst, Kai-Michael (2000): "Nietzsche Pragmaticus. Die Verwandtschaft von Nietzsches Denken mit dem Pragmatismus von William James". In: *Nietzscheforschung* 7, pp. 287–306.
Hingst, Kai-Michael (1998): *Perspektivismus und Pragmatismus. Ein Vergleich auf der Grundlage der Wahrheitsbegriffe und der Religionsphilosophien von Nietzsche und James*. Würzburg: Königshausen & Neumann.
Höffding, Harald (1955): *A History of Modern Philosophy*. New York: Dover.
Hofstader, Richard (1945): *Social Darwinism in American Thought, 1860–1915*. Philadelphia: University of Pennsylvania Press.
Holland, Alan/O'Hear, Anthony (1984): "On What Makes an Epistemology Evolutionary". In: *Proceedings of the Aristotelian Society. Supplementary Volume* 58, pp. 177–217.
Hollingdale, Reginald John (1973): *Nietzsche*. London: Routledge & Kegan.
Holton, Gerald (1993): "From the Vienna Circle to Harvard Square: The Americanization of a European World Conception". In: Stadler, Friedrich (Ed.): *Scientific Philosophy: Origins and Development*. Dordrecht: Kluwer, pp. 47–73.
Holton, Gerald (1992): "Ernst Mach and the Fortunes of Positivism in America". In: *Isis* 83. No. 1, pp. 27–60.
Hussain, Nadeem (2004a): "Nietzsche's Positivism". In: *European Journal of Philosophy* 12. No. 3, pp. 326–368.
Hussain, Nadeem (2004b): "Reading Nietzsche through Ernst Mach". In: Brobjer, Thomas/Moore, Gregory (Eds.): *Nietzsche and Science*. Aldershot: Ashgate, pp. 111–129.
Ibbeken, Claudia (2008): *Konkurrenzkampf der Perspektiven*. Würzburg: Königshausen & Neumann.

Julião, José (2013): "O Perspectivismo de Nietzsche como Relativismo Pragmático". In: *Estudos Nietzsche* 4. No. 2, pp. 181–195.

Karakaş, Tahir (2013): *Nietzsche et William James. Réformer la philosophie.* L'Harmattan, Paris.

Katsafanas, Paul (2015): "Kant and Nietzsche on Self-Knowledge". In: Constâncio, João/Mayer Branco, Maria João/Ryan, Bartholomew (Eds.): *Nietzsche and the Problem of Subjectivity.* Berlin, Boston: De Gruyter, pp. 110–130.

Katsafanas, Paul (2005): "Nietzsche's Theory of Mind. Consciousness and Conceptualization". In: *European Journal of Philosophy* 13, pp. 1–31.

Kaufmann, Walter (1974): *Nietzsche. Philosopher, Psychologist, Antichrist.* Princeton: Princeton University Press.

Kaulbach, Friedrich (1980): *Nietzsches Idee einer Experimentalphilosophie.* Cologne, Vienna: Böhlau.

Kaulbach, Friedrich (1990): *Philosophie des Perspektivismus, 1. Teil.* Tübingen: Mohr.

Kelly, Alfred (1981): *The Descent of Darwin: The Popularization of Darwinism in Germany, 1860–1914.* Chapel Hill: University of North Carolina Press.

Kirchoff, Jochen (1977): "Zum Problem der Erkenntnis bei Nietzsche". In: *Nietzsche-Studien* 5, pp. 17–44.

Lehmann, Gerhard (1987): "Kant im Spätidealismus und die Anfänge der neukantischen Bewegung". In: Ollig, Hans-Ludwig (Ed.): *Materialien zur Neukantianismus-Diskussion.* Darmstadt: Wissenschaftliche Buchgesellschaft, pp. 44–65.

Leiter, Brian (2002): *Nietzsche on Morality.* London: Routledge.

Leiter, Brian (2000): "Nietzsche's Metaethics: Against the Privilege Reading". In: *European Journal of Philosophy* 8. No. 3, pp. 277–297.

Leiter, Brian (1994): "Perspectivism in Nietzsche's *Genealogy of Morals*". In: Schacht, Richard (Ed.): *Nietzsche, Genealogy, Morality: Essays on Nietzsche's Genealogy of Morality.* Berkeley: University of California Press, pp. 334–352.

Loukidelis, Nikolaos (2014): "Nietzsche und die 'Logiker'". In: Heit, Helmut/Heller, Lisa (Eds.): *Handbuch Nietzsche und die Wissenschaften.* Berlin, Boston: De Gruyter, pp. 221–241.

Loukidelis, Nikolaos (2013): *"Es denkt". Ein Kommentar zum Aphorismus 17 aus "Jenseits von Gut und Böse".* Würzburg: Königshausen & Neumann.

Loukidelis, Nikolaos (2006): "Nachweis aus Otto Liebmann, *Zur Analysis der Wirklichkeit*". In: *Nietzsche-Studien* 35, pp. 302–303.

Loukidelis, Nikolaos (2005): "Quellen von Nietzsches Verständnis und Kritik des cartesischen *cogito, ergo sum*". In: *Nietzsche-Studien* 34, pp. 300–309.

Lovejoy, Arthur O. (1911): "Schopenhauer as an Evolutionist". In: *The Monist* 21. No. 2, pp. 195–222.

Lupo, Luca (2006): *Le colombe dello scettico. Riflessioni di Nietzsche sulla coscienza negli anni 1880–1888.* Pisa: ETS.

Marchetti, Sarin (2015): *Ethics and Philosophical Critique in William James.* Palgrave: MacMillan.

Marcuse, Ludwig (1959): *Amerikanisches Philosophieren. Pragmatisten, Polytheisten, Tragiker.* Hamburg: Rowohlt.

Marcuse, Ludwig (1950): "Nietzsche in Amerika". In: *Essays, Porträts, Polemiken aus vier Jahrzehnten.* Ed. H. von Hofe. Zürich: Diogenes, pp. 91–103.

Marinucci, Angelo/Crescenzi, Luca (2015): "M III 1: Nietzsche et le retour éternel. Une nouvelle recherche généalogique et philosophique". In: *Estudos Nietzsche* 6. No. 2, pp. 161–197.

Martinelli, Riccardo (1999): *Misurare l'anima. Filosofia e psicofisica da Kant a Carnap.* Macerata: Quodlibet.

McDermid, Douglas (2006): *The Varieties of Pragmatism: Truth, Realism, and Knowledge from James to Rorty.* London: Continuum.

Mittasch, Alwin (1952): *Nietzsche als Naturphilosoph.* Stuttgart: Kroner.

Mittasch, Alwin (1950): *Friedrich Nietzsches Naturbeflissenheit*. Heidelberg: Springer.
Moore, Gregory (2002): *Nietzsche, Biology and Metaphor*. Cambridge: Cambridge University Press.
Müller-Lauter, Wolfgang (1999): *Nietzsche. His Philosophy of Contradictions and the Contradictions of his Philosophy*. Eng. trans. Urbana, Chicago: University of Illinois Press.
Müller-Lauter, Wolfgang (1978): "Der Organismus als innerer Kampf. Der Einfluß von Wilhelm Roux auf Friedrich Nietzsche". In: *Nietzsche-Studien* 7, pp. 189–235.
Murphey, Murray G. (1968): "Kant's Children. The Cambridge Pragmatists". In: *Transactions of the Charles S. Peirce Society* 4. No. 1, pp. 3–33.
Neuber, Matthias (2014): "Einleitung: Die Welt im Modus des Als Ob – Hans Vaihinger und die philosophische Tradition". In: Neuber, Matthias (Ed.): *Fiktion und Fiktionalismus: Beiträge zu Hans Vaihingers 'Philosophie des Als Ob'*. Würzburg: Königshausen & Neumann, pp. 9–18.
Nohl, Herman (1913): "Eine historische Quelle zu Nietzsches Perspektivismus: G. Teichmüller, die wirkliche und die scheinbare Welt". In: *Zeitschrift für Philosophie und philosophische Kritik* 149, pp. 106–115.
Orsucci, Andrea (2001): *Genealogia della morale. Introduzione alla lettura*. Rome: Carocci.
Orsucci, Andrea (1997): "Teichmüller, Nietzsche e la critica delle 'mitologie scientifiche'". In: *Giornale Critico della Filosofia Italiana* 17, pp. 47–63.
Pihlström, Sami (2009): *Pragmatist Metaphysics*, London: Continuum.
Pihlström, Sami (2007): "Metaphysics with a Human Face: William James and the Prospects of Pragmatist Metaphysics". In: *William James Studies* 2. No. 1, pp. 1–28 [open access: http://williamjamesstudies.org/metaphysics-with-a-human-face-william-james-and-the-prospects-of-pragmatist-metaphysics/].
Pihlström, Sami (1998): *Pragmatism and Philosophical Anthropology. Understanding Our Human Life in a Human World*. New York: Peter Lang.
Pippin, Robert (2010): *Nietzsche, Psychology, and First Philosophy*. Chicago: Chicago University Press.
Ratner-Rosenhagen, Jennifer (2012): *American Nietzsche: A History of an Icon and His Ideas*. Chicago: University of Chicago Press.
Reichenbach, Hans (1951): *The Rise of Scientific Philosophy*. Berkeley, Los Angeles: University of California Press.
Remhof, Justin (2016): "Scientific Fictionalism and the Problem of Inconsistency in Nietzsche". In: *Journal of Nietzsche Studies* 47. No. 2, pp. 238–246.
Remhof, Justin (2015): "Nietzsche's Conception of Truth: Correspondence, Coherence, or Pragmatist?" In: *The Journal of Nietzsche Studies* 46. No. 2, pp. 229–238.
Reuter, Sören (2006): *An der "Begräbnissstätte der Anschauung": Nietzsches Bild- und Wahrnehmungstheorie in* Ueber Wahrheit und Lüge im aussermoralischen Sinne. Basel: Schwabe.
Ribeiro dos Santos, Leonel (2015): "The 'will to Appearance' or Nietzsche's Kantianism According to Hans Vaihinger". In: Hay, Katia and Ribeiro dos Santos, Leonel (Eds.), *Nietzsche, German Idealism and its Critics*. Berlin, Boston: De Gruyter, pp. 282–295.
Riccardi, Mattia (2018): "Nietzsche on the Superficiality of Consciousness". In: Dries, Manuel (Ed.): *Nietzsche on Consciousness and the Embodied Mind*. Berlin, Boston: De Gruyter, pp. 93–112.
Riccardi, Mattia (2015): "Nietzsche's Pluralism about Consciousness". In: *British Journal for the History of Philosophy* 24. No. 1, pp. 132–154.
Riccardi, Mattia (2014): "Nietzsche und die Erkenntnistheorie und Metaphysik". In: Heit, Helmut/Heller, Lisa (Eds.): *Handbuch Nietzsche und die Wissenschaften*. Berlin, Boston: De Gruyter, pp. 242–264.
Riccardi, Mattia (2013): "Nietzsche's Sensualism". In: *European Journal of Philosophy* 21. No. 2, pp. 219–257.

Riccardi, Mattia (2011): "Il tardo Nietzsche e la falsificazione". In: Gori, Pietro/Stellino, Paolo (Eds.): *Teorie e pratiche della verità in Nietzsche*. Pisa: ETS, pp. 57–73.

Riccardi, Mattia (2009a): *"Der faule Fleck des Kantischen Kriticismus". Erscheinung und Ding an sich bei Nietzsche*. Basel: Schwabe.

Riccardi, Mattia (2009b): "Nachweise aus Gustav Teichmüller, 'Die wirkliche und die scheinbare Welt' (1882)". In: *Nietzsche-Studien* 38, pp. 331–332.

Richards, Robert J. (1977): "The Natural Selection Model of Conceptual Evolution". In: *Philosophy of Science* 44. No. 3, pp. 494–501.

Richardson, John (2004): *Nietzsche's New Darwinism*. Oxford: Oxford University Press.

Rorty, Richard (1991a): "Nietzsche, Socrates, and Pragmatism". In: *South African Journal of Philosophy* 10. No. 3, pp. 61–63.

Rorty, Richard (1991b): "Introduction: Pragmatism and Post-Nietzschean Philosophy". In: Rorty, Richard: *Essays in Heidegger and Others. Philosophical Papers*. Vol. 2. Cambridge: Cambridge University Press, pp. 1–6.

Ruse, Michael (1998): *Taking Darwin Seriously: A Naturalistic Approach to Philosophy*. Amherst: Prometheus.

Ryan, Judith (1989): "American Pragmatism, Viennese Psychology". In: *Raritan* 8, pp. 45–55.

Salaquarda, Jörg (1978): *Nietzsche und Lange*. In: *Nietzsche-Studien* 7, pp. 236–253.

Schacht, Richard (2015): "Gehlen, Nietzsche, and the Project of a Philosophical Anthropology". In: Honenberger, Phillip (Ed.): *Naturalism and Philosophical Anthropology. Nature, Life, and the Human between Transcendental and Empirical Perspectives*. Basingstoke: Palgrave Macmilian, pp. 49–65.

Schacht, Richard (2006): "Nietzsche and Philosophical Anthropology". In: Ansell-Pearson, Keith (Ed.): *A Companion to Nietzsche*. Hoboken/New Jersey: Blackwell, pp. 115–132.

Schacht, Richard (1983): *Nietzsche*. London: Routledge & Kegan Paul.

Schank, Gerd (2000): *"Rasse" und "Züchtung" bei Nietzsche*. Berlin, New York: De Gruyter.

Schmid, Josef (2005): "Erkenntnis durch Fiktion. Nietzsche bei Hans Vaihinger und Max Weber". In: Himmelmann, Beatrix (Ed.), *Kant und Nietzsche im Wiederstreit*. Berlin/Boston: De Gruyter, pp. 373–381

Simon, Josef (1989): "Die Krise des Wahrheitsbegriff als Krise der Metaphysik. Nietzsches Alethiologie auf dem Hintergrund der Kantischen Kritik". In: *Nietzsche-Studien* 18, pp. 242–259.

Simon, Josef (1986): "Der gewollte Schein. Zu Nietzsches Begriff der Interpretation". In: Djuric, Mihailo/Simon, Josedîf (Eds.): *Kunst und Wissenschaft bei Nietzsche*. Würzburg: Königshausen & Neumann, pp. 62–74.

Sini, Carlo (1972): *Il pragmatismo americano*. Bari: Laterza.

Skagestad, Peter (1981): "Hypothetical Realism". In: *Scientific Inquiry and the Social Sciences: A Volume in Honor of Donald T. Campbell*. San Franciso: Jossey-Bass, pp. 77–97.

Small, Robin (2001): *Nietzsche in Context*. Aldershot: Ashgate.

Small, Robin (1999): "We Sensualists". In: Babich, Babette/Cohen, Robert (Eds.): *Nietzsche, Epistemology, and Philosophy of Science. Nietzsche and the Sciences II*. Dordrecht, London, Boston: Kluwer, pp. 73–89.

Sommer, Andreas Urs (2012): *Kommentar zu Nietzsches Der Fall Wagner und Götzen-Dämmerung*. Berlin, Boston: De Gruyter.

Stack, George (1992): "Nietzsche's Evolutionary Epistemology". In: *Dialogos* 59, pp. 75–101.

Stack, George (1991): "Kant, Lange and Nietzsche: Critique of Knowledge". In: Pearson, Keith Ansell (Ed.): *Nietzsche and Modern German Thought*. London: Routledge, pp. 30–58.

Stack, George (1983): *Lange and Nietzsche*. Berlin, New York: De Gruyter.

Stack, George (1982): "Nietzsche's Influence on Pragmatic Humanism". In: *Journal of the History of Philosophy* 20. No. 4, pp. 339–358.

Stack, George (1981a): "Nietzsche and the Correspondence Theory of Truth". In: *Dialogos* 38, pp. 93–117.
Stack, George (1981b): "Nietzsche and Perspectival Interpretation". In: *Philosophy Today* 25, pp. 221–241.
Stack, George (1980): "Nietzsche's Critique of Things-in-Themselves". In: *Dialogos* 36, pp. 33–57.
Stadler, Friedrich (2015): *The Vienna Circle – Studies in the Origins, Development, and Influence of Logical Empiricism*. Vienna: Springer.
Stadler, Friedrich (Ed.) (1993): *Scientific Philosophy: Origins and Development*. Dordrecht: Kluwer.
Stadler, Friedrich (1982): *Vom Positivismus zur "Wissenschaftlichen Weltauffassung". Am Beispiel der Wirkungsgeschichte von Ernst Mach in Österreich von 1895 bis 1934*. Munich: Löcker.
Stanzione, Massimo (1981): "Introduzione". In: Campbell, Donald: *Epistemologia evoluzionistica*. Italian trans. Rome: Armando, pp. 7–62.
Stegmaier, Werner (2016): *Orientierung im Nihilismus. Luhmann Meets Nietzsche*. Berlin, Boston: De Gruyter.
Stegmaier, Werner (2012): *Nietzsches Befreiung der Philosophie*. Berlin, Boston: De Gruyter.
Stegmaier, Werner (2008): *Philosophie der Orientierung*. Berlin, Boston: De Gruyter.
Stegmaier, Werner (1987): "Darwin, Darwinismus, Nietzsche. Zum Problem der Evolution". In: *Nietzsche-Studien* 16, pp. 264–287.
Stegmaier, Werner (1985): "Nietzsches Neubestimmung der Wahrheit". In: *Nietzsche-Studien* 14, pp. 69–95.
Stellino, Paolo (2015a): *Nietzsche and Dostoevsky: On the Verge of Nihilism*. Bern: Peter Lang.
Stellino, Paolo (2015b): "Self-Knowledge, Genealogy, Evolution". In: Constâncio, João/Mayer Branco, Maria João/Ryan, Bartholomew (Eds.): *Nietzsche and the Problem of Subjectivity*. Berlin, Boston: De Gruyter, pp. 550–573.
Thagard, Paul (1980): "Against Evolutionary Epistemology". In: *Proceedings of the Biennal Meeting of the Philosophy of Science Association*. Vol. 1, pp. 187–196.
Thiele, Joachim (1978): *Wissenschaftliche Kommunikation. Die Korrespondenz Ernst Machs*. Kastellaun: Henn.
Vollmer, Gerhard (1975): *Evolutionäre Erkenntnistheorie*. Frankfurt: S. Hirzel.
Wiener, Philip P. (1944): *Evolution and the Founders of Pragmatism*. Cambridge: Harvard University Press.
Wilcox, John T. (1986): "Nietzsche Scholarship and 'the Correspondence Theory of Truth': The Danto Case". In: *Nietzsche-Studien* 15, pp. 337–357.
Witzler, Ralph (2001): *Europa im Denken Nietzsches*. Würzburg: Königshausen & Neumann.
Wuketits, Franz (1984): "Evolutionary Epistemology – A Challenge to Science and Philosophy". In: Wuketits, Franz (Ed.): *Concepts and Approaches in Evolutionary Epistemology*. Dordrecht: Reidel, pp. 1–33.

## Other texts

The texts marked with "NPL" are works included in the catalogue of Nietzsche's personal library, according to Campioni *et alia* 2003.

Armstrong, A. C. (1909): "The Evolution of Pragmatism". In: Elsenhans, Theodor (Ed.): *Bericht über den III. internationalen Kongress für Philosophie zu Heidelberg*. Heidelberg: Universitätsbuchhandlung, pp. 720–726.
Berthelot, René (1911): *Un Romantisme Utilitaire. Etude sur le Mouvement Pragmatiste*. Vol. 1. Paris: Alcan.

Campbell, Donald (1979): "A Tribal Model of the Social System Vehicle Carrying Scientific Knowledge". In: *Knowledge: Creation, Diffusion, Utilization* 1, pp. 181–201.
Campbell, Donald (1977): "Comment on 'The Natural Selection Model of Conceptual Evolution'". In: *Philosophy of Science* 44. No. 3, pp. 502–507.
Campbell, Donald (1975): "On the Conflicts Between Biological and Social Evolution and Between Psychology and Moral Tradition". In: *American Psychologist* 30, pp. 1103–1126.
Campbell, Donald (1974): "Evolutionary Epistemology". In: Schlipp, Paul (Ed.): *The Philosophy of Karl R. Popper*. LaSalle: Open Court, pp. 412–463.
Caspari, Otto (1881): *Der Zusammenhang der Dinge. Gesammelte philosophische Aufsätze*. Breslau: Trewendt (NPL).
Darwin, Charles (2008): *The Origin of the Species by Means of Natural Selection, or the Preservation of Favoured Races in the Struggle for Life*. Oxford: Oxford University Press [$^1$1859].
Dewey, John (1908): "What does Pragmatism Mean by Practical?" In: *The Journal of Philosophy, Psychology and Scientific Methods* 5/4, pp. 85–99,
Drossbach, Maximilian (1884): *Über die scheinbaren und die wirklichen Ursachen des Geschehens in der Welt*. Halle: Pfeffer (NPL).
Du Bois-Reymond, Emil (1884): *Über die Grenzen des Naturerkennens – Die sieben Welträthsel. Zwei Vorträge*. Leipzig: Veit & C. (NPL).
Espinas, Alfred (1879): *Die thierischen Gesellschaften. Eine vergleichend-psychologische Untersuchung*. Braunschweig: F. Vieweg und Sohn (NPL).
Fouillée, Alfred (1880): *La science sociale contemporaine*. Paris: Hachette et C.ie (NPL).
Frank, Philipp (1949): *Modern Science and Its Philosophy*. Cambridge: Harvard University Press.
Helmholtz, Hermann von (1925): *Treatise of Physiological Optics*. Eng. trans. New York: Dover.
Helmholtz, Hermann von (1921): *Schriften zur Erkenntnistheorie*. Ed. Schlick, Moritz/Herz, Paul. Berlin: Springer.
James, William (1992): *Writings 1878–1899*. Ed. G. Myers. New York: The Library of America.
James, William (1920): *Collected Essays and Reviews*. Ed. R. Perry. New York: Longmans, Green & c.
James, William (1912): *Essays in Radical Empiricism*. New York: Longmans, Green & c.
James, William (1909): *The Meaning of Truth. A Sequel to "Pragmatism"*. New York: Longmans, Green & c.
James, William (1907): *Pragmatism. A New Name for Some Old Ways of Thinking*. New York: Longmans, Green & c.
James, William (1890): *The Principles of Psychology* (2 vols.). New York: Henry Holt & C.
Kant, Immanuel (2007 [1798]): "Anthropology from a Pragmatic point of View", eng. trans. in: Kant, Immanuel (2007), *Anthropology, History, and Education*, eds. Zöller, Günter and Louden, Robert B., Cambridge: Cambridge University Press, pp. 227–429 ["Anthropologie in pragmatischer Hinsicht" (1st ed. 1798). In: Kant, Immanuel: *Werkausgabe*. Vol. 12. Frankfurt a. M.: Suhrkamp, 2000.]
Kant, Immanuel (1974): "Kritik der reinen Vernunft" (1st ed. 1781, 2nd ed. 1787). In: Kant, Immanuel: *Werkausgabe*. Vols. 3 and 4. Frankfurt a. M.: Suhrkamp.
Kleinpeter, Hans (2011): *La teoria della conoscenza di Mach e Nietzsche*. Italian trans. ed. Gori, Pietro. In: *Giornale Critico della Filosofia Italiana* 7. No. 7, pp. 352–382.
Kleinpeter, Hans (1913): *Der Phänomenalismus. Eine naturwissenschaftliche Weltanschauung*. Leipzig: Barth.
Kleinpeter, Hans (1912a): "Der Pragmatismus im Lichte der Machschen Erkenntnislehre". In: *Wissenschaftliche Rundschau* 20, pp. 405–407.
Kleinpeter, Hans (1912b): "Nietzsche als Schulreformer". In: *Blätter für deutsche Erziehung* 14, pp. 99–100.

Kleinpeter, Hans (1912c): "Die Erkenntnislehre Friedrich Nietzsches". In: *Wissenschaftliche Rundschau* 3, pp. 5–9.
Lange, Friedrich Albert (1882): *Die Geschichte des Materialismus* (2 vols.). Iserlohn: Baedeker [¹1866, ²1875] (NPL the 1887 single-volume "wohlfeile Ausgabe" edition).
Liebmann, Otto (1880): *Zur Analysis der Wirklichkeit. Eine Erörterung der Grundprobleme der Philosophie*. Strasbourg: K. J. Trübner (NPL).
Lorenz, Konrad (1977): *Behind the Mirror*. London: Methuen.
Lorenz, Konrad (1941): "Kants Lehre vom apriorischen im Lichte gegenwärtiger Biologie". In: *Blätter für Deutsche Philosophie* 15, pp. 94–125.
Mach, Ernst (1991): "The Leading Thoughts of My Scientific Epistemology and Its Acceptance by Contemporaries." In: Blackmore, John (Ed.): *Ernst Mach – A Deeper Look*. Dordrecht: Kluwer, pp. 133–138.
Mach, Ernst (1976 [1905]): *Knowledge and Error. Sketches on the Psychology of Enquiry*. Eng. trans. Dordrecht: Reidl [*Erkenntnis und Irrtum. Skizzen zur Psychologie der Forschung*. Leipzig: Barth ¹1905, ⁵1926].
Mach, Ernst (1914 [1886]): *The Analysis of Sensations*. Eng. trans. New York: Dover [*Beiträge zur Analyse der Empfindungen*. Barth: Leipzig ¹1886 (NPL); *Die Analyse der Empfindungen und das Verhältnis des Physischen zum Psychischen*. Jena: Fischer ⁵1906].
Mach, Ernst (1910): "Die Leitgedanken meiner naturwissenschaftlichen Erkenntnislehre und ihre Aufnahme durch die Zeitgenossen". In: *Scientia* 7, pp. 225–240.
Mach, Ernst (1986 [1896]): *Principles of the Theory of Heat, Historically and Critically Elucidated*. Eng. trans. Dordrecht: Reidl [*Die Principien der Wärmelehre historisch-kritisch entwickelt*, Leipzig: Barth 1896].
Mach, Ernst (1919 [1883]): *The Science of Mechanics*. Eng. trans. Chicago, Open Courts [*Die Mechanik in ihrer Entwickelung historisch-kritisch dargestellt*. Leipzig: Brockhaus ¹1883].
Mach, Ernst (1911 [1872]): *History and Root of the Principle of the Conservation of Energy*. Eng. trans. Chicago: Open Court [*Die Geschichte und die Wurzel des Satzes von der Erhaltung der Arbeit*. Prague: Calve 1872].
Mach, Ernst (1895): *Popular Scientific Lectures*, Chicago: Open Court.
Mead, George Herbert (1934): *Mind, Self, and Society: From the Standpoint of a Social Behaviorist*. Chicago: University of Chicago Press.
Popper, Karl (2002): *The Logic of Scientific Discovery*. New York: Harper.
Popper, Karl (1984): "Evolutionary Epistemology". In: Pollard, Jeffrey W. (Ed.): *Evolutionary Theory: Paths into the Future*. London: John Wiley & Sons, pp. 239–255.
Popper, Karl (1972): *Objective Knowledge: An Evolutionary Approach*. Oxford: Clarendon Press.
Popper, Karl (1969): *Conjectures and Refutations*. London: Routledge.
Roux, Wilhelm (1881): *Der Kampf der Teile im Organismus. Ein Beitrag zur Vervollständigung der mechanischen Zweckmässigkeitslehre*. Leipzig: Engelmann.
Russell, Bertrand (1927): *The Analysis of Matter*. New York: Dover.
Russell, Bertrand (1921): *The Analysis of Mind*. London: Routledge.
Schopenhauer, Arthur (1873–74): *Sämtliche Werke* (6 vols.). Ed. J. Frauenstädt. Leipzig: F. A. Brockhaus (NPL).
Spencer, Herbert (1879): *Die Thatsachen der Ethik*. Stuttgart: E. Schweizerbart'sche Verlagshandlung (NPL).
Spencer, Herbert (1879): *Einleitung in das Studium der Sociologie*. Leipzig: Brockhaus (NPL).
Spencer, Herbert (1855): *The Principles of Psychology*. London: Longman, Brown, Green & Longmans.
Spir, Afrikan (1877): *Denken und Wirklichkeit. Versuch einer Erneuerung der kritischen Philosophie* (2 vols.). Leipzig: J. G. Findel (NPL).
Teichmüller, Gustav (1882): *Die wirkliche und die scheinbare Welt*. Breslau: Koebner.

Toulmin, Stephen (1972): *Human Understanding: The Collective Use and Evolution of Concepts.* Princeton: Princeton University Press.

Toulmin, Stephen (1967): "The Evolutionary Development of Natural Science". In: *American Scientist* 57, pp. 456–471.

Vaihinger, Hans (1925): *The Philosophy of As-if.* Eng. trans. New York: Harcourt, Brace & c. [*Die Philosophie des Als-ob.* Berlin: Reuther & Reichard $^1$1911].

# Index

Abel, Günter  50, 57, 77, 83, 130, 137
Anderson, R. Lanier  30, 71, 133
Armstrong, A.C.  109
Avenarius, Richard  58, 67, 104

Bacon, Francis  147
Baer, Karl von  32
Bain, Alexander  19
Baldwin, James  17
Banks, Erik C.  19, 56, 58, 105, 137, 140, 144, 146
Bayertz, Kurt  57
Ben-Menahem, Yemima  123
Berkeley, George  108
Bernstein, Richard  39, 135
Berthelot, René  68, 103, 118–122
Blackmore, John  68, 137
Boltzmann, Ludwig  19
Bornedal, Peter  53
Bouriau, Christophe  103, 112, 117, 122, 152
Bradie, Michael  7–9, 13–15, 24, 26, 36, 40
Brentano, Franz  56
Brobjer, Thomas  72, 137
Brusotti, Marco  57, 137
Buzzoni, Marco  16

Campbell, Donald  6–9, 11–20, 23–25, 29, 32–34, 36, 40
Campioni, Giuliano  18, 57, 164
Čapek, Milič  19 f., 25 f., 106
Caygill, Howard  105
Ceynowa, Klaus  112 f.
Clark, Maudemarie  27, 30, 35, 71, 80, 86, 130 f., 133 f., 153
Clifford, William  104
Constâncio, João  49, 90
Cox, Christoph  27, 76–78, 80 f., 86, 133
Crescenzi, Luca  57

Danto, Arthur  27, 86, 101, 110, 123 f., 130, 133
Darwin, Charles  6, 8–12, 15, 17–23, 25 f., 28, 33 f., 39, 94, 102, 108, 120, 145
De Paz, María  123
Dellinger, Jakob  61, 71–73, 84
Descartes, René  49, 51, 53, 56, 73, 87
Dewey, John  103, 116, 124–127
Dickopp, Karl-Heinz  84
D'Iorio, Paolo  32, 48, 68

DiSalle, Robert  123
Drossbach, Maximilian  48, 62
Du Bois-Reymond, Emil  57
Dudrick, David  71, 131
Duhem, Pierre  147, 149

Emden, Christian J.  30, 94, 130
Erdmann, Johann Eduard  67
Espinas, Alfred  94
Euclid  25, 144

Fabbrichesi, Rossella  92, 101, 136, 145, 150
Fazio, Domenico  102
Fechner, Gustav  34, 56, 68, 133, 138
Ferrari, Massimo  102, 108, 144, 149
Figl, Johann  27, 30, 41, 48, 54, 63 f., 66, 76, 86, 130
Forberg, Karl  115
Fornari, Maria Cristina  94 f., 97, 102, 120
Förster-Nietzsche, Elisabeth  104
Fouillée, Alfred  94
Frank, Philipp  104, 110, 122, 137
Franzese, Sergio  4, 17 f., 102, 123, 145, 147, 150 f.

Gabriel, Gottfried  115
Gemes, Ken  27, 86, 99, 130, 154
Gentili, Carlo  89, 102, 115 f.
Gerber, Gustav  32
Gerhard, Myriam  57
Gerhard, Volker  102, 131, 153
Giedymin, Jerzy  123
Goethe, Johann Wolfgang  104 f., 108
Gould, Stephen J.  22
Green, Michael Steven  32, 48, 68
Grimm, Rüdiger Hermann  27, 80, 86, 130, 133
Guzzardi, Luca  20, 56

Haeckel, Ernst  20
Hahlweg, Kai  12, 16
Halbfass, Wilhelm  58, 67
Hartmann, Eduard von  67
Hatab, Lawrence  83
Heidelberger, Michael  113
Heinzmann, Gerhard  123
Heit, Helmut  57, 137
Heller, Lisa  57, 137
Helmholtz, Hermann von  25 f., 32–34, 133

Hering, Ewald  20
Hesse, Mary  130
Himmelmann, Beatrix  102
Hingst, Kai-Michael  101, 136, 145
Höffding, Harald  24
Hofstader, Richard  17
Holland, Alan  12
Hollingdale, Reginald John  69
Holton, Gerald  108, 137, 144, 149
Hussain, Nadeem  19, 71, 131, 138, 146

Ibbeken, Claudia  79

Jaeschke, Walter  57
James, William  3–6, 16–19, 23 f., 33, 58, 60, 68, 101–103, 108–112, 116–128, 133, 136–138, 140, 144–154
Jerusalem, Wilhelm  108
Jevons, William S.  19
Joly, Henri  17
Julião, José  128

Kant, Immanuel  3 f., 7, 13 f., 17, 20, 24–26, 29, 32 f., 37, 39, 44, 48, 51, 53, 56 f., 59 f., 63, 65, 68 f., 72, 74, 78, 88, 91 f., 102–108, 111–117, 126, 129 f., 134, 137–139, 144, 152 f.
Karakaş, Tahir  101, 118, 136, 151
Katsafanas, Paul  49 f., 90
Kaufmann, Walter  134, 151
Kaulbach, Friedrich  71, 76, 83, 102
Kelly, Alfred  17
Kleinpeter, Hans  68, 103–111, 119, 122, 138, 146

Lamarck, Jean-Baptiste de  13, 20, 24, 94, 120
Lange, Friedrich Albert  17, 25, 30, 32–35, 55 f., 68 f., 78, 86, 113–116, 129 f., 133 f., 137
Lehmann, Gerhard  25
Leiter, Brian  30, 39, 49, 71, 80, 90, 152 f.
Lichtenberg, Georg  137
Liebmann, Otto  68, 91
Locke, John  108
Lorenz, Konrad  12–16, 23–25, 33 f., 36, 40
Loukidelis, Nikolaos  53, 56, 73, 87, 91
Lovejoy, Arthur  29
Lupo, Luca  47, 80, 83, 90 f., 93 f., 96

Mach, Ernst  4–6, 19–23, 25, 32, 39, 56, 58 f., 67–69, 104–108, 110, 113–115, 121–123, 137–141, 143 f., 146–149
Marchetti, Sarin  123
Marcuse, Ludwig  136
Marinucci, Angelo  57
Martinelli, Riccardo  25, 51, 56
McDermid, Douglas  117
Mead, George Herbert  91
Mittasch, Alwin  57, 137 f.
Moore, Gregory  97, 137
Müller, Johannes  34, 68, 113, 133
Müller-Lauter, Wolfgang  30, 81, 133
Murphey, Murray G.  102, 121

Neuber, Matthias  112
Newton, Isaac  57, 69, 104, 137
Nohl, Herman  72, 84

O'Hear, Anthony  12
Orsucci, Andrea  68, 72 f., 84, 87, 94
Ostwald, Wilhelm  147, 149
Overbeck, Franz  87

Paulsen, Friedrich  115
Pearson, Karl  104, 144
Peirce, Charles Sanders  4, 17, 103, 109, 111, 115–117, 119
Piazzesi, Chiara  38, 45 f., 66, 73, 85, 127
Pihlström, Sami  127, 152–154
Pippin, Robert  52
Planck, Max  20
Plato  1 f., 48, 54, 85, 89, 98, 108, 127, 143
Poincaré, Henri  4, 19, 58, 117, 121–123, 144
Popper, Karl  6–12, 14, 16 f., 19, 21, 23, 25 f., 33, 36, 40

Quine, Willard Van Orman  130

Ratner-Rosenhagen, Jennifer  103, 109, 151
Rée, Paul  120
Reichenbach, Hans  104
Remhof, Justin  133
Reschke, Renate  102
Reuter, Sören  25, 30
Riberio dos Santos, Leonel  115
Riccardi, Mattia  30, 48 f., 62, 68, 72, 84, 86, 88, 90 f., 93, 105, 131, 146
Richards, Robert J.  9
Rickert, Heinrich  115

Riemann, Bernhard  57
Rorty, Richard  102f., 109
Roux, Wilhelm  81, 94, 96
Royce, Josiah  121
Ruse, Michael  6, 8f.
Russell, Bertrand  19, 56
Ryan, Judith  108

Salaquarda, Jörg  25, 56, 68
Schacht, Richard  40, 45, 65, 100, 127, 129, 133
Schank, Gerd  79, 95
Schiller, Ferdinand  5, 104, 115f., 144, 146f.
Schopenhauer, Arthur  29, 93, 108, 115, 129
Simon, Josef  27, 76, 86, 102, 118, 127
Sini, Carlo  17
Skagestad, Peter  15
Small, Robin  72f., 84, 93, 105, 146
Sommer, Andreas Urs  66, 73
Spencer, Herbert  6, 10f., 13, 16–20, 23–26, 33f., 36, 94–97, 120f.
Spir, Afrikan  32, 48, 68
Stack, George  6, 25, 27, 29, 33, 36, 56, 68f., 71, 78, 86, 101, 122, 133, 146
Stadler, Friedrich  69, 104, 137
Stallo, John  104

Stanzione, Massimo  17
Stegmaier, Werner  40, 42, 66–68, 76, 85, 102, 129
Stellino, Paolo  44, 47, 50, 76, 80, 83, 128, 132

Teichmüller, Gustav  38, 48, 61f., 68, 72–74, 84, 87–89, 92f., 105
Thagard, Paul  9
Thiele, Johakim  144
Toulmin, Stephen  8, 11

Überweg, Friedrich  34

Vaihinger, Hans  5, 92, 102f., 111–117, 121f., 134, 149
Vollmer, Gerhard  12f.
Vrba, Elisabeth S.  22

Wiener, Philip P.  17, 102
Wilcox, John T.  27, 86, 101, 133
Wittgenstein, Ludwig  130
Witzler, Ralph  89
Wuketits, Franz  24
Wundt, Wilhelm  115

www.ingramcontent.com/pod-product-compliance
Lightning Source LLC
Chambersburg PA
CBHW080638170426
43200CB00015B/2882